3D for Graphic Designers

ELLERY CONNELL

WILEY

John Wiley & Sons, Inc.

Acquisitions Editor: Mariann Barsolo
Development Editor: Lisa Bishop
Technical Editor: Keith Reicher
Production Editor: Liz Britten
Copy Editor: Sharon Wilkey
Editorial Manager: Pete Gaughan
Production Manager: Tim Tate
Vice President and Executive Group Publisher: Richard Swadley
Vice President and Publisher: Neil Edde
Media Associate Project Manager: Jenny Swisher
Media Associate Producer: Josh Frank
Media Quality Assurance: Doug Kuhn
Book Designer: Caryl Gorska
Compositor: Kate Kaminski, Happenstance Type-O-Rama
Proofreader: Sheilah Ledwidge, Word One
Indexer: Ted Laux
Project Coordinator, Cover: Katherine Crocker
Cover Designer: Ryan Sneed
Cover Image: © Slavenko Vukasovic / iStockPhoto

Dear Reader,

Thank you for choosing *3D for Graphic Designers*. This book is part of a family of premium-quality Sybex books, all of which are written by outstanding authors who combine practical experience with a gift for teaching.

Sybex was founded in 1976. More than 30 years later, we're still committed to producing consistently exceptional books. With each of our titles, we're working hard to set a new standard for the industry. From the paper we print on, to the authors we work with, our goal is to bring you the best books available.

I hope you see all that reflected in these pages. I'd be very interested to hear your comments and get your feedback on how we're doing. Feel free to let me know what you think about this or any other Sybex book by sending me an email at nedde@wiley.com. If you think you've found a technical error in this book, please visit http://sybex.custhelp.com. Customer feedback is critical to our efforts at Sybex.

Best regards,

Neil Edde
Vice President and Publisher
Sybex, an Imprint of Wiley

To Monica, Kyrstin, Zoe, and Gwendolyn

Acknowledgments

I would like to thank a number of individuals and institutions that have made this book possible. Special thanks to DV Garage and Arroway Textures for their contributions to the materials included in the book. I would also like to thank Luxology for their continued support, wonderful customer service, and a fantastic 3D application. ■ There are many members of the 3D community who have been helpful throughout this process, and I would like to thank them. Alex Lindsay, who has been a mentor and hero of mine for years, has been a great support throughout this process. Thanks, Alex! Jim Berton (www.source3d.net), who is a great community activist and champion of all things 3D, has given me support and encouragement over the past months. I would also like to thank Andy Carr. Andy is one of my greatest colleagues and oldest friends. He has been available to talk and give an extra push when I needed it. Thank you, Andy; your friendship has meant more to me than I can express. ■ Most of all, I would like to thank my family. I thank my mom and dad for their support and encouragement as I dove into this field from an early age. I cannot give enough thanks to my beautiful wife, Monica. Your help and loving support have made this work possible. Finally, I would like to thank my wonderful children: Kyrstin, Zoe, and Gwendolyn. They have given up time with Daddy and put up with me when I have drudged through mornings after long nights. Thanks to all of you. Without you, I could not have made this happen.

About the Author

Ellery Connell is a seasoned professional with well over a decade of experience in interactive media, film, television, web, print, and game design. His personal clients cover the United States, the United Kingdom, and Europe. Some of his notable credits include work for CBS Broadcasting, Inc., Simon & Schuster, *Star Trek* Magazine, the Utah Jazz, Caesars Palace, the Bellagio, and CGChannel.com. Ellery has created numerous professional training series and taught seminars (both live and web-based) covering a wide variety of subjects related to motion graphics, visual effects, 3D modeling, animation, and postproduction.

Ellery spent six years as a bilingual (English/Spanish) graphic designer for Dex Media, now known as Dex One. During his time at Dex, Ellery fulfilled his regular duties and added his expertise to the company by creating training materials, writing Photoshop scripts to enhance and speed artist workflow, and completing various special projects that utilized his unique skill set.

Ellery has a passion for teaching. He has often sought opportunities to work in instructional design. Since 2009, he has been employed as a full-time assistant professor of multimedia at the University of Wisconsin-Stout. During his tenure at Stout, he has helped to develop, update, and enhance courses in 3D modeling and animation, motion graphics, digital narrative, and game design. Ellery has spent years improving his skills in all aspects of his field. He holds an MFA from the Academy of Art University in San Francisco with an emphasis in animation and visual effects.

CONTENTS AT A GLANCE

Contents

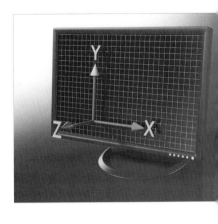

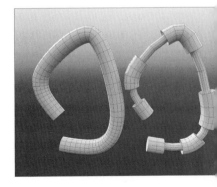

Introduction

Over the years working as a 3D artist, I have noticed that many of my best clients have been competent (even fantastic) artists. They have had a wonderful grasp of design principles and produce excellent work for clients large and small. The time that I have spent working as both a 3D artist and a graphic designer have lead me to the realization that one key element is missing in the workflow of the modern graphic designer: 3D skills. Clearly, the needs of a graphic designer do not include the depth of knowledge needed by a production 3D artist for film, television, or game design, but a basic understanding can set an artist apart in the field. These skills will open doors for both artists and their employers or clients. This can also save money by dispensing with the need to outsource simple to moderate 3D sections of larger projects. When more-complex needs arise, a solid foundation of 3D design techniques will allow you to interface more easily with 3D artists and streamline the collaborative process.

As an educator, I have found this same lack of 3D instruction within digital foundation courses. In fine arts course layouts, 3D skills are usually included for all artists regardless of their target medium and area of study. The addition of sculpting, pottery, or metalwork classes helps to add breadth to the education of a painter, but that same breadth is rarely offered as an option to artists in graphic design, multimedia design, or other digital mediums. This book is intended to fill that crucial gap as a text for related courses in a digital media curriculum.

This book uses Luxology modo as the software for demonstration purposes. If you are completely new to 3D, I highly recommend modo for its power, modern user interface, ease of use, and high-quality rendering. If you are already using another 3D software package with a moderate level of fluency, most of the skills will transfer to any modern application. If the features demonstrated in the sections of this book are not available in your 3D program, a demo of modo is available for you to use as you work through the exercises in the book. You can download it at www.Luxology.com/trymodo.

Who Should Read This Book

Graphic designers are the main audience for this book. Any artist who may use 3D for visualization or illustration purposes will find the information they need to create great 3D art to support or augment their current workflow. Designers who are outsourcing portions of their current projects, looking to expand their current capabilities, or wanting an advantage in the current job market will benefit greatly from this book. In addition to graphic designers, industrial designers and interior designers can use this book to help increase their capabilities for creating advanced visualization of their designs.

With the increase of 3D usage in marketing, photography, and visualization, the skills taught in this book will be of use to beginning 3D artists who are looking to improve the quality of their output and find new venues for their work. Just as graphic designers can use the lessons to add 3D workflow, 3D artists can use this as a guide to find new clients among graphic designers and businesses looking for these services. In addition, novice 3D users will find that this book is useful for more-concrete training in this subject. Anyone interested in learning 3D modeling, texturing, lighting, rendering, and animation with practical and marketable outcomes should study the projects in this book.

What You Will Learn

3D for Graphic Designers covers many of the basic principles of 3D design. In this book, you will learn to create many types of 3D models for use in illustration, product visualization, and architectural visualization. The techniques used to add textures to 3D models are also covered for various applications as well as advanced texturing beyond the basics. Scene setup and lighting as well as final render settings will be covered to make high-quality finished works. Even though animation is not a key topic in this book, at times it is useful for graphic designers to know, so a chapter has been dedicated to the basics of setting up simple animation. Upon completing the exercises and reading the chapters in this book, you will be able to create professional-quality works for various purposes.

Hardware and Software Requirements

Hardware requirements for 3D modeling, rendering, and animation are some of the most demanding for any type of computer usage. As a general rule, the best system for your budget is what you should use. Special emphasis should be given to three areas: CPU, RAM, and GPU (graphics card). A fast processor will allow you to make your finished rendered images more quickly and also let you work more smoothly in general. The amount of RAM you have will determine the size and complexity of scenes that you can work with and will also affect the resolution of the final images you can produce. The GPU determines the interactive abilities of your system, so a faster GPU will allow you to model more-complex objects, sculpt with higher-resolution models, and paint 3D textures with greater fluidity and resolution. Since RAM is usually the easiest thing to upgrade, I highly recommend adding as much as your system can handle to make your work more productive and enjoyable. For minimum requirements, see the website of your 3D program. If you are new to 3D and using modo (or trying modo as a new 3D solution), visit the Luxology website at `www.Luxology.com`.

Most modern computer systems will run modo and other 3D applications for at least basic functions relatively well. So as you begin to work in 3D modeling, rendering, and animation, no major purchases are required to get started!

How to Use This Book

The first section of this book, comprising Chapters 1–4, covers the basics of 3D scene creation. The first two chapters act as an introduction to 3D space, creating and moving objects, and the 3D viewports. Chapter 3 continues to cover basic texture and material creation as well as the creation and implementation of simple UV maps. Chapter 4 finishes this section with a basic look at lighting and rendering a simple but complete 3D scene.

Product visualization is the topic for the second section (Chapters 5–7). In the modeling process, subdivision surface modeling is covered in depth. Chapter 5 covers the processes of object creation and modification, including falloffs, action centers, and edge weighting. In Chapter 6, more-complex texture creation is discussed, including opaque, reflective, and transparent materials. Chapter 7 focuses on lighting appropriate to each type of material in a manner similar to real-world photographic lighting.

The third section (Chapters 8–11) covers modeling, texture creation, lighting, and rendering for architectural visualization. The projects in this section include workflows for both interior and exterior scenes. The modeling in this section is mainly polygonal but also includes the use of subdivision surfaces where appropriate. Efficient use of materials is covered to allow you to make and modify complex material settings quickly. Lighting and rendering appropriate to both interior and exterior scenes completes each of the projects in this section. Chapter 8 details the modeling process for an interior space. Chapter 9 adds texture and lighting to complete the interior visualization. In Chapter 10, the focus is the creation of a building exterior. This includes using reference images, blocking in basic geometry, and using the base geometry to create a complete and detailed model. Chapter 11 continues with the model created in Chapter 10 to add texture, lights, and scenery appropriate to this type of visualization.

The fourth section (Chapters 12 and 13) is aimed at helping you move beyond the basics covered in the first part of the book. Chapter 12 presents advanced material creation to allow you to improve and add complexity to the techniques covered in previous chapters. Post-processing is an important part of any 3D workflow. Efficient postproduction allows a 3D artist to make changes and adjustments in seconds that would take many minutes or even hours if another finished render had to be made. These skills will allow artists to adapt to client needs in a timely manner. Basic animation can be helpful for many graphic design projects, so Chapter 13 covers the basics of adding motion to the work from previous chapters.

How to Contact the Author

You can contact the author at www.sm-graphics.com. You may also go to the book's website at www.sybex.com/go/3dforgraphicdesigners.

CHAPTER 1

Working in 3D

The initial impulse for someone interested in learning 3D graphics is to immediately jump in and start building—trust me, I have been there! While there is definitely something good to be said about diving right in, if you spend a little time creating a foundation of skills, you will have less need to break bad habits later. Before you start creating anything, you need to understand the canvas you will be working with and the elements that will be used in the creative process.

This chapter covers the following:

■ **Understanding 3D space**

■ **Exploring a 3D scene**

■ **Navigating the modo user interface and its viewports**

■ **Maneuvering views and objects in space**

Understanding 3D Space

Maneuvering in 3D space can seem easy at first glance. After all, only one dimension has been added to the standard page layout, and that dimension is what we experience as we move around every day. However, believe it or not, the addition of this dimension can make navigation harder to get used to for the novice 3D artist. If you don't grasp some foundational principles from the outset, you can become disoriented and lose track of your model and scene. The addition of a third dimension adds much more than just another arrow on the monitor.

A standard page layout has two axes: x and y. If these equate to the horizontal and vertical directions, respectively, then the third axis (z) extends off the screen, toward the viewer (see Figure 1.1).

This works well for starters, but let's take it a step further and look at space in terms of a map or other top-down design. In this case, the plane defined by the x and z axes makes up the Cartesian plane. More specifically, the negative z-axis is north, and the negative x-axis is west, in relation to the middle of our workspace (see Figure 1.2).

The center of space (called the *origin*) will be the starting point for all of our design work unless we specifically need to work in a different area of the scene. Even in this case, it is often best to create an object at the origin and then move it to the desired location, because this will enable you to work with symmetry, easily locate objects, and move the mesh layer, which can then be reset or animated much more easily.

Figure 1.1

Three dimensions from a screen perspective

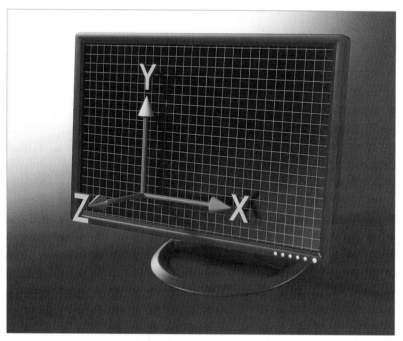

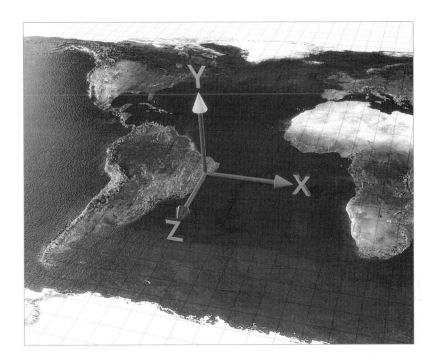

Figure 1.2

Three dimensions from a map perspective

Luxology's modo and many other common 3D applications work by default with the y-axis pointing up. Some applications, however, use z as the up-axis. The modo program allows you to customize this aspect in its preferences. Choose System → Preferences → Input → Accuracy And Units. From the heading marked Coordinate System, you can change the up-axis to z, y, or even x to suit your needs.

You can view a 3D scene through either an orthographic or a perspective view. An *orthographic view* offers a completely flat vantage point of objects, and placement without perspective of any kind. This means that objects located farther from the viewer will not appear smaller as the distance increases. An orthographic view is similar to a floor plan or elevation in architecture. Because it lacks the distortion associated with perspective, this type of view is ideal for creating and aligning objects.

Modo offers different interface layouts under its viewport tabs. Model Quad gives us three orthographic views and one perspective view. Although these two-dimensional views are initially set to Top, Front, and Right views, they can be changed to any other angle (Bottom, Left, or Back) and to views that include three-dimensional perspective.

Perspective views enable you to see objects and scenes with real depth. There are options to use an arbitrary perspective (the default in the Model Quad layout), camera perspective (based on the default scene camera or any additional cameras that have been added in the creative process), or light perspective. You can completely adjust the first option without changing the scene in any way, but it is important to note that both camera and light perspectives are tied to actual objects in 3D space. Thus, if you move these views, you will actually be moving (or rotating) objects and changing the makeup of the scene. Movement in camera and light perspectives can be reversed with the Undo command, but movement in the generic perspective view cannot be undone.

A common analogy is that if an Adobe Photoshop (or other 2D graphic) image is like a painting, a 3D document is like a sculpture. Two-dimensional art forms (digital and analog) use space, form, and color to create the finished image. Depth and dimension are created through color variation for simulation of light and shadow. Three-dimensional art adds volume to the mix, which offers more-concrete simulation of real light and shadow. Because 3D provides added levels of realism, you need to consider additional parts of the creative process in order to create compelling 3D art.

Exploring a 3D Scene

The next things to consider when beginning to work in 3D are the individual pieces of a 3D scene and the steps in the creative process that will result in a finished project (a model, still image, animation, and so forth). This space is filled with points, edges, and polygons that create the objects. Materials and textures control the appearance of objects. Lights add shading and highlights to the scene. The camera provides the vantage point for the finished scene. Let's look at each of these in more depth.

Points, Edges, and Polygons

At the heart of any model that you will create are three basic elements: points (also called *vertices*), edges, and polygons. Points represent a single location in space. The initial impulse is often to think of these as being analogous to pixels in a raster image, but this is not the case. Because a vertex represents a single point in space, it is infinitesimally small and therefore does not appear in a finished 3D render. The fact that the vertex is the basic building block of the 3D creative process means that it is visible only when several are combined to create edges and polygons.

Edges make up the next level in the 3D food chain. When two points are joined together, an *edge* is created. This edge now exists in one dimension and is still invisible to the finished rendering. Once again, this should not be confused with a line in a 2D image file. For both edges and points, it is better to consider a vector illustration without any line weight assigned. Individual points and lines may appear on the page, but they will not print unless some thickness is attached to these elements. To see these elements, you must have a combination of at least three of them (points and edges), which creates a polygon.

A simple triangle represents the *polygon* at its most basic level. Three points (with three edges connecting them) creates a defined surface. For the most part, four-sided polygons, also known as quads, will be the basis for your models. The reason for this will become clear when modeling is discussed in the coming chapters, but suffice it to say that many forms can be more easily defined by quads than by triangles. By combining and blending together multiple polygons, objects take form.

SINGLE-SIDED POLYGONS

Polygons exist as two-dimensional elements within the three dimensions of a scene. The flat surfaces of polygons face in a single direction. Just as the points are infinitesimally small, so polygons are infinitely thin. This means that they are invisible when viewed from the back. Some thickness must be added in order to make the geometry appear from all angles.

Materials and Textures

After polygons are created, they must be assigned surface attributes to define their appearance. A *material* contains the basic description of how light interacts with a surface. The key components of a material are color, reflection, transparency, refraction, absorption, and emission of light. A material creates these attributes at a very basic level that is defined by either a color or a percentage (depending on the attribute). Proper combination of these properties can create a wide variety of looks and styles. To achieve something beyond the evenly distributed appearance of a basic material, additional layers must be added.

Textures add additional detail to surfaces. Textures are made from either rasterized 2D images or mathematical functions that display colors based on various inputs. Images can be placed on the surface of 3D models and offer a high degree of customization. You can place details exactly where you want them and edit them either by using an application such as Photoshop or by using texture painting inside of modo. The downside of image textures is that they can become pixilated if they are not of a high-enough resolution. Mathematical textures (known as procedural textures) are free from resolution and have a fairly wide range of styles, from simple grids and gradients to complex fractal algorithms. These textures, however, cannot be edited directly, so placement of detail is random.

These textures can be used to modulate any aspect of a material. Color can be applied to add variation as well as to colorize reflections or transparent tints. Other possibilities include changing the amount of reflection or transparency, the shininess, the translucency, or even adding the appearance of depth on a surface (see Figure 1.3).

Figure 1.3

A few examples of possible textures

Lights

There are two methods of adding light to your 3D scenes: using computer representations of real lights (*standard lighting*) or casting light from the environment and textures in the scene (radiosity). The former is relatively easy to compute and delivers results more quickly. The latter uses more-complex computation and slows the finished image but results in lighting with more subtlety, nuance, and realism. Figure 1.4 shows a simple scene with standard lighting, and Figure 1.5 shows that same scene using radiosity.

Figure 1.4

A scene using standard 3D lights

Figure 1.5

A scene using radiosity for lighting

Traditional lights in 3D space use simple math to add brightness based on an area of influence, light color, and intensity. These lights come in common variations that are seen in most 3D applications. *Distant lights* (sometimes called directional lights) are similar to the sun. The actual light comes from infinitely far away and is adjusted by the angle it enters the scene. *Spotlights* simulate their real-world namesake. Point lights are similar to lightbulbs and cast light outward from a single point, in all directions evenly. *Area lights* are similar to soft boxes used in studios. Other lights are more situational and are covered in depth (along with the other lights mentioned here) in the following chapters.

Radiosity is also known as global illumination, because illumination comes from other angles than just the direct light source. In this lighting model, light is based on light particles (known as *samples*), which project into a scene much like real-world light. As with light particles in the real world, these samples can bounce off surfaces to provide illumination in areas where a light does not have a direct effect. Each bounce of light adds an order of complexity to the calculation and, as a result, causes a slower render time. Because light samples are blended together for the final result, using more of them creates a smoother finished look and (like other quality-improving options) slows the final image production.

In general, a combination of both lighting types gives the best quality and control. However, there are times when using just one or the other can deliver excellent results.

The Camera

The camera in a 3D scene gives the viewpoint for finished images. Cameras appear only as representations in the scene and will not appear when a finished image is rendered (so you don't have to worry about them showing up in reflections). Cameras offer control over many of the options that physical cameras have. You can control focal length, lens distortion, f-stop, film back, and shutter speed. Although they are simple, cameras are the window into a scene, so using them properly will improve your art and add impact to your designs.

Navigating the modo User Interface

Modo offers visual cues that enable us to keep things straight from an orientation standpoint. In the bottom-left corner of each viewport window, a small axis indicator shows, in the orthographic view, the two axes making up the plane of view. The colored lines point in the positive direction, and the colors always correspond to a particular direction (red for x, green for y, and blue for z). These same colors will appear in tool handles after modeling begins. In the perspective view, indicators are displayed for all three axes. As in the orthographic view, each line indicates the positive direction. In the perspective view, there is also a light gray square that aligns itself to the two axes that are most perpendicular to the current view. This square indicates the orientation of the work plane, which is presented in more depth in Chapter 2, "Creating Objects." By staying aware of these markers, we can more easily keep the scene aligned.

In addition to the axis widget, the perspective view offers a gradient background that helps to keep us from looking at our scene upside-down (or enables us to more easily get there if that is our desire). The background consists of a two-color gradient: a light blue-gray color indicates up, in the positive y direction (think of the sky); and a darker shade of the bluish color fills the negative y direction (indicating the ground). Because we spend a lot of time rotating around our objects to get the best view, staying aware of this gradient ensures that we keep our feet on the ground, so to speak.

Before you move on to navigating this space, you need to know about scale. You may notice that there are no document boundaries in 3D space as there are in a page layout document, at least not visible ones. What we do have to consider is the depth that the computer is able to re-create. This is called *draw distance*. A good example of a short draw distance can be seen in older racing video games. As you drive along a course and look into the distance, objects (such as buildings, trees, and mountains) will appear rather suddenly instead of growing from small points on the horizon. Although modern 3D applications are much more capable of handling distance than those games were, we want to keep draw distance in mind and create our scenes at (or near) actual scale.

In the bottom-right corner of each modo viewport, a display shows the scale of the small grid boxes. By default, the three orthographic views are linked together, but the perspective view is independent. Because modo uses physical scale for many aspects of lighting and texturing, it is important to check your scale as you begin to create models in 3D space. I have seen many students (and, regrettably, myself) create large sections of scenes only to realize that the pencil onscreen is as large as an oak tree—or bigger! In the 3D view, you will also see a light-colored grid that changes position and orientation based on your perspective. This is the Work Plane, and it is a huge help when you begin modeling objects.

Figure 1.6 is a breakdown of the modo user interface (UI) with labels for the features that are pertinent to this section.

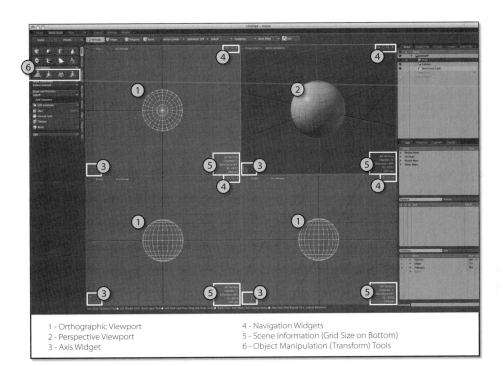

Figure 1.6

**The modo user
interface**

1 - Orthographic Viewport
2 - Perspective Viewport
3 - Axis Widget

4 - Navigation Widgets
5 - Scene Information (Grid Size on Bottom)
6 - Object Manipulation (Transform) Tools

Maneuvering in 3D Space

Now that you have a basic understanding of our canvas, you are ready to start maneuvering the viewports to get the best view for any part of the creative process. In a 2D application, the view controls are simple and are limited to panning, zooming, and rotating the canvas. Interestingly, the addition of just one more navigational feature significantly complicates the way that we interact with the environment.

Panning and zooming are relative to the perspective of the user, so they do not change much. There are two ways to pan in 3D space: by clicking and dragging on the pan icon in the upper-right corner of the view or by holding Alt (Windows) or Option (Mac) while clicking and dragging.

Zooming can be achieved via one of three methods. As with the pan tools, there is a zoom widget in the upper-right corner (this one zooms directly toward the center of the view). Holding Alt+Ctrl (Windows) or Option+Control (Mac) while clicking and dragging zooms based on the position of the cursor. By using this method with the right mouse button, a zoom area can be selected. This creates a box, and the area inside will zoom to fill the view after the mouse button is released. Finally, you can zoom with the scroll wheel. This last option is also context sensitive and will zoom toward the cursor position.

> While in the camera view, using the Alt+Ctrl / Option+Control key combo with the right mouse button adjusts the focal length of the camera and enables you to zoom in and out, as opposed to actually moving the camera in and out in space.

The real complication comes with rotation. Rotation works based on the combination of two axes. Consider the way we rotate in two dimensions. With the x and y axes covering the screen horizontally and vertically, we can rotate along the perpendicular axis (in this case, z). Because only two axes are present, we can rotate in only one dimension. The addition of the third axis adds two more possible rotation options, as we now have three planes to consider (xy, xz, and yz). As if this did not complicate things enough, there is one more point to consider: the center of rotation. In a 2D layout, we rotate relative to the center of the document. If we were to rotate only in relation to the origin (center of space), we would be very limited in our access to the work area.

To move freely in a 3D workspace, we need to rotate our viewport dynamically. So there are three types of rotation to deal with:

- Around the view focal point
- On a virtual tripod
- Rolling around the axis perpendicular to the perspective

Figure 1.7 shows a model from the front. Figure 1.8 shows that same object with the view rotated to show the depth of the model.

Figure 1.7

Flat front view of a model

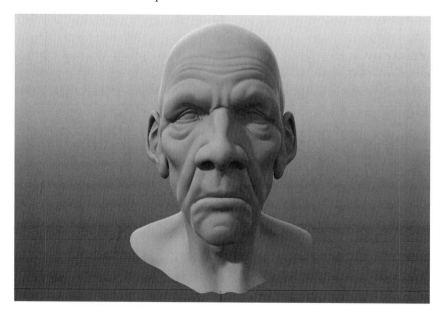

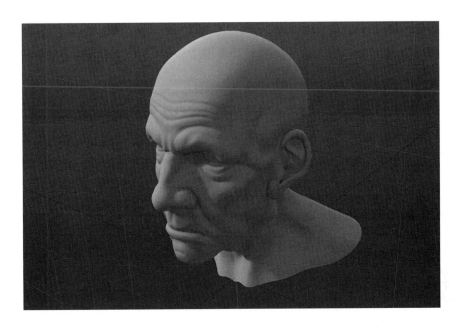

Figure 1.8

Perspective view of a model

First, let's look at the rotation based on the center. This type of rotation is accessed by pressing the Alt/Option key while clicking the left mouse button, or by clicking and dragging the rotation widget in the top-right corner of the viewport. As you drag up, down, left, and right, the view shifts around the focal point. This rotation technique keeps a set distance from the center of view and always faces that point in space until another focus is selected.

To rotate the view from a tripod, press Alt/Option and the right mouse button. The tripod rotation works exactly like a real tripod: the orientation of the view is changed, but the position of the view remains constant. This can be quite useful when working on large scenes or architectural interiors. One thing to remember is that this option is specific to views from cameras and lights, so the basic perspective view is not able to use tripod-based rotation.

QUICK TURNTABLE

Using the right mouse button to rotate in the perspective view enables the view to rotate on its own. As soon as you release the button, the view continues to spin, with the speed based on the mouse speed when the button was released. Moving slowly allows for slow and subtle rotation, while a quick flick of the mouse sends the view spinning rapidly. There is a falloff of speed, and then the view comes to rest. This can also be done with the question mark (?) key, which gives a single revolution around the scene.

Finally, by holding Alt/Option and using the middle mouse button (or scroll wheel button), the view can spin perpendicular to the viewport. This can be useful if the current view is upside-down and needs to be flipped over quickly. This is also useful when aligning a view that is slightly skewed and requires a minor rotation to see a level view of the scene.

The three movement tools work well when the view is focused on either your entire scene or a specific selection. The A key is used to center on all visible items in the scene. You can use the rotation tool to spin around your entire scene, and press Shift+A to focus on a selection. By selecting the area you are interested in or working on, you can center your perspective and rotate around the area in question. Subsequent chapters cover selections in more depth, but you can get started selecting by simply clicking and dragging across some surfaces (polygons, edges, or points) in your scene. After you select something, pressing Shift+A will center your view on that selection.

Practice: Navigating in Space

Open the file Navigation_Practice.1xo from the included DVD. Spend a few minutes moving around the scene. The more you navigate the space, the more comfortable it will become. Start by moving around the objects generally, and then choose various sections of the objects and manipulate the perspective until you get a good view of them. See if you can get a side view showing all three objects aligned in the view. Remember to utilize all of your newly learned navigation tools. Rotate, pan, and zoom your view. Use the A key and Shift+A centering tools to center your view on an area of interest.

The practice file starts out with the viewport containing all three objects from an angle, as seen in Figure 1.9. Try to duplicate the view shown in Figure 1.10. A few minutes practicing with a simple scene such as this will reduce frustration when you have a more complex scene and are still familiarizing yourself with the controls.

Moving Objects in 3D Space

Now that we have discussed moving around, you can begin to look at moving the objects that you create. There are three methods for basic object manipulation: move, scale, and rotate. Each of these tools (known as *transform tools*) can be activated by clicking the corresponding button on the left side, toward the top of the user interface, or by using their hot keys. Each transform tool has some quirks or additional features that will speed your workflow if you take advantage of them.

After a transform tool is activated, a property tab appears in the bottom-left corner. The fields in this tab enable you to enter numeric values for each of the transform functions as well as control of some additional options for each tool. These values can be entered by clicking in the fields and entering a value, by clicking on the arrows to increase or decrease the values by small increments, or by clicking and dragging the arrows.

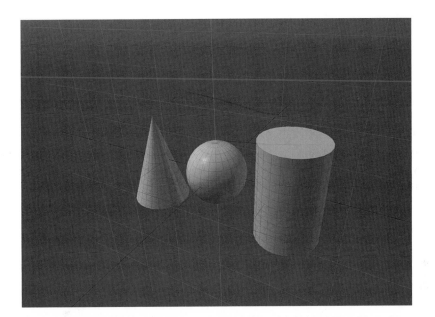

Figure 1.9
Starting perspective

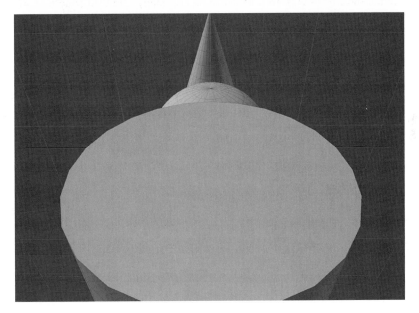

Figure 1.10
Goal after navigating the perspective view

If a value is entered in a numeric field, holding the Ctrl / Control key and pressing the Enter key (on the Mac, Tab or Enter) will change the other values proportionally. In other words, if all fields read 100% for scale and you enter 10% in the X value, the other two values will be changed to 10% automatically.

First, let's consider the Move tool. When activated, the tool handles appear at the center of the selection and show arrows that align to each axis (x, y, and z) and circles that float between the arrows in free space. For reference, the colors of the arrows correspond to the axis of movement. To move in a single axis, click and drag on the individual arrows. When the axis is active, the arrow turns yellow. Clicking and dragging anywhere but on the tool handles in the perspective view causes the handles to snap to the click point, and dragging moves the object on the Work Plane. Clicking and dragging on the circles moves the object perpendicular to the axis of the same color (red, green, or blue for x, y, and z, respectively). While in the orthographic views, clicking and dragging on the handles produces the same behavior as in the perspective view, and clicking off the handles moves the object along the plane in view. The hot key for the Move tool is W.

CENTERING THE TOOL HANDLES

The default behavior of the tool handles to align to a click point is controlled by the Action Center, which is set to Automatic when modo starts up. I cover Action Centers in depth in future chapters, but for now, if the behavior is difficult to use, you can click Action Center above the viewports and select Selection Center Auto Axis. This ensures that the tool handles remain in the center of the object and still align to the x, y, and z axes.

Next, let's consider the Rotate tool. The handles for this tool are circles. Each circle is colored like the circles on the Move tool. Clicking and dragging on these rotates the object perpendicular to the axis of the corresponding color. Again, the active handle turns yellow. Clicking off the handles snaps the tool to the click point, and dragging free-rotates the object in all directions at once. This type of rotation is very difficult to control and is not recommended. The gray circle that encompasses the rest of the handles rotates the view and rotates the object perpendicular to the current view. In the orthographic viewports, the gray circle is no different from the colored handles, but in the perspective views, this will rotate variably based on the angle of view. This is a pretty special use, but when it is needed, it can come in quite handy! Because rotation by its very nature takes place around an axis, there is no way to rotate in a single direction, and so there are no separate axes at one time (as with the Move tool). The hot key for the Rotate tool is E.

Pressing and holding the Ctrl / Control key prior to clicking a rotation handle causes the angle of rotation to snap to 15-degree increments. This is useful when precise rotation is required.

The Scale tool changes the size of the selected object or objects. The handles for the Scale tool are similar to those of the Move tool. The Scale tool is visually differentiated by the ends of the tool handles, which are boxes instead of arrows. Just as on the Move tool, the handles scale in one direction, and the circles scale in two directions (one plane). Clicking off the handles scales based on the work plane. Because clicking in open space still scales the object independently, it is usually preferable to use the planar circles and scale uniformly in two directions. Unlike the Move tool, the Scale tool has another behavior controlled by the cyan-colored circle at its center. This circle scales the object uniformly in all directions. The hot key for the Scale tool is R.

The Transform tool is a combination of all three of the other transform tools (Move, Scale, and Rotate). The question you may ask is, "Why on earth would I use individual tools when the Transform tool does it all?" The answer is that it really doesn't do it all. Although the tool does provide the basic function of the Move, Rotate, and Scale tools, it lacks several key options. The move portion of the Transform tool does not have planar handles. The scale portion lacks both planar handles and the uniform scale option. Because the tool has to act on one axis at a time, it is often more productive to switch tools and be able to scale or move in multiple (or all) directions at once. The Transform tool comes in most handy when making quick adjustments to both movement and rotation. Mostly, this comes down to a matter of personal preference. Try the tools and see which ones make the most sense to you and allow you to work the most efficiently. The hot key for the Transform tool is Y.

Tools in modo are "sticky" and will remain active until the tool is dropped. A tool can be dropped by pressing the spacebar, the Q key, or the Esc key. On subsequent presses, the spacebar will switch modes between vertex, edge, and polygon. The Esc key will (with additional strokes) clear out the tool pipe. I cover these functions in the next few chapters, but because the Q key is bound only to dropping a tool, it is often the first choice for this function.

Transform tools applied in vertex, edge, or polygon mode will alter the position of geometry and cannot be reset with the exception of centering the selection by using the Center Selected tool (under the transform tools on the left side of the screen). Objects can be centered on any axis or combination of axes. When transforming objects in Item mode, the changes are logged under the properties for the mesh layer. The Properties tab at the bottom-right corner of the screen contains numeric fields for position, scale, and rotation. After a change has been made, it can be adjusted or reset in the numeric fields on this tab.

Practice: Moving Objects

Open the file Transform_Practice.1xo from the included DVD. The file contains six cubes in individual layers. When in individual layers, each object can be moved separately when in Item mode.

1. Enter Item mode by clicking the Items button above the viewports (next to Vertices, Edges, and Polygons).

2. Select a layer either by clicking on it in a viewport or by clicking on it in the Items list tab on the upper-right side of the screen.

3. To move more than one layer at a time, Shift+click on it in the item list.

4. Use combinations of the Move, Rotate, Scale, and Transform tools to get the cubes into the positions shown in Figure 1.11.

Figure 1.11

Final position and orientation of the six cubes

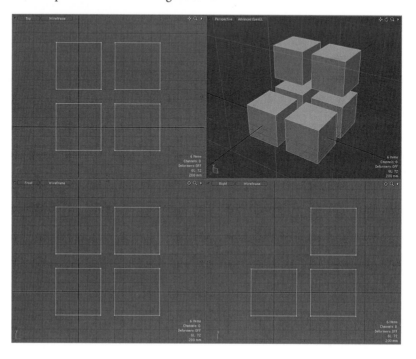

Review

This chapter has covered an intro to 3D space as well as the basics of moving around our viewports and objects in three dimensions. You have looked at some of the basic sections of the user interface (UI) and learned some important hot keys. With the large number of tabs, menus, and buttons in the interface, learning hot keys can be important to a quick and efficient workflow. Here are the hot keys, to recap:

- Alt+Shift+click / Option+Shift+click = pan view

- Alt+Ctrl+click / Option+Control+click = zoom view

- Alt+click / Option+click = rotate view

- A = center view on all visible items

- Shift+A = center view on selection

- W = Move tool
- E = Rotate tool
- R = Scale tool
- Y = Transform tool

In the next chapter, you will start creating 3D objects. You will look at object primitives and all of their options that enable you to control their size proportions and structure. This will also give you the opportunity to explore some additional sections of the modo user interface.

On the DVD for this chapter are practice files and videos covering the topics discussed in the previous pages. These short videos show tools and procedures in action to help accelerate the learning process.

CHAPTER 2

Creating Objects

Now that you have learned the basics of 3D space and covered the basics of a 3D workflow, you can start creating objects that will be the basis of your first scene. There are several ways to create models. In this chapter, you will learn to create basic shapes and to manipulate them to create more-complex forms.

This chapter covers the following:

- **Handling objects in modo**
- **Exploring the Work Plane**
- **Creating and editing primitives**
- **Making selections**
- **Using the transform tools**
- **Understanding action centers**
- **Using falloffs**

Handling Objects in modo

Individual elements of a scene are known as *items*. In modo, items consist of cameras, lights, reference images, meshes (models), replicators, and various types of locators (place-holders used for textures, organization, and animation). These can be found in your Items list on the upper-right side of the screen (see Figure 2.1).

Figure 2.1

The Items list shows a breakdown of all the components in your scene.

With the exception of mesh items, each of these elements make up individual items. Mesh items differ in that they act as containers for models. You can create as many models inside of an individual mesh item as you like. The simple analogy is a Photoshop layer. You can add as many pixels, shapes, and colors as you would like into a Photoshop layer, but there comes a point where it is easier to add multiple layers and flatten them (if needed) after the composition is complete.

When you create new geometry, it will appear in the currently selected mesh item. You can copy or cut geometry from one mesh item and paste it into another at any time. As you create models, you may find it easier to temporarily move sections of polygons into new mesh items to keep things separate and then place them back in one layer when the edits are made. Additionally, it becomes important to spread your models across multiple layers in order to group and organize them more effectively.

Exploring the Work Plane

One of the huge advantages to modeling in modo is the Work Plane. This simple but highly effective tool will help you to efficiently and accurately create geometry, keep your objects aligned in space, and even model easily on strangely angled surfaces. Initially, this plane is fixed, but the user can edit it to allow for numerous working options. In this first look, you will start with the basics and look at more-detailed options when they are needed in future projects.

The *Work Plane* is the light-colored grid in the 3D viewport. This grid snaps to align itself to either the xy, xz, or yz plane as the perspective rotates to stay roughly perpendicular to the current perspective. When creating geometry, this is key to knowing what is happening in the viewport. If you choose to create geometry in the perspective view, clicking in open space can be quite ambiguous. After all, the depth of the view means that the point you clicked could be represented by a nearly infinite number of points between the screen and the ongoing space that falls under your cursor. The Work Plane takes away the guessing. When clicking in a 3D viewport, new geometry will be created on the Work Plane. So, if you want to create something on the ground plane, you will need to rotate your view to be roughly downward facing (looking down the y-axis). This also works with the x and z axes.

The Work Plane can be manually positioned and oriented to any point in space or it can be aligned to any existing geometry. Re-orienting the Work Plane in this manner will not only rotate and position the white-colored plane itself, but will also reset the orthographic views to make them correspond to this new world center. At the beginning, the Work Plane will be a useful tool for making object creation simple, so it is best to get used to it now. In more-advanced modeling, good use of this option will enable you to create your models and scenes more quickly, with better accuracy, and increase your options when facing difficult modeling challenges.

Creating and Editing Primitives

All 3D programs offer a common array of basic geometric shapes known as *primitives*. Modo offers five basic primitives: cube, sphere, cylinder, cone, and torus. Each one has options that enable you to modify it to suit your needs.

Figure 2.2 shows modo's primitive palette. In addition to the five geometric shapes, the primitive palette contains the Tube tool, the polygon Pen tool, and the Text tool. Each of these can be created interactively or by dropping a preset-sized object into the current layer or a new layer. Simply clicking one of these icons starts the tool and enables you to interactively create any of the objects.

Holding the Ctrl/Control key and clicking a primitive icon creates a *unit primitive*. Figure 2.3 shows the change of icon indicating a unit primitive option. This is an object with the default dimensions and settings. Holding the Shift key and clicking a primitive icon creates a unit primitive in a new mesh item (see Figure 2.4).

Each primitive has its own options such as position, scale, and number of subdivisions. Also, there are additional meshes that can be created by clicking and holding the buttons for each item. Before you start modeling specific objects, let's look at each of the basic tools in the 3D arsenal. Understanding these will help you create more-complex forms in the future. For the most part, the function of these tools is self-explanatory, but there is a lot in the details that should not be overlooked.

The Cube Tool

When you activate any tool in modo, the bottom-left area of your screen will populate with a set of options specific to that tool. In this section, you will look at the options for the *Cube tool* (see Figure 2.5). The options for the Cube tool are pretty simple and serve as a good introduction to the way that tool properties work.

Figure 2.2

The primitive palette

Figure 2.3

Unit primitives are created by holding the Ctrl/Control key and clicking a primitive icon.

Figure 2.4

Holding the Shift key and clicking a primitive icon creates a unit primitive in a new mesh item.

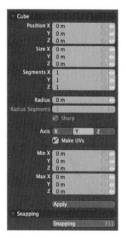

The first two sets of fields in the options menu correspond to the position and size of the primitive that will be created. If you enter these values manually and then click the Apply button, a cube will be placed in the scene that cannot be edited using this menu. By clicking and dragging in the viewports, you can manually draw out a cube. Right-clicking and dragging up and down, or right and left, adds or subtracts edges to the mesh vertically or horizontally, respectively. This can also be accomplished by changing the fields for Segments, only while the cube is in interactive mode. Adding Segments you to create lines or a grid to divide the faces of the cube.

> If you want to use numeric size and position but still adjust the other options interactively, simply start creating an object in the viewport and then enter values in the desired numeric fields. After you begin entering values, the object will adjust in real time.

Figure 2.5

The Cube tool options

The Radius field adds rounding to the edges of the cube to remove the harsh-looking edges. Radius Segments adds additional edges to make the rounding smoother. The Sharp toggle adds one more set of edges along the flat faces (adjacent to the rounded edges), and this enables the mesh to be changed to Subdivision Surface mode without losing its form. I cover subdivision surfaces (or *SubDs*) in a later chapter, but for now I can say that this is a method of creating smooth geometry that does not have the blocky nature of regular polygonal models. In most cases, when using SubDs, the rounding options will be irrelevant. However, if you intend to create a simple cube for your scene and will not add many modifications, using this method can be a good alternative to having sharp, artificial edges.

For the Cube tool, the Axis options do not really take effect because the cube is a simple six-sided object with no real horizontal or vertical area. You will see the Axis options come into play with other objects. The Make UVs option can be helpful if you do not intend to significantly modify the mesh. A *UV* is a 2D representation of the 3D object that can be used to attach images to your model. Think of this as a box the way it was printed: unwrapped and flattened out. As with subdivision surfaces, UVs are a subject for another chapter.

The final sets of fields (labeled Min X, Y, and Z and Max X, Y, and Z) give you another way to indicatethe size and position of the object. If you know the starting and ending boundaries for the object, these can be entered here. If the size and position have already been set in the Size and Position fields, the Min and Max fields will automatically be filled.

The Sphere Tool

The *Sphere tool* basics are much like those of the Cube tool, as you can see in Figure 2.6. Note that the second field denotes radius (not diameter), so entering 500 mm in these fields will result in a sphere that is the same size as a cube with 1 m in each dimension. Sides and Segments will divide the geometry much like the segments on the cube, but they are in relation to the poles of the sphere (in the default Globe mode). Sides are the radial divisions

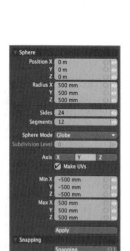

Figure 2.6

Sphere tool options

(longitude), and segments make up the concentric divisions (latitude). The Axis defines the direction that the poles face.

Unlike the Cube tool, the Sphere tool has several modes: Globe, Quadball, and Tesselation. These sphere types are illustrated in Figure 2.7. The Globe mode works as previously discussed and represents a typical polar globe. The Quadball is essentially a cube that has been divided and smoothed based on a subdivision level. The base level of 0 has only six sides and is smoothed via subdivision surfaces. Going up to level 1 will divide each of the six faces into four (for a total of 24 faces). Again, this is smoothed with SubDs by default. Increasing the subdivision level will always quadruple the number of faces making up the sphere. The positive side to this for a sphere is that it is made entirely of four-sided polygons and subdivides very well. On the negative side, it will always have a little bit of a cube shape (not an exact sphere). The Tesselation sphere is made entirely of interlocking triangles (think Epcot at Walt Disney World in Florida). At a base level of 0, the form is an icosahedron (consisting of 20 equilateral triangles). Each subdivision level will, like the Quadball, quadruple the number of polygons. Like the Quadball, this provides an even surface but does not smooth well with SubDs and must have the desired amount of smoothing added when the sphere is created.

Figure 2.7

Globe, Quadball, and Tesselation types of spheres

The Cylinder Tool

The *Cylinder tool* works much like the Sphere tool. Size is set by Radius fields, the Sides field defines the number of subdivisions around the Axis (radial), and Segments defines the subdivisions perpendicular to the Axis of the object. Overall, the Cylinder tool is quite simple. However, clicking and holding the icon for a second will reveal an interesting option: the Capsule tool. This tool acts as a hybrid between the Sphere and the Cylinder.

By choosing the Capsule tool, two additional fields are activated: End Segments and End Size. The former controls how far out the spherical cap will reach, and the latter determines how many edges define the cap. The Capsule creates smooth, even geometry and makes an excellent start for any model shaped like…well…a capsule! This does also come in handy with some more-complex models, where you can use pieces of a simple primitive to form the shape of something else. A good amount of modeling skill comes with recognizing the simple forms that add together to make up the shape of your desired form. The options for the Cylinder tool are shown in Figure 2.8.

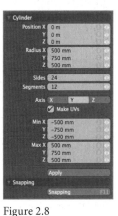

Figure 2.8

Cylinder tool options

The Cone Tool

Because the *Cone tool* carries the same options as the Cylinder tool, we will deal with it very quickly. Think of the Cone construction as a cylinder that is tapered to a point. Subdivisions work in the same way as for the Cylinder and the Sphere tools. This one is simple enough. Now we will move on to a primitive that has some overlooked options that make it quite useful and powerful.

The Torus Tool

The *Torus tool* is deceptively simple on the surface. However, by adjusting some of the settings, you can easily create a wide variety of forms. Figure 2.9 shows the options available for the Torus tool.

This tool, in its simplest form, creates a kind of donut. This can be useful for any ring-like shape. You can set the radius of the cross section as well as the size of the inner ring (Hole Size). In this case, sides are the divisions that run around the ring, and segments are the number of sides on the circles that make up the cross sections.

The real power of the Torus tool comes in the next two fields: Bulge Top and Side. The Bulge Top option enables you to flatten the cross sections, making them more like rounded squares. A higher value in this field makes for sharper edges of the cross section. The Side field makes the overall ring shape more square-like by moving the edges closer to the corners. These values can also be driven into the negative range in order to make a star-like shape for both of these categories.

Figure 2.10 shows some of these options in action. This very powerful tool can be the basis for a wide array of shapes. Spend some time exploring the options, and you will be glad you did!

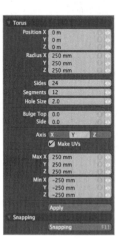

Figure 2.9

Options for the Torus tool

Figure 2.10

Some of the possibilities with the Torus tool

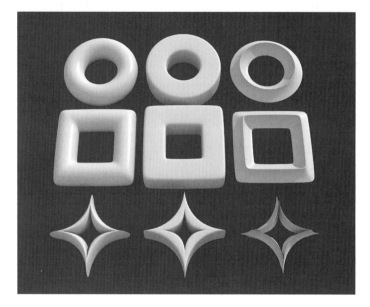

The Tube Tool

The *Tube tool* (see the options in Figure 2.11) acts a bit like the Cylinder tool, with individual segments added by clicking in space. Each click in the viewports adds another node to the tube. The position coordinates are specific to the current point that is indicated on the screen in yellow (all other points appear in blue). You can go back and adjust previously plotted points by simple clicking on them. New points will be added after the current point, so if you have made some changes to previous points, make sure you have reselected the last point before continuing—unless, of course, you want to add additional points between the ones you have previously plotted. The Mode defaults to Add, which lets you place points at will and adjust points if you click directly on them.

The other two settings (Edit and Delete) work pretty much as you would expect. The Sides and Segments settings work very much like those on the Torus tool, where Sides identifies the cross-section subdivisions and Segments defines the number of edges between the points. Radius once again refers to the cross-section radius. The next two options give you control over the way your shape terminates. Caps adds polygons at the beginning and end of the tube, while Closed creates one last segment between wherever your last point is located and the starting point. As with other primitives, there is an option to make UVs. The UVs created by the tool are quite good and will probably save you a lot of time.

Figure 2.11

Tube tool options

A new set of options appears with the Tube tool: Profiles. This option appears in other tools in modo, and you will take a more in-depth look at it in future chapters, but this is a great way to get an introduction to this powerful subtool. The idea behind Profiles is to add additional detail to an otherwise smooth surface (in this case, the body of the tube).

To add a profile to your tube, simply click on one of the thumbnails. The profile is based on the polygons between tube placement nodes (by default) or along the entire curve of the tube (by deselecting the Repeat option). Both the direction of the profile along the tube and direction of the inset can be changed by selecting the corresponding option boxes.

Because profiles are based on an abstract curve, not every one will work in every situation, but they are very worthwhile if you see one that is close to your intended form. This option is "sticky" and will remain on with subsequent iterations of the tool, but you can quickly remove it by clicking the left-facing arrow above the profiles themselves. Figure 2.12 shows an example of two simple tubes with and without profiles attached.

Along with the Tube tool is the *Solid Sketch tool*. The basic idea here is much like the Tube tool but with the option to create multipronged forms. This could be anything from a simple stick figure to a fairly complex tree. The options are simple. One setting enables you to move, edit, or rotate points, and the other deletes nodes that you have already created. Each node can have its own size and orientation that can be edited when the node is created or by going back and selecting a previous one. Auto Align and Auto Merge options adjust the orientation of each node and merge closely placed nodes in order to maintain smooth transitions, respectively. Finally, the Negative option creates a node that pushes against the previous node. This can be used to create indents in the model. It should be noted that this last option should mostly be used at the end of a chain, because adding new nodes after a negative node will cause holes in the mesh.

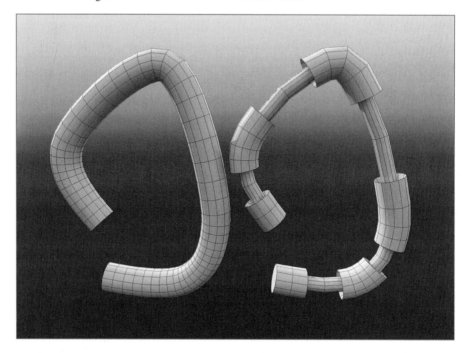

The Pen Tool

At its core, the *Pen tool* in modo behaves much like the corresponding tools in Adobe Photoshop or Illustrator. Plotting points creates a polygon. Position values are specific to the current point. Points that have already been placed can be edited either by selecting them in the viewport or by using the current point field. The tool is capable of creating regular polygons, subdivision surface shapes, spline patches, or simple placement of points and edges. For most purposes, the Polygon option will suffice (this can always be converted to subdivision surfaces after creation). Other simple options include the ability to flip the created polygon(s) so they face the opposite direction, to close the polygon, or to merge nearby vertices to keep a smooth surface. All of these options work very similarly to the Tube tool.

This default behavior, however, does not demonstrate the real power of the Pen tool. You can use the Make Quads option, for example, to create a strip of polygons. The first two vertices created will create one side of a four-sided polygon, and subsequent clicks will create edges that are perpendicular to the previous one, and this makes the foundation of a strip of polygons. This can be useful for blocking out shapes while keeping an even division of polygonal topology.

The Wall mode offers a fantastic way to build architectural geometry very quickly. Walls can be set inside, outside, or on both sides of the plotted points. The Inset option rounds corners on walls based on the distance (radius) entered. This rounding is highly useful in architectural situations. Segments will define the subdivisions that make up the rounding. Because architectural models like this are rarely made in SubDs, it is usually best to add ample segments to ensure a smooth appearance. You will look at this tool more when creating architectural visualization models in the coming chapters. Figure 2.13 shows the options for the Pen tool.

The Text Tool

To quickly add text to your 3D scene, the *Text tool* is a great option (see Figure 2.14).

This tool gives you basic control over the size and spacing of text. Characters you wish to display are entered into the Text field. Tracking is usually best handled visually, because it is based on real-world scale (meters, millimeters, and so forth) instead of points.

There are two handles for this tool in the viewports. The vertical handle adjusts the size of the text (proportionally), and the horizontal one adjusts tracking. The Location and Justification settings set the text in relation to the position of the tool.

Text is created based on multisided polygons (known as *n-gons*). The Split field determines whether the text polygons will be grouped together as one polygon (Line), by individual words, or even as individual characters. This will enable you to select words or characters separately, after the tool is dropped and modeling operations need to be performed. Because the Text tool has limitations to its layout and character styling, it is often best to import an EPS file if more control over the text layout is desired.

Making Selections

To modify objects in 3D space, you first have to select them. This may sound like an overly simplified statement, but making selections in 3D can be as nuanced and as complex as making complex selections in a 2D image. There are various forms of selecting objects and their components (vertices, edges, and polygons). By using all types of selections, you will be able to work with your geometry effectively. For the most part, selections work the same for vertices, edges, and polygons. The major exception is the double-click behavior. With vertices and polygons, a double-click selects all of the corresponding elements that are attached to the surface. In Edge mode, a double-click selects the entire loop of edges but not every edge on the surface.

Modo uses a click-and-drag selection style for all components. Using the left mouse button to click and drag over an area will select anything that you drag across. Using the right mouse button will act as a lasso selection: any polygons that are completely inside the lasso area will be selected. In a shaded viewport, the selections will be constrained to the visible elements. If you want to select all the way through an object, you can select it in a wireframe view. To add to a selection, hold the Shift key and click or lasso-select. To

Figure 2.13
The Pen tool options

Figure 2.14
Text tool options

remove something from the selection, hold the Ctrl/Control key and click on the elements you wish to remove. These two options are mutually exclusive, so you can add or subtract from your selection without fear of doing the opposite. Two additional keys that are helpful with general selections are the bracket keys. The [key inverts your selection, and the] key selects everything connected to your current selection.

Selecting Loops

Selecting loops can be an important part of a good modeling workflow. Selection of edge loops is simple. As previously mentioned, a double-click selects the loop. With points and polys, you have an additional step. The L key selects a loop based on your current polygon or vertex selection. To define the direction in Vertex mode, select two vertices. This defines the direction of the loop. Pressing the L key selects the loop. Loops of polygons can also be selected in the same manner. Setting the direction by selecting two adjacent polygons will enable you to invoke the loop selection with the L key. This also works with edges, but because an edge is made up of two vertices, the direction is already defined. The left- and right-arrow keys will select the next or previous loop of vertices, edges, or polygons on the object surface. Pressing and holding Shift along with the left- or right-arrow key will add those loops to your current selection.

Pattern Selections

Modo can also select in patterns to speed up the modeling and editing process. For example, you can select a polygon on a surface, skip a polygon, and then select the next polygon to set the pattern. The up-arrow key adds to the pattern, and the down-arrow key subtracts from the pattern. This works in instances where there is a simple, recognizable pattern. These patterns work with all components (vertex, edge, and polygon). Holding Shift along with the up- or down-arrow key expands or shrinks your selection, respectively. Expanding and shrinking the selections is done either by adding all of the adjacent elements to the outer edge of the selection or by removing the outer edge itself.

Another type of pattern is defined by two selected components. By choosing one polygon and then selecting another polygon that is a few polygons away, you can select everything between those polygons by using the Between command (from the Select menu) or with the Shift+G key shortcut. This works in a linear fashion for vertices, edges, and polygons, but polygon selection also has additional functionality. By allowing the two selected polygons to serve as maximum and minimum locations, the Between command will create a selection grid between those polygons in two dimensions along the surface (see Figure 2.15).

Selection Sets

Sometimes you will spend a great deal of time precisely selecting groups of polygons, edges, or vertices. In a dense mesh, this is a process that you would likely want to avoid repeating if possible. This is where *selection sets* come in extraordinarily handy!

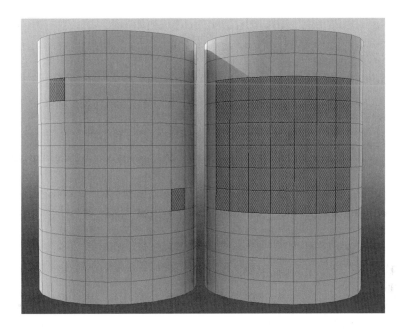

Figure 2.15

Two initial selections (left) and the resulting selection after running the Between command (right)

After deciding on a selection set, go to the Select menu and choose Assign Selection Set. A dialog box displays, enabling you to create a new selection set, add to an existing set, or subtract from an existing one. After you have created a selection set, you can recall that selection by using the Use Selection Set command from the same menu. From the command window, you can either add a set to your current selection or subtract a set from your selection. There is also a menu option to delete selection sets, but these take up very little memory, so it is often best to keep them just in case. Even if your model has changed since the set was made, this can still get you started and save a lot of time.

Statistical Selections

There is one additional method of making selections, which can be very useful in some instances. From the Lists tab in the lower-right corner of the screen, you can add to or subtract from selections by using a wide variety of options. This series of drop-down lists includes selections for vertices, edges, polygons, and items of all types. You can select based on material settings, groups, selection sets, or types of elements (polygon, subdivision surface, and so forth). You will use this method when we begin to create scenes; this way of making selections is better covered in depth after the context of the options have been discussed.

Making selections effectively is a core skill for any 3D artist. By knowing what tools you have at your disposal and using them creatively, you will speed up your workflow and increase the quality of your final product. Although not all of these tools will be needed on every project, knowing that they are there and how to use them will allow you the flexibility to work in the manner that best suits you.

Using the Transform Tools

In modo, as in all 3D applications, there are controls to move, rotate, and scale objects. These tools are collectively known as *transform tools*. When activated, tool handles appear onscreen. The handles for Move and Scale are a set of axes. The center of the axes represents the center point, from which the action will originate (known as the Action Center). The two tools are differentiated by the widgets at the end of each axis. For the Move tool, the axes terminate in arrows, and the Scale tool handles end in boxes. The orientation of the handles (the axis) controls the direction that transformations are applied when using the tool handles. These handles can be changed based on a number of parameters discussed in the next section. The Rotation tool consists of three circles (one for each axis). Like the Move and Scale tools, you can change the center and the axis by adjusting the Action Center.

Aside from editing using the axes, the transform tools also feature additional handles. The Move and Scale tools can be adjusted by using planar handles (the circles that are set in space at the intersection of the handle endpoints). Dragging these handles will adjust the selection in two dimensions at once. Additionally, the Scale tool features a central handle that scales in all axes simultaneously. Rotation is already based on a plane (as opposed to an axis, like the other transform tools) so there is not a different set of handles for planar rotation. There is, however, a gray handle for viewport rotation. This handle always rotates the selection on the plane that is perpendicular to the current perspective.

Understanding Action Centers

Another piece of the modeling puzzle focuses on the point from which transformations (move, rotate, scale) take place and the orientation of the axes that drive them. *Action Centers* are made up of a center and an axis. Action centers can be changed through the menu located at the top of the screen, next to the component modes (Vertex, Edge, Polygon, and Items). By default, the Action Center is set to Automatic, which initially places the action center in the middle of the selection, with the axes aligned with the world orientation. Clicking on the transform handles will re-center the center to the click point. In an orthographic view, this will center at the click point for the two dimensions visible in the view and at the origin in the third axis. In a perspective view, the tool will center to the position on the Work Plane under the mouse location. The axis will remain aligned to the world axes regardless of the center. Here is a quick rundown of the other action center presets:

Selection In this setting, the tool handles center on your current selection, and their orientation is based on the average direction the polygons are facing in the selection.

Selection Border This preset finds the open edge of the selection and is defined by the average position and orientation of that edge.

Selection Center Auto Axis This setting behaves much like the Automatic Action Center but will not be moved by clicking the transform handles. The center is locked to the center of the selection.

Element This very useful setting aligns the position and orientation of your tool handles to any vertex, edge, or polygon in your scene. Simply activate a tool and click on the desired element. The elements will be highlighted when the cursor rolls over, and the tool will align when clicked. This can be recentered at will.

Screen In this setting, the handles of a tool are aligned to be perpendicular to the viewport. The position of the tool will align to your mouse click.

Origin This setting does exactly as you would expect. The position and orientation of your tool snap to the origin and the world axis.

Parent If object hierarchies are established, this setting will align the tool handles to the center of the current object's parent item.

Local This setting applies transforms to each connected group of polygons based on their own orientation. This setting acts much like the Selection Action Center but enables you to transform large, individual selections en masse.

Pivot This setting centers the handles at the pivot point, which defaults to the origin unless the item is moved or the center has been repositioned.

Pivot Center Parent Axis This setting works like the previous Pivot Action Center but aligns the handles of the tool to the center of the current object's Parent setting.

In addition to these presets, you will notice drop-down menus for Center and Axis. These menus allow you to combine any two action centers: one to control the center of transformation, and the other to control the axis of transformation.

Using Falloffs

Falloffs fade out your tools and let you feather your transformations in various ways. These tools work like gradients, where one end is normal transformation, and the other end of the gradient is no transformation. The direction, shape, and slope of the falloff can be customized to fit the need at hand perfectly. The following is a list of the available falloffs:

Linear The Linear falloff works in a simple point-A-to-point-B format. Each end can exist anywhere in 3D space.

Cylinder This falloff fades out in two directions from the center to the outer edge. The falloff is projected along the third axis into space.

Radial This falloff fades off in all three directions.

Airbrush This falloff gives you some simple sculpting ability. Right-clicking and dragging enables you to set the size of the airbrush. Clicking enables the brush, and dragging "paints" areas where the falloff is active. Pressing Ctrl/Control while clicking and dragging inverts the effect of the falloff.

Screen This falloff works in a similar fashion as the Airbrush falloff, but the brush is not persistent. Size is set with the right mouse button. Clicking enables the tool, but dragging will simply use the Transform tool that is active. Subsequent clicks define a new area of transformation each time.

Element This falloff simply focuses on an individual vertex edge or polygon. The element is highlighted when the cursor moves over it, and clicking on the element activates the current tool for the selected element.

Noise This falloff is based on a simple fractal noise pattern (like Photoshop's Clouds filter). The only control given is the scale of the noise. This is an excellent method for adding random geometric detail very quickly.

Vertex Map This falloff fades based on the selected vertex map. Vertex maps are covered in another chapter, but suffice it to say that any individual vertex on the mesh can be given a percentage value, and this falloff uses those values.

Path This is one of the more finicky and esoteric falloffs. The idea is that a curve is plotted and a distance is set. The point where the curve intersects your surface will receive 100% of the transformations applied, and then at the extent of the distance set (controlled by the numeric field labeled Size), the falloff will equal 0%. This falloff works best if you set your Action Center to Origin, enable the transform tool of choice first, and then choose the falloff. After a curve is plotted, you will be able to use your transform tool(s) to add additional points to the curve and adjust the size while the tool is live. This falloff can be used to create nice, clean shapes on your surfaces, and it works quite well with the Move tool.

Lasso This falloff is quite simple and powerful. The setup is much like making a selection in Photoshop. You can choose from lasso (free-form), rectangle, circle, or ellipse shapes. Right-click and drag to define your area, set your soft border size if desired, activate your transform tool, and you will see the shape appear in the transformation.

Image This falloff requires that an image file be loaded into the image palette. After the image is loaded, click on the screen, and the image will fill the view. You can move the image position by using the center circle, scale it with the box on the left, and rotate it with the circle on top. After the image is in place, the brightness values will provide the falloff information. Brighter areas will have a high effect on the mesh, and darker areas will have little effect on it. You can choose a UV map for placement (if one is defined) instead of the viewport placement by clicking the Use Selected UV Map check box.

Selection Given a selected set of vertices, edges, or polygons, this falloff creates a border. The outer edge receives 0% and then fades in to 100% based on the number of steps that are set.

The Shape preset identifies the slope of the falloff. Linear creates a transition directly from 0% to 100% values. Ease-In weights the curve on the 100% side and scoops toward 0%. Ease-Out does the opposite and inverts the curve. Smooth creates an S-curve type of transition. The Custom setting enables you to set your own input and output values to precisely define the falloff shape.

Using falloffs will turbocharge your modeling workflow. Because most of these are easier to understand by seeing them in action, the enclosed DVD contains video demonstrations of each falloff type.

Practice: Modeling a Water Bottle

Now you will use the action centers and falloffs to create a simple bottle. This will be the start of a complete scene designed as a walk-through of a simple and introductory version of the entire 3D creative. This exercise will allow you to move on to more-complex scenes in future sections.

You will start by creating a cylinder. Begin with something roughly the size of a water bottle, so under Radius set the x and z values both to 35 mm and the y value to 100 mm. Additionally, this object should sit on top of the grid, so set the y position to 100 mm. Remember that a cylinder deals entirely with radius values, so setting that value to the same value as the y size will rest the cylinder precisely on top of the grid. For the Sides and Segments values, set both to 24. This will give you a good starting point for the geometry.

Next, you will use falloffs to create the tapers at the top, bottom, and middle of the mesh. To set the falloff for the top of the bottle, do the following:

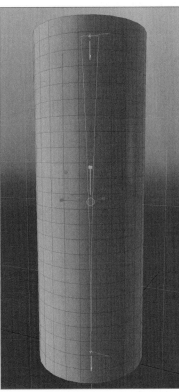

Figure 2.16

Setting the Linear falloff to the proper orientation

1. Click the Falloff option and choose Linear.

2. In the Linear Falloff properties (in the lower-left of the screen), set Auto Size to y. This creates the taper along the height of the model.

3. Enable the Scale tool by clicking its icon or using the hot key R. This shows the scale handles and makes the falloff appear.

4. Check the direction of the falloff and make sure that the wide end of the falloff is at the top of the model (see Figure 2.16). If it is upside down, click the Reverse button under Auto Size.

5. Now set the area of the falloff. Drag the lower falloff handle to an appropriate place on the mesh for the bottom of the upper curve of the shape (this corresponds to the Start y and End y values). I used 180 mm as the start point and 135 mm as the end point.

6. Now scale in on the x and z axes by using the green scale circle (this is easy to do from the top view). Set the scale to 33% for these dimensions.

7. Set the Shape Preset to Ease-Out so the shape is rounded instead of a flat angle.

8. Drop the Scale tool by pressing the Q key and leaving the falloff enabled.

To set the bottom falloff, drag the Start point down to a y value of 0 and the End point to a value of 15 mm. Activate the Scale tool again and scale x and z to 80%.

Now for the center inset area, you will use a slightly different technique:

1. Select two adjacent horizontal polygons in the middle of the bottle.

2. Press the L key to select the entire loop around the bottle.

3. Hold the Shift key and press the up-arrow key five times to increase the selection so that it covers the label area of the bottle.

4. Set the Falloff to Selection.

5. In the Selection Falloff properties, set Steps to 1 and Shape to Linear.

6. Enable the Scale tool, and scale the x and z axes to 92.5%.

7. Press the Q key to drop the Scale tool and then press Esc to clear the falloff.

8. Hold the Shift key and press the down-arrow key to decrease the selection by one row on either side of the selection.

9. Enable the Scale tool (R key) and scale on the y-axis to 135%. This tightens up the edges of the label area.

Now that the general shape of these three sections is set, you should have something resembling the mesh in Figure 2.17.

With this general shape formed, we can start creating a smooth shape and adding a few details. Modo features two types of subdivision surfaces: native (which we will call *SubDs* from here out) and the latest implementation of Catmull-Clark subdivision surfaces, which are technology from Pixar (referred to as *PSubs*). PSubs feature a more advanced method of creating smooth surfaces and offer a few additional controls over the model. The trade-off is in the speed department. PSubs tend to render slightly more slowly than regular SubDs. In general, this speed difference will be quite small and, for the purposes of this book, the difference is relatively negligible, so in most instances, we will use PSubs. The Tab key is the hot key to toggle SubDs on and off, and the Shift+Tab combination toggles PSubs.

With that quick explanation, press Shift+Tab to turn on PSubs. You will notice that the top and bottom of the bottle are now rounding off a bit

Figure 2.17

The general bottle shape after using the Scale tool on three sections

harshly. The top is easy to deal with: because the top of a bottle has a hole, simply select the polygon on top and cut it out (Ctrl+X or Command+X).

DELETING POLYGONS

For deleting polygons, use the typical "cut" operation. Pressing the Delete key gets rid of the polygon but keeps the vertices associated with the polygon. This command (known as the Kill Polygon command) is sometimes desirable when the vertices are needed, but the polygon is not. However, this method of removing polygons typically results in a large number of empty vertices and should be avoided.

The bottom of the bottle needs some added detail, so you will create that now. To start, you need to add more geometry to get the proper shape. To add the necessary divisions in the mesh, you will use two tools that are very common in 3D modeling: Bevel and Loop Slice.

Start by selecting the bottom polygon on the bottle. The Bevel tool is located in the Polygon section on the left side of the modeling tabs (the tabs running vertically in this window) or by pressing the B key. Bevel the polygon by dragging the red square handle inward. Set the inset to 15 mm. Then hold Shift and click in the viewport (not on the tool handles) to start a new bevel. This time, bevel in just 2.5 mm. This will create a good start for adding edges and will help keep the bottom polygon from becoming distorted.

N-GONS

Using *n-gons* (polygons with more than four sides) in modeling must be done carefully. Creating a ring of four-sided polygons around the n-gon will ensure that the surface renders properly. The second bevel will keep the bottom surface of the bottle clean and smooth.

Now you will use the Loop Slice tool to add a couple of extra edges around the bottom of the bottle. Select two polygons running around the bottom of the bottle, leaving the bottom polygon and the surrounding loop alone. Run the Loop Slice tool from the Mesh Edit section or with the Alt/Option+C hot key. Set Count to 2 and click the Uniform button in the tool options. This creates two additional edges around the bottom of the mesh. With this geometry created, selecting the right polygons and simply moving them can detail the bottom of the mesh very quickly. Do the following to start the bottom:

1. Select the bottom polygon and press Shift+up-arrow.

2. Select one polygon around the perimeter of the current selection.

3. Skip over three polygons and Shift+select another in the same loop.

4. Hold the up-arrow key until the rest of the pattern is selected around the loop.

5. Repeat steps 2–4 for two more polygon loops so that you have the center polygon, a loop around that, and six groups of three polygons surrounding the center selection.

6. Activate the Move tool and pull the selection up (y-axis) 8 mm. This creates six extensions that give the bottom of the bottle a defined shape.

With these steps completed, you should have a relatively complete bottle shape. Adding some thickness to the model and a little cleanup will give you something that you can texture, light, and render in the upcoming chapters.

Adding thickness is quite simple. Double-click on one of the polygons to select the entire model and activate the Thicken tool, which is located in the Polygon section. Click in the viewport to activate the tool. Set the Offset to –1 mm, leave the scale at 100%, and change Max Smoothing to 175 degrees (this will fix some errors at the bottom of the bottle).

Sharpening some of the edges comes next. Three sections need to be a little more crisp: the top at the opening, the borders of the label area, and the feet at the bottom. We will get into some more-detailed principles of subdivision surfaces in a later chapter, but for starters, adding some additional loops of edges will help to create sharper edges. Select two polygons around the top of the bottle and enable Loop Slice (Alt/Option+C). Set Count to 2 and set Mode to Symmetry. Click and drag until the edges are at 10% and 90% (for the symmetrical edge). Do the same thing with the angled polygon loops at the top and bottom of the label area.

For the feet, a slightly different approach is needed. Add a single loop slice at the bottom of the neck area to create a more creased contour. Finally, select the polygons that make up the flat bottoms of the feet and run the Bevel tool (press the B key). Drag the red square handle to scale in the newly beveled sections until you reach the desired shape (I chose about 3.5 mm). Repeat these steps on the inside of the bottle to firm.

Now, you will remove some edges to clean up the mesh a bit. Select the horizontal edges running around the middle of the label area. This can be done quickly by selecting one on each loop and then pressing the L key. Leave one loop on either side of the section to keep the geometry defined. Press the Delete key to remove these edges and create long, straight polygons connecting the two halves of the bottle. Once again, do the same thing to the inside of the bottle, and the model is complete! At this stage, you should have a model looking something like the one pictured in Figure 2.18.

ADDING EDGES AND THE THICKEN TOOL

These sharpening and cleanup actions can be done before thickening the bottle. However, these steps create some geometry that is very close together. Often this will cause serious problems with the Thicken tool that take a significant amount of extra time to clean up.

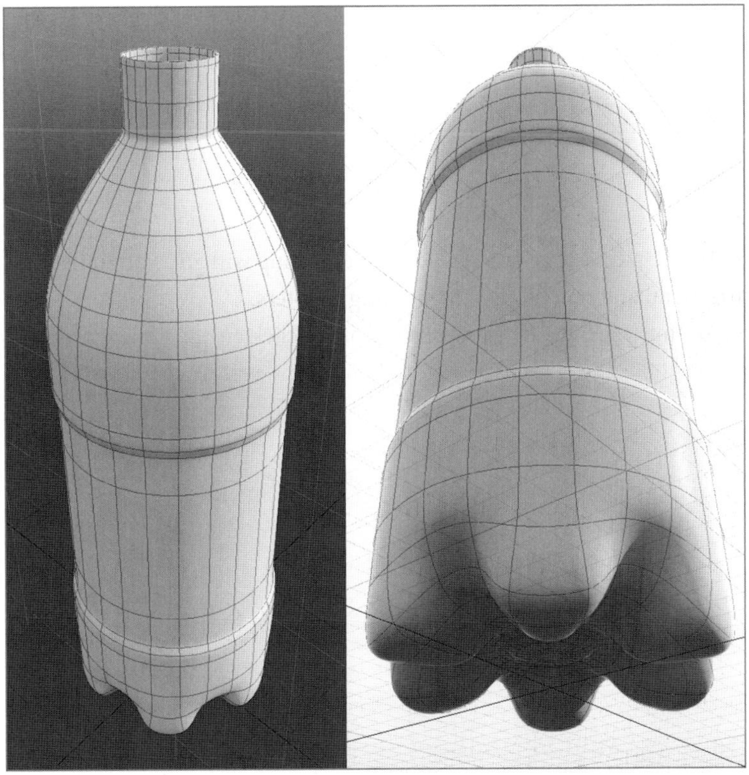

Figure 2.18

Bottle mesh at the end of this stage

Review

In this chapter, you have looked at the basics for creating 3D geometry. Let this chapter serve as a reference for the various types of primitive objects. Knowing the structure of primitives can be crucial to creating clean models very quickly. Using sections of these shapes will allow you to form complex meshes in a fraction of the time that it would take to create them from scratch.

Selection methods, Action Centers, and falloffs are amazing tools that we will revisit over and over. They will enable you to complete multiple complex operations quickly and precisely without spending large amounts of time fine-tuning the position of individual elements. By starting off learning to create shapes cleanly and with good polygonal flow (or topology), you will be able to make much more complex forms that are clean and precise.

FEATURE VIDEOS

The accompanying DVD provides video explanations of the process of modeling the bottle as well as a completed model for you to examine. The videos also contain some additional tips for adding some extra detail to the model.

CHAPTER 3

Creating Textures

With a model created, you are ready to make those polygons look like something in the real world. When light hits a surface, many things can happen. The light can reflect back, pass through, be absorbed into the surface, or even scattered. The result of this interaction between light and surface defines color, reflectivity, transparency, and other surface attributes. This chapter serves as an introduction to re-creating those effects on a 3D model.

This chapter covers the following:

- **Understanding surface attributes of real-world objects**
- **Creating textures in 3D**
- **Using texture layers**
- **Using UV mapping**
- **Creating image-based textures**
- **Understanding texture channels**

Understanding Textures in the Real World

When you look at an object in the real world, what you see is the result of light particles leaving a light source and bouncing around on everything that they contact. Opaque materials either absorb light or bounce light back at the viewer. Different materials absorb different wavelengths of light, and the wavelengths that are bounced back define the color of the surface. If everything is reflected, we see white; if everything is absorbed, we see black. A similar thing happens with transparent materials. However, much of the light passes through the surface instead of being absorbed or reflected. Mirrorlike reflection is associated more with the roughness of a surface. Surfaces that are smooth (on a microscopic level) will result in a visible reflection, while a rough surface will just show color. Figure 3.1 shows examples of opaque, transparent, and reflective (mirror) surfaces.

Figure 3.1

Photographic examples of opaque (left), transparent (middle), and reflective (right) surfaces

When surfaces have more than microscopic roughness, this reads as physical depth. A good example of this is concrete or tree bark. In cases such as these, the actual surface is made up of many small variations in surface color and quality. With the differences in texture packed closely together, the end result is one complex texture. Differences in highlight, reflectivity, color, and roughness give character to these materials that often have an organic or aged appearance. Figure 3.2 shows detailed close-ups of some rough surfaces.

Translucent materials are surfaces that act as a hybrid between opaque and transparent materials. Light passes through the surface, is scattered throughout the area underneath, and then either continues through the surface or returns toward the viewer. The result is a material through which light passes but that

Figure 3.2

Photographic examples of uneven surfaces

is still not transparent. This is similar to how a piece of white paper reflects all light but shows no reflection. Translucent surfaces are seen heavily in skin, wax, and even marble. Figure 3.3 shows translucent surfaces.

Figure 3.3

Photographic examples of three translucent surfaces

Creating Textures in 3D

To create believable 3D textures, you will start by looking at the basic settings available for a simple material. To set a new material, press the M key. This applies a new material to any selected polygons (in Polygon mode) or objects (if in Object mode). If nothing is selected, the material will be applied to everything in the current mesh layer. A field appears in the resulting pop-up window, enabling you to name the new material or to choose a material that already exists in the scene (by using the arrow to the right of the Name field). From this window, you can also set a basic color and other attributes. We will discuss Diffuse, Specular, and Smoothing settings shortly. The final check box sets the current texture as the default. When this texture is set, that material will be attached to any new object that is created.

After a material is set, you can adjust a wide variety of parameters from the material's Properties tab in the lower-right corner of the screen. However, editing materials is best handled in the Render tab. From this tab, you will have control of all texture attributes, access to material presets, a view of the scene, and a high-quality preview of the final render (see Figure 3.4).

Figure 3.4

Render tab

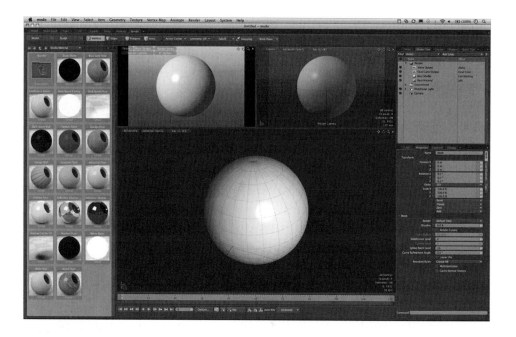

With a basic material, you can adjust uniform settings on any surface. The control over these attributes is broken into two main categories: Material Ref and Material Trans. Material Ref refers to reflective attributes or settings that return light to the viewer. Material Trans deals with settings for light that goes into or passes through the surface of the material. There are some additional settings in each of these categories that you will look at now.

Material Ref Settings

The Material Ref panel is broken into two sections: BRDF and Surface Normal, as shown in Figure 3.5.

The upper section of the panel is the BRDF section. *BRDF* stands for Brightness Reflective Diffuse Fresnel. The Diffuse Amount and Diffuse Color options work together in their effect. The Diffuse Color sets the basic color of the material. The Diffuse Amount is a multiplier of the Color, so setting this field to 100% will make it so a pure white light on the object will return the actual Diffuse Color. Setting the Diffuse Amount to 0% makes the object appear black. The settings between 0% and 100% mix black with the Diffuse color for the final output. The Conserve Energy option acts as a check for all of the material settings to ensure that exactly 100% of the light rays that hit the surface are reflected, absorbed, or transmitted. Generally, this effect can be achieved by balancing the amounts manually, and that way you can compensate slightly to better customize the look of the material.

The rest of the BRDF section deals with direct reflectivity in one way or another. Specularity is essentially the reflection caused by lights in the scene. Because conventional 3D lights placed in the scene do not appear as physical objects, they do not appear in reflections. Specular Amount controls the strength of this type of reflection. The Reflection Amount option controls the actual (mirrorlike) reflections on the surface. Because these two options actually control the same thing (just for different sources), it is usually best to keep the settings the same for both. For this reason, modo 501 has added the Match Specular option to make the reflection settings match the specular settings. The Fresnel option adds control over the reflective settings as the surface becomes more perpendicular to the viewer. Setting this option to a value of 100% will make the surface completely reflective on the perpendicular surfaces, and that amount will taper as the surface faces the camera. Figure 3.6 displays this effect in action.

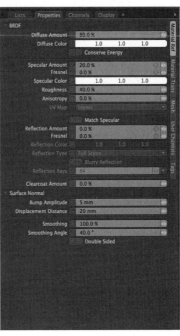

Figure 3.5

Material Ref properties panel

The Reflection Color option allows the reflections to take on a tint. When this option is set to white, reflections appear with coloration identical to that of the actual reflected object(s). Adding color to reflections tints them so that they appear less pure. Usually a good starting point for this setting is the same value as Diffuse Color with some white added in (lightened color). Varying levels from the diffuse color to white will work best for most objects, but setting Reflection Color to a color that is contrasting to Diffuse Color can produce some interesting effects. Reflections can be set to reflect everything or just an image-based environment. This is controlled through the Reflection Type option. Although full-scene reflections take longer to render, they give a more accurate and realistic effect—and with the speed of most modern computers, reflections calculate quickly enough to use this better-quality setting on pretty much every image.

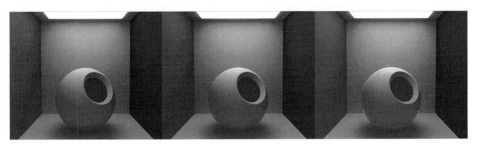

Figure 3.6

The Fresnel setting set to 0% (left), 50% (center), and 100% (right)

The Roughness and Anisotropy options control the sharpness and regularity of reflections, respectively. Roughness settings at low values are associated with a smooth surface that will evenly reflect the environment. A higher Roughness setting decreases the legibility of reflected objects and causes them to blur. Blurriness increases as the reflected object gets farther from the surface. When the Blurry Reflection check box is selected, the Reflection Rays field will become active. Lower settings in this field make rougher blurs that render more quickly, while higher settings increase the quality of the blur at the expense of render time. Anisotropy is the effect of stretched reflections. There are several ways to achieve this, and different techniques will be discussed later chapter. Generally, setting the Anisotropy option to positive percentages tightens the reflections on one axis, and setting the value to negative percentages causes the effect to occur perpendicular to a positive setting. This setting can be used to achieve anything from simple brushed metal to complex effects such as carbon fiber and machined metal.

BLURRY REFLECTIONS

Roughness will affect the reflection only if the Blurry Reflection check box is marked, but roughness will always affect specular reflections.

The final setting in the BRDF section is Clearcoat Amount. This setting will add a small amount of clear reflections that increase in intensity as the surface becomes more perpendicular to the camera (Fresnel effect). This adds a layered effect to the surface and works particularly well in conjunction with blurred or anisotropic reflections. A good real-world example of this is car paint. The initial coat of paint often has softly blurred reflections and contains the color information of the paint. On top of the base coat is a thin and highly reflective coat that gives the paint job its crisp, reflective appearance. Figure 3.7 shows the effect of Clearcoat Amount on a surface.

Figure 3.7

The Clearcoat effect set to 0% (left), 50% (center), and 100% (right)

The Surface Normal section affects the physical roughness of the material. The roughness created in this section is more like the visible unevenness on a surface. The Bump Amplitude option sets how strong bump materials appear. Displacement Distance sets the actual distance that a displacement map can be raised from the surface of the material. Once again, I cover this in depth later, but *bump* refers to a surface trick that makes the surface appear to have depth without actually adding to the amount of polygons in the scene. Displacement adds detail (and polygons) to the surface. These two options represent a typical trade-off between quality and speed. Displacements look more realistic on many surfaces but take longer to render. In many cases, a well-designed bump map will save valuable resources and still achieve the desired effect.

The Smoothing option makes shading even across polygons. When set to 100%, this option makes all polygons appear as one surface. A setting of 0% shows all of the individual polygons on the model and gives a faceted look. The Smoothing Angle is the threshold for smoothing to occur. If the angle between polygons is less than the smoothing angle, the polygons will be smoothed. Sharper angles will result in the appearance of a crease in the surface. Finally, selecting the Double Sided check box enables you to see both sides of a polygon. When this is not selected, polygons appear to be invisible when viewed from the back.

Material Trans Settings

While the Material Ref settings handle light bouncing off the surface, the Material Trans settings deal with, essentially, everything else (see Figure 3.8). We will consider each of these headings individually because the way light penetrates a surface can produce very different effects.

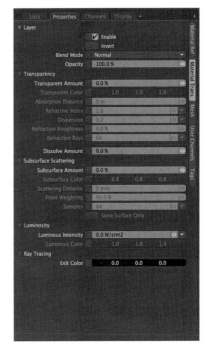

Figure 3.8

Material Trans properties

Layer

The Layer setting handles the general blending of a material with other materials. This is done in a way that should be familiar to any Photoshop user. The Enable check box is a toggle for the visibility of the material. When Enable is off, the base material will appear by default, but other materials can be layered underneath if necessary. The Invert check box simply inverts the Diffuse Color only. The Blend Mode option also shows the base material and blends the current layer based on the mode. The layer modes available in modo are as follows:

- Normal
- Add
- Subtract
- Difference
- Normal Multiply
- Divide
- Multiply
- Screen
- Overlay
- Soft Light
- Hard Light
- Darken
- Lighten
- Color Dodge
- Color Burn

These modes work very much like blend modes in Photoshop. The Opacity option is like a fader for the Enable check box (think of it as the Opacity slider in Photoshop if the Enable option is like Photoshop's layer visibility toggle).

Transparency

This setting handles the direct transparency of a surface. The Transparent Amount option sets the percentage of light rays that can pass through the surface. Transparent Color controls the tint of the transparent material.

Transparent materials have little to no diffuse amount, so coloration needs to be done via the Transparent Color option.

Absorption Distance sets the depth that a light ray has to travel into a surface before returning the Transparent Color. If a surface is thinner than this value, the material will be lighter and less colored than the Transparent Color. Thicker surfaces will look darker and more saturated. The default value of 0 mm will always return the Transparent Color and will not vary based on the thickness of the model.

Every transparent object (besides air in a vacuum) bends light very slightly. The amount of bending is called the *refractive index*. These are mathematical descriptions, and a list of many refractive indices can be found with a simple Internet search. Modo has some common indices on file. These preset values for the Refractive Index can be found by clicking the arrow to the right of the numeric field. When light is slowed (bent) through a material, it can also be separated slightly into its component colors. This prismatic effect shows a rainbow on refractions. This is a very nice effect that adds a lot of realism to transparent models, but it should be used carefully because it increases render time significantly.

Many transparent materials do not allow light to pass evenly through the surface. Fogged glass is a good example of this effect. Refraction Roughness gives the ability to blur the transparency of an object. Much like roughness affects blurred reflections, a higher value here will make the effect more blurry, while a lower value will make it less blurry. Refraction Rays controls the quality of the effect and, like many other options, a higher setting will result in a better quality with an increase in render time. This is a calculation-intensive effect, so it should be handled carefully.

Dissolve Amount controls the overall opacity of the entire material. This includes all settings, and unlike transparency, can make an entire object disappear. Setting Transparent Amount to 100% will leave refractions, specularity, any diffuse color, or reflection, but a setting of 100% in Dissolve Amount will make the material completely invisible. Figure 3.9 shows some of the effects of transparency settings.

Figure 3.9

The effect of various transparency settings

Subsurface Scattering

Some objects allow light to pass through without being transparent. This allows light values to be seen through the surface but will not show details on the other side. This translucent effect is often found in cloth, wax, skin, and many other surfaces. The reason for this effect is that when light hits a surface, it penetrates the material, but instead of passing straight through (or bending as with refraction), it is scattered in many directions. This physical phenomenon is known as *subsurface scattering* (or SSS for short).

Just as with transparency, an amount and color can be set for the effect. The Scattering Distance works much like Absorption Distance but sets the distance that light can penetrate a surface. Very slight values in this field will increase the perceived scale of the object, while higher values will make an object appear much smaller. A setting of 0 mm will result in simple translucency that is unaffected by the thickness of the object. The Front Weighting setting controls the amount of light that is bounced back toward the viewer. High values in this setting will cause most of the light to be scattered toward the front of the object and cause the Subsurface Color to appear relatively evenly across the surface. Low values will result in the Subsurface Color staying near the edges of the object. The Samples option works the same as with other quality settings. The final check box, Same Surface Only, will not calculate the effect on geometry with different materials applied. This can increase speed when selected but will result in problems with intersecting geometry.

Luminosity

This setting handles materials that glow or cast light on their surroundings. This self-illumination can simply allow materials to appear when no light is cast on them. When Global Illumination is enabled (which is covered in Chapter 4, "Lighting"), surfaces with Luminous Intensity added will actually light up nearby objects. This will allow for very advanced and realistic lighting. The value entered here is the same as values given to lights. A color can be set to tint the effect.

Ray Tracing

Light in a 3D scene can be bounced a certain number of times before stopping and resulting in black pixels. Modo defaults to eight bounces for reflection and eight for refraction (transparency). When that limit is reached, the light ray will not be calculated any further. Although this limit is often plenty, at times more depth is needed (especially with transparency). Because black portions of a transparent object can be a problem and turning up the number of bounces can result in increased render times, the Exit Color field can be used to cheat the effect of more ray bounces. The default setting of black will essentially do nothing, but setting a color here will make semitransparent areas that are tinted with the Exit Color. This is a simple workaround that can increase the quality and visual appeal of transparent materials without adding gratuitous amounts of time to the final render.

Using Texture Layers

By adjusting the various controls on a basic material, some excellent materials can be created. However, only so much can be done by using blanket, uniform adjustments to material settings. In many cases, values need to modulate across the surface of a 3D model. To increase the possibilities of textures, additional layers need to be added. Layers can be placed in the Shader Tree (see Figure 3.10). The Shader Tree is divided into four sections: Render, Environment, Lights, and Cameras.

Figure 3.10
The Shader Tree

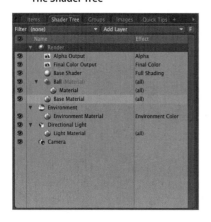

Render

The Render setting is the largest part of the Shader Tree. This setting contains Render Outputs (Alpha and Final Color by default), Shaders, Materials, and Textures. The Render Outputs option determines what images will be created when the final render is completed and can be an extremely powerful tool for creating complex edits after the image is rendered. Shaders handle the way light interacts with the scene and how the scene is rendered, and gives some fine-tuned control over scene rendering. Materials can be placed individually or in groups with textures. Textures can be mathematical or image-based and provide added detail to surfaces.

Clicking the Add Layer menu enables you to place additional layers. This menu includes categories for various types of textures, materials, shaders, and grouping options. There is no limit to the number of layers that can be added. However, when using many layers, it is often best to group items for better organization. Building layered materials will allow you to have a great deal of freedom and power to create any type of surface.

Environment

The Environment setting gives access to the background of your scene. The environment exists like a sphere that is infinitely far from the rest of the scene. By default, the environment consists of a gradient that has values shifting from up (positive Y direction) to down (negative Y). The gradient can be changed from four colors (default) to two colors or it can be a constant color. There are also options to mimic an overcast sky or daylight. Textures can be added to the environment just as they are on objects. Photographic environments can be used to add light and reflections, or they can act as a backdrop to the scene and add an extra level of realism to finished renders.

Lights and Cameras

Lights and cameras are listed individually in the Shader Tree. Lights have materials assigned to them, which can control the color of light and shadow much like the materials used on objects control the final color. In addition to color control, light materials also control the way the light interacts with different aspects of materials in the scene. Light can even be visible in the scene via volumetrics. This mimics the effect of light that hits tiny pieces of particulate matter in the air. Just like environments and materials, textures can also be used to control many aspects of the light.

The Camera options have many controls, just like real-world cameras. There are three types of cameras in modo: Perspective (like a standard camera), Orthographic (cameras with no perspective), and Spherical (shows everything around the camera position). For most purposes, the Perspective camera is the only one needed. Some effects can also be applied in the Cameras option. These include Depth Of Field, Motion Blur, and Stereoscopic. The details of lights and cameras are covered in future chapters.

Adding Procedural Textures

Textures provide a way of adding detail to surfaces. One of the ways to create this type of texture variance is by applying mathematical procedures to different channels that create more-complex effects. These procedural textures can be added as layers to any material. Values placed in these layers will override the settings in the main material (as discussed in the preceding section) unless opacity is reduced, a mask is added, or a blending mode is used. Many 3D applications employ a set of similar procedural textures, so we will look at the common ones first. These procedural textures can be added by clicking the Add Layer drop-down menu in the upper-right corner of the Shader Tree tab.

Basic Textures

The bottom section of the Add Layer drop-down menu is Textures. This contains a good variety of options to get started creating textures. Looking at the texture options in depth will make exploring the remaining options much easier because many procedural textures share common settings. The basic textures are Cellular, Checker, Dots, Grid, Noise, Ripples, Weave, and Wood. Examples of each of these styles and their settings are presented in the following sections.

Cellular

The Cellular texture uses individual "cells" that are placed by using a fractal algorithm to create a pattern. Circles or varying polygonal shapes can be used as the cells. Colors can be assigned to both the cells and the area between the cells (Filler Color). In addition, an alpha can be assigned to each of these, to fade the cell or filler to whatever is underneath the cellular layer. Cell Width sets the amount of space that a particular cell can take up. A setting of 100% will result in very little filler, and a setting of 0% will make the actual cells disappear. The Transition Width defines the amount of blur between the cells and the filler. Multiple iterations of the pattern can be added to increase complexity by increasing the frequencies. Frequency and Amplitude Ratios are used to affect the amount of downward scaling and the amount of fading applied to each subsequent frequency. The Smooth Tops function affects cellular color when multiple frequencies are in use. When set to

Figure 3.11

The Cellular texture

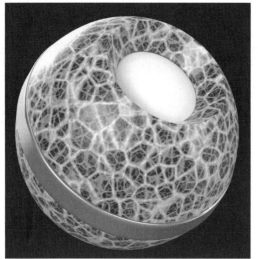

0, this function will allow all other frequencies to show through the cells; when set to a value of 1, nothing will show through (in this case, frequencies are visible only in the filler area). Setting the value higher will cause the additional frequencies to fade from the filler area as well. The variation settings (Value, Hue, and Saturation) add variation to individual cells. Finally, the Bias and Gain settings control the shift from foreground to background and the contrast, respectively. Figure 3.11 shows the Cellular texture.

Checker

The Checker texture is a simple pattern that is easy to control. Just like the Cellular texture, colors can be set for the two parts of the pattern, but these correspond to the grid squares. Alpha works the same way with these two values as with the Cellular texture.

The Type option decides whether the texture exists on a single plane (Square) or is projected from all directions (Cube). The Transition Width sets the amount of blur between checkers. Bias and Gain also work as they do with the Cellular texture. Figure 3.12 shows a simple version of the Checker texture.

Dots

For the most part, the settings for Dots are the same as those covered in the previous two textures. Dot Width and Transition Width control the size and amount of fade between dots and open space, respectively. For the Type setting, Square and Cube work the same as with the Checker texture. The added setting (Hexagon) staggers alternating rows so that the grid is offset. This can be useful for creating machined holes in a surface, which often do not follow a direct grid pattern. Figure 3.13 shows this hexagon version of the Dots texture.

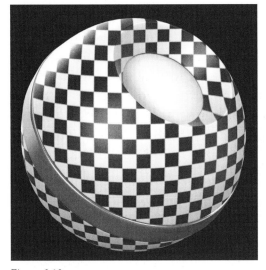

Figure 3.12

The Checker texture

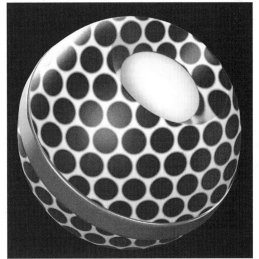

Figure 3.13

Hexagonal Dots texture

Grid

For the most part, the Grid texture contains options that are found in the other procedural textures discussed thus far. You can set Line Color, Filler Color, and their corresponding alpha amounts, which adjust the transparency of the element. There are settings for Line Width and Transition Width, and also controls for Bias and Gain. The Type menu allows access to grids that are Square, Hexagonal, and Cube. These options work similarly to the other textures already presented. In addition to these types of grid textures, the Grid texture adds Triangle (which consists of interlocking triangles) and Line (which projects lines on any one axis). Figure 3.14 shows the triangle Grid texture.

Figure 3.14
The triangle Grid

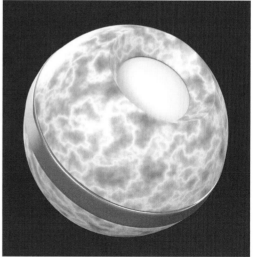

Figure 3.15
The turbulent Noise texture

Noise

The Noise texture behaves similarly to the Photoshop Clouds filter. This is a fractal pattern, which varies between two colors and two alpha values. The default type of noise is a fractal noise. This uses a mathematical algorithm to create the variation between the two colors. This can be set to varying levels of complexity with the Frequencies option. Setting Frequencies to 1 will result in a simple and smooth fractal pattern. Setting it to a higher value will increase the subtle variances in color. The Simple type of noise is essentially equal to the Fractal type set to a single frequency. The third type of Noise is Turbulence. Turbulence behaves more like the Difference Clouds filter in Photoshop. This final version has stronger peaks and is generally brighter in appearance than the other two types. Both the Fractal and the Turbulence types allow for control over the number of frequencies as well as the Frequency and Amplitude ratios. Smooth Tops gives control over the visibility of the underlying frequencies. These three settings behave nearly identically to the settings in the Cellular texture. Figure 3.15 shows a turbulence Noise texture with the default settings and Bias increased to 80%.

Ripples

As the name suggests, the Ripples texture can be used to create the effect of ripples on a watery surface. Controls are given for the value at the peak of the wave (Crest) and at the bottom of the wave (Trough). As with other textures, there is also a transparency control given to these values. Instead of using a fractal algorithm for creating the variance in this texture, there is a control for the number of sources that create the ripples. Wavelength controls the distance between each wave and is essentially used for scaling the effect.

Phase controls the position of the individual waves. This option has more to do with animation, because animating the Phase value will cause the ripples to move. The default settings of the Ripples texture are demonstrated in Figure 3.16.

Weave

Simple and versatile, the Weave texture can be used to create the effect of cloth, woven wood textures (such as a basket), or even chain-link fencing. In this texture, the color controls are for the color of the woven material and the color of the space in between. Yarn Width controls the size of the weave and inversely controls the size of the gaps. Roundness controls the depth of the woven material. So, a high value given to Roundness will result in deeper shadows and a heavier look, while a low value will flatten the appearance of the weave. The example in Figure 3.17 shows the weave texture with high Yarn Width and low Roundness values to create an effect similar to a woven basket.

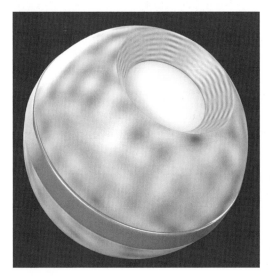

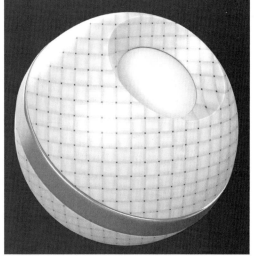

Figure 3.16

The Ripples texture

Figure 3.17

A simple start of a basket created with the Weave texture

Wood

Wood is the only one of the basic textures that defaults to colors that are not black and white. This is probably because the primary use for this texture is to create simple wood materials. As with the other textures, there are controls for two color values (which default to varying shades of brown) and corresponding alpha values (for transparency). This texture features more options than many of the other procedural textures, but they are relatively self-explanatory. Ring Scale gives simple adjustment over the size of the texture. Waviness and Wave Scale control the distorted variations in the ring texture. Graininess and Grain Scale give roughness to the surface and break up the smooth gradation between the Ring Color and Filler Color. Although the materials created with the Wood texture are rarely photorealistic, the precise control over scale, coloration, and distortion make this an excellent choice for creating the look of wood on secondary surfaces. You can see the default values of the Wood texture in Figure 3.18.

Additional Procedural Textures

In addition to the basic textures covered in the previous section, modo ships with a group of visualization-based textures labeled Bentley Procedural Textures and a more complex and varied group of procedurals called the Enhance: modo Textures. These textures offer the ability to create a vast array of materials. However, each of these textures relies on the same basic principles discussed in the previous section. In general, control is given to two colors, alpha values, and Bias and Gain. By adjusting the numeric values in each of these textures, you can create the look of water, tiles, metal plates, skin, and even digital readouts. Figure 3.19 shows a selection of these textures in action.

Figure 3.18

A simple wood material created with the Wood texture

Figure 3.19

Various procedural textures

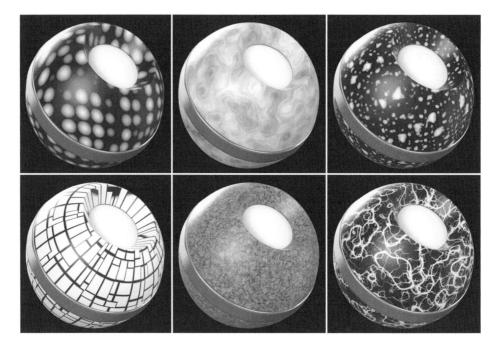

Processing

The Processing setting contains textures that are more closely tied to the geometry of the model than mathematical algorithms. For the most part, these textures are very simple, but the fact that they adapt to the geometry of the scene or model makes them extremely powerful and useful. Starting with the simplest, the Constant texture applies uniform color. The Process texture acts like a Photoshop adjustment layer and can modulate the values of any other texture layer in the scene. The Gradient texture allows you to create simple and complex gradients and to apply the values of the gradient to a wide variety of surface and texture attributes. The Weight Map texture applies color values based on user input per vertex as governed by a weight map. These textures are covered in depth in Chapter 12.

Occlusion is based on the principle of Ambient Occlusion. Ambient Occlusion uses even ambient lighting to emphasize convexity, concavity, slope, and even reflective angle. Because this texture is actually based on a type of lighting, control is given to the quality of the finished texture. Increasing the Occlusion Rays setting will smooth the texture and create a higher-quality finished look. Occlusion Distance controls the depth of the effect. Variance and Variance Scale enable you to disturb the smooth gradation and create a more mottled look. Spread Angle and Max Cavity Angle control the sensitivity of the texture to geometric contours.

Special

The textures and other options available in the Special setting give you control over both more-complex and more fine-tuned aspects of your scene and your materials. The Special setting houses shaders and render outputs. Fur materials enable you to create the look of hair, fur, and other fibers. Surface Generators work in conjunction with Replicators. This powerful scene-creation option allows you to place massive amounts of duplicated models in your scene without the tremendous decrease in render speed that has been previously associated with such scale and complexity. Replicators are covered Chapter 9.

Using UV Maps

Procedural textures are extraordinarily powerful. They enable you to create many types of materials and services, but they are limited because the placement of color values is based on mathematical algorithms that cannot be precisely controlled by the user. To make more-exact textures, it is often necessary to use images as textures. Unfortunately, images are two-dimensional, and their placement in three-dimensional space can be problematic because many models are much more complex than simple cubes, spheres, or cylinders. To gain precise control of two-dimensional texture placement in three-dimensional space, 3D models must be flattened into two dimensions. The creation of a two-dimensional representation of a three-dimensional form produces what is known as a *UV map*.

UV maps enable you to place image-based textures onto your models, gain additional control over the placement of procedural textures, and open up options for painting and sculpting directly on the surface of your models. Geometry created with basic shapes will automatically have an associated UV map. Simple edits to this geometry will not damage the UV. After extensive modeling processes are carried out on a model, the original UV map will lose its integrity and will need to be either repaired or replaced. Geometry that is created from scratch will often have no associated UV at all, in which case one will need to be created.

The UV tab gives access to all of the tools necessary for creating clean and usable UV maps. The basic idea behind the creation of these maps is similar to removing the wrapping from a package. This can be done via simple projection methods (that is, planar, spherical, or cubic) or by selecting edges that act as seams, where the model can be separated and unwrapped and flattened into two-dimensional space. After an initial UV unwrap has been performed, you can use various tools for aligning the individual pieces, edges, and vertices as well as optimizing the placement of these pieces. The creation of UVs can be a complex and daunting process, but it is essential to many aspects of the design process. The exercise at the end of this chapter includes a simple introduction to this technique. A more complex look at UV creation is featured Chapter 6.

Creating Image-Based Textures

Image-based textures will grant you increased artistic freedom as well as the ability to use photographs as textures. While images can be placed with simple projection methods, it is typically necessary to create UV maps for proper placement. Many times 3D models are created to showcase packaging, label design, or other two-dimensional pieces of work. In these cases, it is imperative for these images to appear on the surface of 3D models. Using image-based textures enables you to use your creative prowess in 2D design and showcase it in realistic 3D scenes, on 3D models, and in compelling environments.

In addition to the ability to incorporate graphic designs into 3D scenes, the use of photographic image-based textures can heighten the realism and believability of a 3D scene. Photographic textures can be used directly to color objects or to add variations in reflectivity, shininess, transparency, and even surface contour. Often, these variations can be subtle, but they allow for the inclusion of details that would be difficult, time-consuming, or even impossible to create with procedural textures or by hand. Figure 3.20 shows an example of a simple 3D scene that utilizes photographic textures and painted textures to create the final look.

Figure 3.20

A simple scene is greatly enhanced by texturing.

Using Texture Channels

Up to this point, you have looked at textures as they pertain to controlling the surface color of models and scenes. There is, however, much more to a compelling texture than the simple surface color. Textures can be added to any aspect of the material. This means that any of the attributes defined in the Material Ref and Material Trans properties can be controlled with texture layers. A list of available texture channels appears in the Effect column of the Shader Tree (located on the right side of the Shader Tree, opposite the Name column). By default, all textures are assigned to the Diffuse Color channel. Right-clicking on this setting enables you to access the other available channels and assign the texture to one of them. The majority of these attributes are found under the Basic

Figure 3.21

Texture maps set to (from left to right) Diffuse Color, Bump, Reflective Fresnel, and all three combined

Channels heading. In addition to these channels, there are headings to control attributes of Fur, Surface Particles (Replicators), Surface Shading (Bump and Displacement settings), and Special Effects such as stretched (anisotropic) reflections. Figure 3.21 shows the effect of textures in various channels individually and their combined effect in a finished material.

Practice: Texturing the Water Bottle

Now that you have a model to work with, let's take a look at the application of textures to the water bottle created in the practice section of the previous chapter. If you have not created a model and would like to practice the texturing process, an untextured model is included on the DVD for this chapter (Bottle_Texture_Start.lxo). The water bottle model will need several textures to complete its look. You will need opaque texture for the cap, transparent textures for the bottle itself and liquid inside, and an image-based texture for the label. You will also need to create a UV map for proper placement of the image on the label.

Setting Basic Materials

The first thing you'll need to do in order to set up textures for the scene is to assign individual materials to each section of the model. You'll need individual textures for the transparent bottle, for the opaque cap, and for the label, which will be placed on the bottle later. The liquid inside is placed on its own layer so it will be easier to assign any material to it. To assign materials to each of the individual sections of the model, follow these steps:

1. While in Items mode, select the Liquid mesh item.

2. Press the M key and enter a name for your liquid material.

3. Move to the bottle mesh item and enter Polygons mode.

4. Double-click on the cap to select it, press the M key, and assign the material.

5. Double-click on the bottle itself, press the M key, and assign a name for your clear plastic material.

6. Finally, double-click on the label and assign the material as with the previous sections.

Now you're ready to begin work on the material values themselves. To make material selection more intuitive, you can simply click on a section of your model in the Render Preview window, and its corresponding material will become highlighted in the Shader Tree. In a simple scene like this one, using Render Preview can save a significant amount of time. In a complex scene with dozens of materials, this can be an absolute lifesaver.

Start by clicking on the cap in the Render Preview window to access the cap material. This is a simple white plastic material, and the default settings are close to our desired finished result. The main difference is that the default material is too shiny for our purposes. Leave Diffuse Color and Diffuse Amount at their default settings. The specularity on a material such as this is very low, so change Specular Amount to 3% and Fresnel to 25%. Any highlights on this dull, rough plastic will be very broad, so increase Roughness to about 80%. As previously mentioned, reflection and specularity are essentially the same thing, so select the Match Specular option to keep these two values tied to each other, and select Blurry Reflection to soften the reflections on the material.

With the basic color and surface attributes set for this material, you will move on to add a procedural texture, to create a slightly rough surface. Choose Add Layer and select the Noise texture from the Textures heading. By default, this maps to the Diffuse Color channel. To better visualize the placement and scaling of this texture, leave it assigned to Diffuse Color for now. To create the desired scale, choose the Texture Locator section under the texture's Properties tab and set the size for X, Y, and Z to about 0.5 mm. When the scale of the Noise texture seems appropriate, right-click on Diffuse Color under the Effect channel and from the drop-down menu, select the Surface Shading section and assign the texture to Bump. At first, the effect will be far too strong. To decrease the amount of bump, go to the Texture Layers section and set Value 2 to about 3%–5%. Your material should now look something like the image shown in Figure 3.22.

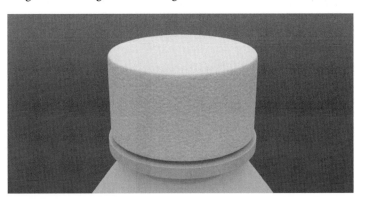

Figure 3.22

The cap material

At this point, it would likely be beneficial to hide the liquid mesh layer to more clearly see the transparent plastic material. Simply click the eye icon next to the liquid mesh item to hide that layer.

Click on the bottle itself to begin work on the clear plastic material. Most transparent materials reflect very little light back to the viewer, so decrease Diffuse Amount to about 5%. Because the plastic is clean and smooth, it will likely hold some reflections. Setting Specular Amount to 10% and Fresnel to 60%, and selecting the Match Specular check box should give a good start to this plastic.

Next, switch to the Material Trans section to start work on the transparent attributes of the material. Although this is a relatively clear plastic, a setting of 1 will likely look a bit too invisible. Setting Transparent Amount to 95% will give a more appropriate result. With this done, the bottle will all but disappear from view, showing only slight reflections. Setting the Refractive Index will cause the bottle to reappear. A good refractive index for many simple plastic materials is around 1.4.

For this very basic plastic, leave the other settings zeroed out. Before moving on to the liquid material, select the label material and select the Double Sided check box. Because the label will require a UV map, you will deal with that object last, but it may be important for it to be visible before you continue. The now empty bottle should look similar to the image in Figure 3.23.

Now select the Liquid layer (make it visible if you have it hidden) and select the corresponding material in the Shader Tree. Many of the basic settings for the liquid material will be similar to the clear plastic material. To use the clear plastic material as a starting point, right-click on that material in the Shader Tree and choose Copy, and then right-click on the liquid material and choose Paste. By simply changing the refractive index to 1.33 (the refractive index of water), the bottle will suddenly appear to be full. If you want the appearance of a different liquid (for example, a colored one), changing the Transparent Color setting will allow you to achieve a wide variety of styles. Figure 3.24 shows the bottle filled with water.

Creating a UV for the Label

To place an image on the label, you will need to create a UV map that will tell the two-dimensional image how to map onto the three-dimensional object. Start by clicking on the UV tab; then under the Lists tab (on the middle right-hand side of the screen, where you find the Properties viewport), select the Texture UV map under the UV Maps section. What you'll see in the UV space on the left-hand side of the viewport is pretty much a mess. When the initial shape for the bottle was created as a cylinder, a clean UV map was created with it, but throughout the modeling process, that UV map has been essentially rendered useless.

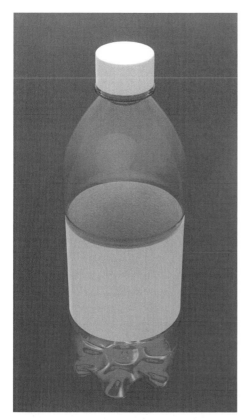

Figure 3.23

A plain-labeled, empty bottle

Figure 3.24

The bottle is now full of water.

To use this UV map, you first need to clear out all of the existing data. On the left side of the screen, you will find a list of possible operations for the creation and editing of UV maps. One section is labeled Edit UVs. The options in this section enable you to copy, paste, and delete existing UV data. Refrain from simply using the standard cut or delete operations, because these operations will remove the polygons (your mesh) rather than simply removing the UV maps. Use the Edit UV options to delete all of the existing UVs.

> After deleting the existing UVs for the bottle, you will still see some geometry and UV space. These are the UVs used for the liquid mesh layer. By moving to that mesh layer, you will be able to delete or edit those UVs as well.

Now that you have a clear UV space, double-click on the label polygons and press Shift+H to hide the rest of the model. Because you need to map an image onto only the label, you can hide the rest of the bottle while working on the UVs.

Because the label consists of a simple cylinder shape, the UV Projection tool will be your best option for creating clean UVs. Click the UV Projection Tool button at the top of the UV controls. Set the Projection Type to Cylindrical and the Axis to Y. Click in the UV workspace to engage the tool.

With these settings, the label geometry will be spread out evenly across UV space. One problem with this type of UV creation is that the resulting UV map will not be at a one-to-one ratio with the geometry in 3D space. In other words, the image map will be stretched (in this case vertically) to fill the square UV space. Even though the label will fit cleanly into a square, the image map that you need to create for this label will still need to be proportionate to the label in 3D space. It is possible to scale the UVs vertically so that the label in UV space is proportionate to the label in 3D space. However, this will result in a mapping issue when creating the image for the label: to fit the label into the square UV space, there will be empty space in the UV map. You would need to create corresponding empty space in any image map that would be mapped using this UV. By creating an image map that has the correct proportions for the label model and using the stretched UV map, the image will map correctly onto the model. After creating this UV map, you can add a new texture layer to the label material and load the image map for the label. When this is completed, your model should look something like the image shown in Figure 3.25.

Figure 3.25

The bottle with all textures in place

Review

This chapter presented many of the basic options available for creating materials on 3D models. In this chapter, we have really only scratched the surface of material creation, but we've still laid the groundwork for techniques that will be used to create more-complex and compelling textures in future chapters. After reading this chapter and completing the practice section, you should be able to do the following:

- Create opaque materials
- Use procedural textures to add depth to materials

- Adjust color and reflective properties
- Create transparent materials
- Adjust the tint to transparent objects
- Create simple UV maps
- Apply image maps to 3D models

You will continue to look at material creation in future chapters and use a layered learning approach to add complexity to the simple techniques learned here. Remember that there is no limit to the number of layers that can be added to the material, and no limits to the number of materials that can be applied to a model. Observing and analyzing real-world materials and photographic references will enable you to create more-realistic textures in 3D. Take the time to examine the world around you, and you'll begin to notice the attributes of color, reflectivity, transparency, and so forth in the objects that you see every day.

CHAPTER 4

Lighting

When taking a good photograph, lighting is key to the overall success of the image. Studio shots require a careful balance of light and color created by artificial sources. Outdoor (natural) shots are dependent on getting the right time of day, a good surrounding environment, and even the careful use of reflectors and bounce cards to get just the right touch. To achieve good results in 3D, similar (but not identical) considerations must be taken.

This chapter covers the following:

- **Using lights in 3D**

- **Creating a basic light setup**

- **Setting up environments**

- **Rendering basics**

Using Lights in 3D

As discussed in Chapter 1, "Working in 3D," there are essentially two broad categories of lights in 3D. One is a category of lights that attempts to mimic physical lights and is based on mathematical descriptions of a light's brightness, direction, and size. These "traditional" lights (sometimes referred to as *Direct Lights*) have been used in 3D computer graphics for many years. The other category of lights is based on a much more complex math called radiosity and results in a much more natural and realistic lighting. Although the typical trade-off between quality and speed exists between these two lighting categories, there is actually a more complex issue here since the two types of light can be used in conjunction. In many cases, a combination of traditional Computer Generated lights and radiosity is needed to provide the best results.

Traditional 3D Lights

Even though traditional CG lights lack a fair amount of complexity and realism, it is important to understand them in order to effectively light a scene. The types of lights found in modo are common to many 3D applications, and understanding them in modo will allow you to work effectively with lights in most 3D applications.

Before looking at individual types of lights, we should note that all lights have three options for the type of shadows they cast. The default (Ray Trace) offers realistic and accurate shadows. Deep Shadow Map provides slightly faster render times. The None option disables the light shadows entirely. In most cases, the default setting is used because the speed increase of using shadow maps is minimal on modern computer systems. Next, we will consider each of the types of lights available in modo and how to use them effectively.

LIGHT RADIUS

All traditional lights have the option for a Spread Angle or Radius (to soften shadows and lighting). With these options enabled, two fields become active: Samples and Simple Shading. Samples controls the overall quality of shadows by using more light rate calculations to smooth the effect of the softened light. Simple Shading (on by default) calculates the light from a single point for Diffuse and Specular values. Disabling Simple Shading causes Diffuse and Specular values to be calculated along with the shadows. This results in higher quality and slower render time.

Directional Light

The default light type (*Directional Light*) essentially mimics the sun. This type of light does not originate from anywhere inside 3D space but rather from a point infinitely far from the scene. As a result, the position of this light is irrelevant, and the only parameter of light placement that needs to be considered is its direction (angle).

The Directional Light has control over Radiant Exitance (brightness), Shadow Type, and Spread Angle (which controls the sharpness of shadows). These controls are typical to most lights. Because this type of light does not originate from within the 3D space, there is no calculation of decay. This means that objects closer to the light will not receive any difference in brightness than objects farther from the light.

One of the most powerful options for the Directional Light is the ability to turn it into a Physical Sun light. When Physical Sun is enabled, a new set of controls decides the angle color and quality of light emitted. By setting the time of day, the day of the year, and the physical location on Earth, this option can mimic real daylight on Earth. By default, the negative Z direction is designated as North, but this direction can be shifted by using the North Offset field. Figure 4.1 shows an example of a Physical Sun model in a simple scene.

Figure 4.1

Physical Sun can mimic real daylight in a scene.

HIDDEN OPTIONS

Because screen size differs from computer to computer, some options and properties may not always fit onscreen. When this happens, modo places a small box with a pair of arrows in the bottom-right corner of the particular panel. Clicking this icon will show the hidden options in a pop-up window.

Point Light

The *Point Light* is a simple light, which differs significantly from the Directional Light. With this type of light, angle of rotation is irrelevant because the light is emitted in from a single point in space. If the Directional Light is similar to the sun, the Point Light is analogous to a lightbulb.

Like the Directional Light, the Point Light has control over its intensity. Because the Point Light comes from one point in space, it also has a falloff assigned to it. By default,

Falloff Type is Inverse Distance Squared. This is the way light naturally falls off in the real world. The setting can also be changed to Linear falloff (which makes light fall off more gradually) or None (which makes the light intensity equal at any distance from the source).

At its default settings, light is emitted from an infinitely small point in space. The Radius controls the volume of space from which the light is emitted. Increasing this value makes the light come from a sphere as opposed to a point. This increases the realism of shadows by making them softer. Figure 4.2 shows the effect of a Point Light with default settings and with the Radius setting increased.

Figure 4.2

A Point Light with default settings (top) and with the Radius increased (bottom)

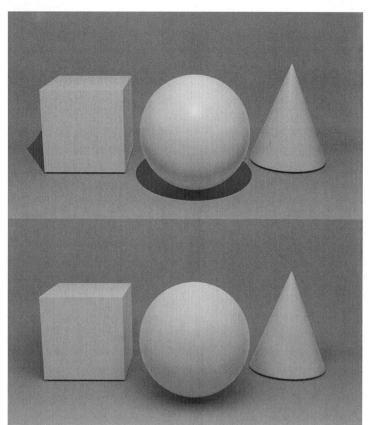

Spot Light

The *Spot Light* derives its name from its real-world counterpart. This light shines from a single point in space in one direction and has an angle that defines the area illuminated by the light. Like the Point Light, the Spot Light has controls for Radiant Intensity, Falloff Type, and Radius. The Spot Light also controls the angle of the cone from which the light is projected and the Soft Edge, which gives a slight blur at the edge of the projection area (similar to the effects of a real-world spotlight). Figure 4.3 shows examples of Spot Lights with different Soft Edge settings.

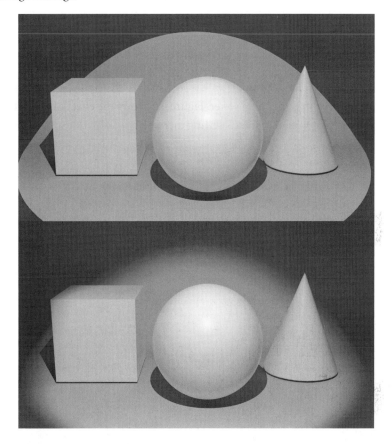

Figure 4.3

Spot Lights with no Soft Edge (top) and with Soft Edge set to 5° (bottom). Note that the shadows are unchanged because the radius has not been changed.

Area Light

The *Area Light* offers a great degree of realism but is also one of the more expensive types of lights to render. By default, the Area Light (as the name suggests) casts light not from a single point in space but from a defined area. By adding dimensionality to the projection area of the light, the Area Light produces even lighting and soft shadows more easily than other light types. Area Lights can be either rectangular or elliptical in shape. Width and height of these lights can be set with the corresponding fields or by dragging on the handles on the light in 3D space (see Figure 4.4).

Because Area Lights come from more than a single point in space, the number of light rays must be set by adjusting the Samples field. The default setting of 64 will produce relatively balanced results (speed versus quality), but for many finished renders, a higher number of samples is required. Figure 4.5 demonstrates the realistic lighting produced by Area Lights.

Figure 4.4

Area Lights can be scaled by using the handles shown here.

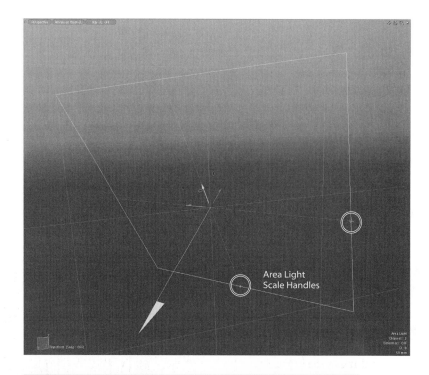

Figure 4.5

Area Lights offer realistic, soft illumination and shadows. Simple Shading (top) renders all but shadows from a single point, while disabling this option results in softer shading with slightly longer rendering times (bottom).

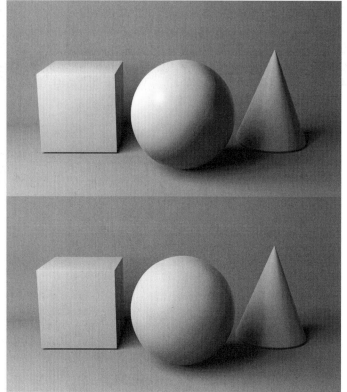

Cylinder Light

The *Cylinder Light* is a derivative of the Area Light. This type of light projects from a volume of space as opposed to a point or a plane. The cylinder can be defined by Length and Radius to produce soft and even lighting in a scene. The behavior of this light is in many ways similar to a florescent lightbulb. As with the Area Light, setting Samples to a higher value will produce a smoother and higher-quality result. The intensity of the Cylinder Light is directly tied to its radius. Increasing the radius of this light type results in higher intensity. Figure 4.6 shows an example of a Cylinder Light with Simple Shading disabled.

Dome Light

Another variation of the Area Light is the *Dome Light*. As its name suggests, the Dome Light projects light from a hemisphere surrounding the scene. Using the Scale tool can control the size of the hemisphere. With the Dome Light, Simple Shading will typically produce unwanted results. Instead of enabling this option, it would be beneficial to use a Directional Light with a high Spread Angle. The Dome Light projects light from all around the scene to simulate global illumination, where the environment itself illuminates everything in the scene. Often, the number of samples required to create an even lighting solution will result in a relatively high render time, so in most cases using global illumination is preferable. The Dome Light does produce soft, realistic lighting from a highly diffused source, as seen in Figure 4.7.

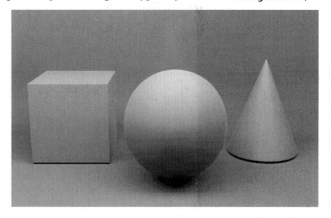

Figure 4.6

The Cylinder Light (with Simple Shading disabled)

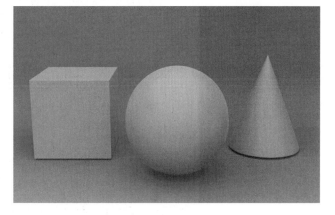

Figure 4.7

The Dome Light

Photometric Light

A *Photometric Light* is an interesting type of hybrid between a Point Light, Area Light, and real-world engineering. The brightness, falloff, and light pattern are governed by mathematical lens descriptions known as Illuminating Engineering Society (IES) files. These files act as a digital profile of how the light behaves in the real world. As a result of this mathematical description, an IES light casts extremely realistic light and adds subtle nuance to an image. IES files can be found freely on the Internet, and some are available on the sharing section at www.luxology.com.

In addition to the realistic falloff properties of Photometric Lights, volumetric lighting can also be applied. It should be noted, however, that these lights might require a high number of samples to render cleanly, so they should be used carefully to avoid extensive render times. The example in Figure 4.8 shows a simple scene led by a traditional Spot Light in the same scene with the Photometric Light.

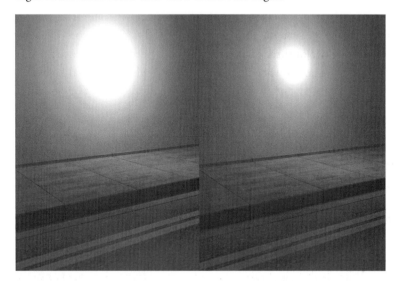

Figure 4.8

A scene with a Point Light (left) and the same scene with a Photometric Light (right). Note the subtle effect on realism that the Photometric Light adds.

Radiosity

Lighting with *radiosity* (or global illumination) adds a significant amount of photorealism to a 3D scene. Radiosity takes into account light from indirect sources (such as the environment), light bouncing/bleeding, and light from luminous textures. There are a number of ways to light a scene when using global illumination. Scenes can be lit with traditional CG lights as main lights and allow bounce lighting to create secondary illumination. Lighting can come from simple environments such as gradients or even from image-based light files using high dynamic range (HDR) images. Lighting can even be produced by increasing the Luminous Intensity on textures for objects that would cast light in the real world (TVs, computer screens, and so forth). Most realistic scenes take advantage of this type of rendering to produce accurate and natural light.

Doing the following enables global illumination: On the Shader Tree tab, click the Render item. Click the Properties tab, and then click the Global Illumination section on the right side. Under Indirect Illumination, select the Enable option. After Indirect Illumination is enabled, the default settings for Global Illumination will provide you with a decent radiosity solution. Next, you will take a look at several samples that utilize different methods of lighting using radiosity.

Traditional Lights and Radiosity

First, you will look at a scene that uses a Directional Light set to Physical Sun and multi-bounce global illumination to fill out the lighting. The Indirect Illumination properties allow you to set the number of bounces the light ray can take to illuminate the scene. With Indirect Illumination enabled, the default is one bounce, but this can be increased to achieve more-accurate lighting. Take into account the increased calculations required as the number of bounces increases, because higher numbers will adversely affect render time. Typically, the setting of two or three bounces is all that is needed to produce the desired lighting effects. In the example shown in Figure 4.9, a single Directional Light is pointed into the scene through the window, and global illumination is used to fill out the light and the rest of the room.

Figure 4.9

Physical Sun with global illumination added produces good daytime lighting.

Environmental Lighting

In many ways, environmental lighting produces a similar effect to that of the Dome Light. With the basic Environment Material (4 Color Gradient), Ambient Light will be cast using the colors of the gradient. By default, the environment is set to a 4-color Color Gradient with different colors for the zenith, sky, ground, and nadir. The colors used in the default gradients are neutral grays and will give balanced lighting to the scene.

The image shown in Figure 4.10 is a good example of a simple global illumination. Note that this example looks similar to the previous example of the Dome Light (just a little brighter). Because global illumination has been highly optimized in modo, this scene actually renders much more quickly with this complex lighting style. The Dome Light sample took around 1 minute and 15 seconds to render, whereas this sample took less than 15 seconds. In addition, much of the grain and noise from the Dome Light to render is not present in the global illumination sample.

Figure 4.10

**Basic global illumi-
nation using the
default environ-
ment gradient**

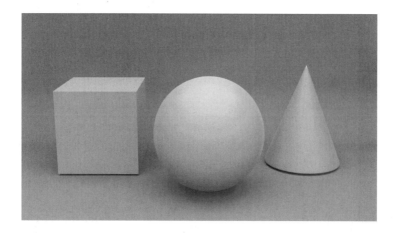

Image-Based Environments

Just as images can be used to create textures on objects, images can be used as the environment for a scene. By using high dynamic range images (or HDRIs) to surround the scene, lighting can be derived from the environment. Modo ships with several preset environments. These presets can be accessed in the Preset tab on the left side of the render interface. Simply click on the drop-down menu at the top of the preset viewer and choose Environments. Environment presets are broken into three categories: indoor, outdoor, and studio. Each of these categories holds various ready-made HDR environments. Double-clicking on one of these presets adds it to the scene. If global illumination is already enabled, the image will automatically light the scene. Figure 4.11 shows an example of a studio preset in use.

In addition to these preset environments, many photographic HDR environments can be found for free or purchased on the Internet. It is also possible to create your own HDR environments by using bracketed photos at various exposure levels.

Luminous Textures

Adjusting the Luminous Intensity setting on a material causes it to cast light on the scene when global illumination is enabled. This can be used to simulate a broad range of lighting—from television and computer screens, to photographic lighting equipment, to simple glowing objects. Because the global illumination engine is highly optimized, using luminous objects and textures can produce high-quality, realistic, and fast rendering solutions.

In the example shown in Figure 4.12, Environment Material is set to Constant, with Zenith Color set to black, and Luminous Intensity on the sphere material is increased to 1.0. The resulting image is lit entirely by geometry and the luminous texture. With a little bit of adjusting, the sphere can appear to be a lightbulb illuminating the scene.

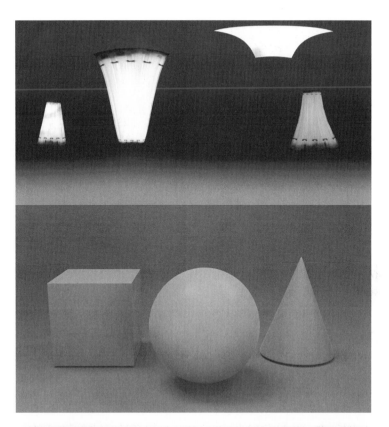

Figure 4.11

A studio environment (top) and the scene with this environment in use (bottom). Note the subtle reflections from multiple light sources.

Figure 4.12

A simple luminous material on the sphere causes it to light the scene.

In Figure 4.13, a gradient was added to the luminous amount that allowed it to fall off gently toward the edges of the sphere, and some reflections were added to give it a glassy finish. In many cases, lighting with this type of global illumination will produce more-polished results in less time. For instance, each of the renderers with the glowing spheres took less than 20 seconds to complete.

Figure 4.13

With some adjustments, the sphere is turned into a glass lightbulb for added realism.

Figure 4.13

With some adjustments, the sphere is turned into a glass lightbulb for added realism.

Creating a Basic Lighting Setup

Now you will look at how to set up the lighting in a simple scene. To start off with a firm grasp of lighting concepts, you will first explore lighting using traditional lights alone and then move on to more complex lighting schemes. The ability to light a scene properly by using traditional lights is key to understanding the lighting process and the tools at hand. In this section, you will create a simple three-point lighting scheme. After the lighting rig is created, you will move on to see how this setup can be adapted to provide a wide variety of lighting options.

Using Three-Point Lighting

Three-point lighting is a common technique in photo, film, and 3D. As the name suggests, the light that is set up (or rigged) consists of three elements: the key light, the fill light, and the rim light. The key light provides the majority of the illumination for the scene and is typically positioned in front of the subject (seen in Figure 4.14). The fill light is used to balance out the shadows left by the key light. Finally, the rim light is added to accentuate the silhouette of the subject. In Figure 4.15, the fill light is shown alone. In Figure 4.16, the rim light is demonstrated.

The use of these three lights will allow you to cleanly and evenly illuminate your model. Any two of these lights will illuminate the model but leave heavy shadows or undefined boundaries. Figure 4.17 shows various combinations of these lights.

The fully illuminated model is shown in Figure 4.18. The lighting rig in this image uses a key light behind and to the left of the camera, a fill light coming from the right side of the camera, and a rim light nearly opposite the camera and on the far side of the model.

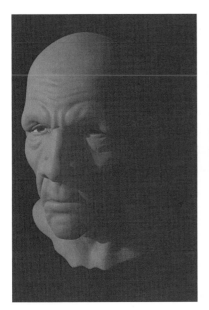

Figure 4.14

The key light alone in a scene

Figure 4.15

The fill light (isolated) balances out the shadows left by the key.

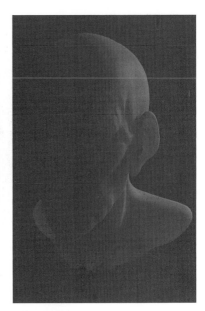

Figure 4.16

The rim light provides definition to the subject.

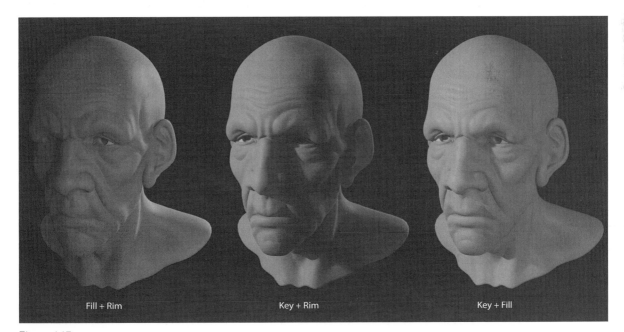

Fill + Rim

Key + Rim

Key + Fill

Figure 4.17

Various combinations of these lights will illuminate the subject but leave undesirable shadows or undefined edges.

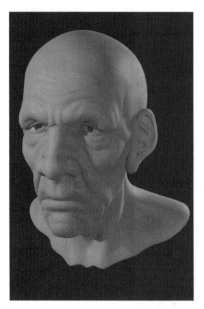

Figure 4.18

**The fully lit model
with all three light
sources enabled**

With this in mind, you will now build a simple three-point light rig and then add some controls that will make it easier to edit. Open the file 3_Point_Starter.1xo from the DVD. This is an item from the stock content with some texture and details added. To start, set up the scene by doing the following:

1. Right-click on the Directional Light that already exists in your Items list, and choose Change Type → Spot Light. This turns your existing light into a Spot Light, which is aimed at the origin. Leave the default settings on this new spotlight. This will act as your key light.

2. Right-click on the Spot Light in the Items list and choose Duplicate.

3. In the Action Center tab, choose Origin and rotate the light roughly 135° on the y-axis (green rotation handle) and down about 90° on the x-axis (red handle).

At this point, your scene should look something like the image shown in Figure 4.19.

Now you can create the rim light by duplicating one of the existing lights and rotating it behind the subject. I chose to rotate the light upward to fill in the shadows at the top of the head and over the shoulder of the model. Figure 4.20 shows the addition of this light. Note the definition added to the top of the head and shoulder.

With these three lights in place, you should have a fairly even lighting scheme. To add more interest, you can adjust the color, intensity, and radius of these lights. Making these adjustments will provide a less washed-out appearance and help to accentuate the details on the model.

Let's start by looking at color. Move to the Shader Tree tab and click the arrow by your first Spot Light to reveal the light material for your key light. As we've previously discussed, light materials can be changed and edited just as the materials on objects. Click on the color swatch for the light color, and the color picker appears (see Figure 4.21). The color values can be changed by using the color wheel as with any other material, but one control that is of particular importance to light color is Kelvin, which controls the color temperature. Selecting lower Kelvin values will result in warmer colors, while higher numbers will push the color into the cooler color tones. Alternately, color temperature can be set by clicking the Set Temperature (Kelvin) button. This option enables you to enter the color temperature numerically, but it will not give you a real-time preview the way changing this value on the color picker does. Continue to adjust the color values for the fill light and the rim light until you've come to a color balance that you like.

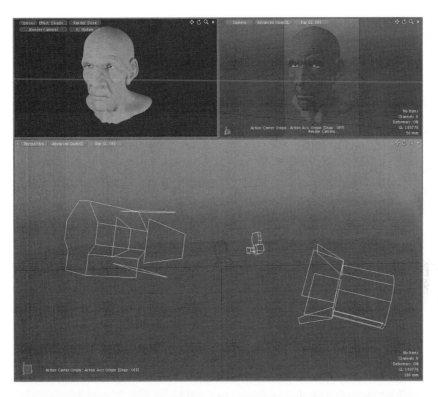

Figure 4.19

Key and fill lights in place

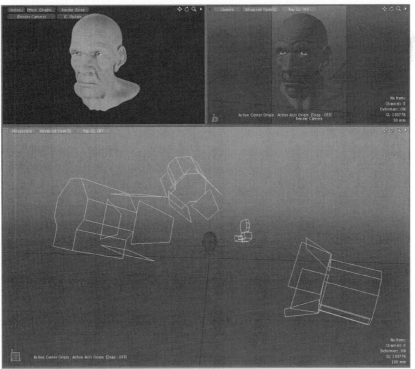

Figure 4.20

The rim light is added to the scene.

Next, look at the Radiant Intensity settings for the lights. The default Radiant Intensity of 3 is usually adequate for a key light. The same setting, however, is probably too strong for the fill light. Select the fill light and lower its Radiant Intensity to soften its effect (in

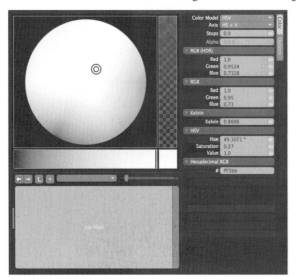

most cases, a setting of 0.5 to 1.0 will provide good results). To give the rim light some added effect, increase its value significantly. A setting of 10 to 12 is not uncommon for a rim light, because this will help add emphasis to your model (the strong but confined effect of this type of rim light is why it is sometimes called a *kicker*). With these adjustments, you should have something like the image shown in Figure 4.22.

With light color and intensity set, adjusting the radius of the lights will provide a nice finishing touch. Select the key light and change the Radius to 250 mm. This gives the key a tight focus and keeps the highlights relatively strong. The rim light can be a little larger (about 500 mm). This helps smooth out the effect of the light. Finally, the fill light can be set significantly larger

Figure 4.21
The color picker

to mimic the effect of environmental light. In this case, I set the fill light to 1 m. With all of these lights, I have disabled the Simple Shading option. This round of adjustments helps to add soft realism to the lighting and helps to complete the image. In Figure 4.23, you can see the improvement in shadows across the entire image.

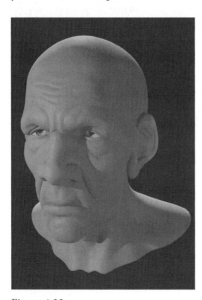

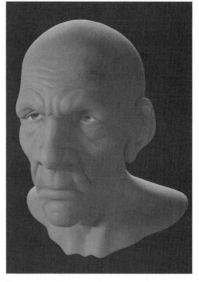

Figure 4.22
Light color and intensity have been adjusted.

Figure 4.23
Increasing the radius of the lights helps add realism to the finished image.

Setting Up Controls for the Light Rig

After your basic light rig is completed, it can be beneficial to add some control so that you can more quickly adjust your lighting style. To create good control for this rig, you will create a simple hierarchy.

First, create a new locator in the scene. By default, this locator will be placed at the origin with its rotational values set to 0 for the x, y, and z axes. In the Items list, select one of your lights and drag it onto this new locator. If you wish, you can right-click on the locator and change its name to denote the light that is now parented to it. Create more locators for the remaining lights in your scene and drag your lights onto them. With this first set created, you will be able to simply select a locator and rotate it to move the position of the corresponding light. The light will always remain focused, and this will allow you to make quick changes to the individual lights within the rig.

To gain more control over the rig as a whole, create another locator and drag each of the three locators that you previously created onto this new "Master Control" locator. With this next level of hierarchy created, the entire rig can be rotated easily. Simply changing the rotational values for x, y, and z on the last locator will allow you to change moods very quickly. Figure 4.24 shows some of the possibilities that can be quickly created by rotating the entire light rig in this manner.

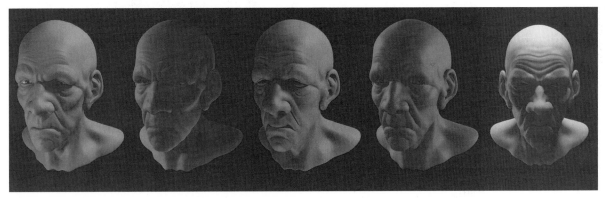

Figure 4.24

Various looks that can be quickly achieved by rotating the light rig. Remember, all that changes in these images is the light (OK, except the last one—I couldn't help myself!).

Setting Up Environments

A good environment can be key to the success of a rendered image. An environment can provide light, color, and subtle reflection to help ground the subject. To see the effect of an environment, you will use some of the environments that ship with modo and apply them to the model used in the previous section.

Start by disabling the Spot Lights in your scene and enable global illumination by clicking the Enable check box for Indirect Illumination. At first, nothing will happen because there is nothing illuminating the scene. To quickly see the effects of global illumination, go to the Environment section and double-click on an environment. Start with a simple studio environment because this will make it easier to make adjustments to the textures. The image in Figure 4.25 uses the environment Black Studio 01.

You may notice that the image looks a bit odd. Lighting is soft and realistic, but the skin now looks dry, chalky, and lifeless. There are a couple of reasons for this sudden change: reflection and subsurface scattering. The original texture has no reflective values (only specular). To quickly remedy this problem, click the Match Specular check box

Figure 4.25

Global illumination with no changes to the texture

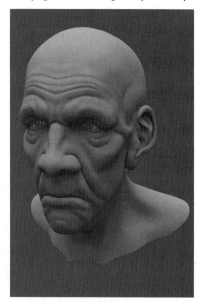

for the reflections on the skin shader. This brings back highlights but leaves the character looking too shiny and wet. Turning on Blurry Reflections causes the reflections to soften the same way the specular highlights did in the previous renders. If you want, you can also add some Fresnel to help add subtle increase in reflections at steep angles to the camera.

The reflections should look decent now, but the overall skin still looks dead. To bring back the effect of the subsurface scattering, it has to be enabled for indirect lighting. Return to the Global Illumination settings and look at the Subsurface Scattering drop-down menu. By default, this is set to Direct Only, and no global illumination will work properly. Changing this to Indirect Affects SSS will bring back the lively tones in the skin.

INDIRECT LIGHTING AND SUBSURFACE SCATTERING

The Subsurface Scattering option can also be set so that indirect lighting can be affected by SSS (like light filtering through thin curtains) or so that both indirect lighting and SSS affect each other. However, often the difference is minor and the impact on render times is significant, so leaving this set to Indirect Affects SSS will give a good balance of quality and speed.

A new render will result in an image like the one in Figure 4.26. This will probably be a lot more along the lines of what you would expect to begin with.

Now that the shaders have been updated properly to take into account the reflective nature of environmental lighting, you can begin to explore more options with environments and texture settings. By adjusting the roughness on the skin shader, you can achieve dry and oily skin types quickly. Decreasing the roughness will provide shinier skin and add the appearance of moisture. This can also be controlled via an image map so that some areas of the skin appear drier and others appear oily. You will look at the use of image maps for this type of application Chapter 13. Try looking at different environment images to see the effect that these preset scenes have on the lighting, color, and mood of the subject. Figure 4.27 shows examples of outdoor and indoor lighting on the scene.

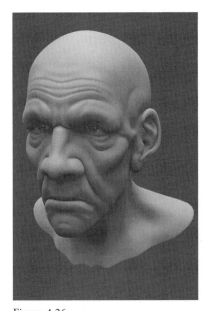

Figure 4.26

The skin shader adjusted for use with global illumination

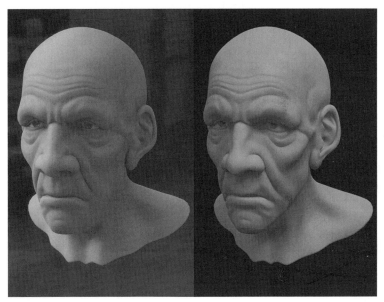

Figure 4.27

Changing the environment can quickly change the mood of a render. With materials set up properly, environments can be changed easily.

Rendering Basics

After lighting is completed, it is time to create some rendered images. Even though clicking the Render option in the Render menu or pressing F9 will give you a rendered image, there are some things that should be considered from both artistic and technical standpoints. As you begin to set up the final image for rendering, take into account framing, pose, and other layout considerations as you would with any design. Remember that you can adjust the camera in terms of position, focal length, and even lens distortion to give you the exact final look that you are going for. Although these aesthetic options will vary from shot to shot and from artist to artist, there are a few common settings that you should consider when setting up your camera for rendering.

Aesthetic Considerations

When you select the camera in the Items list, you will be presented with several options to adjust. On the right-hand side of the camera properties, you will see Camera View and Camera Effects.

The Camera View section gives you control over common camera adjustments that you would make with a real-world camera. These include Focal Length, Angle Of View, and even the camera's Projection Type. A perspective camera is the default Projection Type and acts like a real-world camera. There are also options to use an orthographic camera (which lacks perspective) and a spherical camera that can be used to capture an entire scene in one image (this is especially useful when creating custom environments).

The Camera Effects section allows you to control depth of field, motion blur, and stereoscopic rendering. Although stereoscopic rendering can be useful in some situations (such as rendering for stereo 3D print and film), the two main settings to consider are motion blur and depth of field. Depth of field enables you to create a realistic camera focus, including the Bokeh effect (the tendency for blurred areas to show aperture-shaped artifacts). The Focus Distance can be set manually or by clicking the Autofocus button, which will set the distance based on the geometry directly in front of the camera's view. Further control is given over the F-Stop (which controls the amount of blur), the type of iris (number of blades and rotation), and Edge Weighting (which controls the focus of the Bokeh effect in areas blurred by depth of field). These options will be covered in Chapters 9 and 11, where simulation of real-world cameras becomes more critical.

Another issue that needs to be considered is the control that is desired after the image is rendered. By creating additional render data, a wide variety of post-processing options become available. Camera focus, reflection strength, and even object color can be edited easily if initial steps are taken when setting up the rendered image. Render Outputs are the key to gaining control over your image after the rendering is complete. In some instances, the effects achieved in postproduction will not be adequate for a true finished render, but the ability to change settings instantly (in an image-editing program) will allow you to experiment with finished looks without waiting for a complete render each time. These results can then be used to adjust the final render of the completed scene.

Technical Considerations

After making decisions regarding the visual appearance of the image, you need to adjust various options to optimize quality and rendering time. These options fall into three categories:

- Resolution (the number of pixels in the image)

- Anti-aliasing quality (the level at which individual pixels are subdivided to produce a smooth render)
- Calculation of light rays both for traditional lights and global illumination (the number of rays used by the rendering engine to create the lighting solution)

The majority of these options are housed in the renderer properties. The Frame section offers control for the width and height of the frame as well as the Dots Per Inch (DPI) setting.

Using anti-aliasing smooths the appearance of jagged lines in areas of high contrast. The higher the setting, the more *subpixels* are calculated and then averaged to provide the finished pixel. In the Settings section, the Antialiasing Filter menu contains different styles of anti-aliasing. The default, Gaussian, offers a balanced final image and is appropriate in most cases. For slightly sharper images, the Catmull-Rom filter can be used, and the Mitchell-Netravali filter is best for images with problematic areas of high detail and moiré patterns. Refinement Shading Rate and Refinement Threshold are used to further define the anti-aliasing of the image. Lowering the Refinement Shading Rate value will result in a more finely anti-aliased image. Refinement Threshold determines the amount of contrast necessary between pixels for anti-aliasing to be implemented. Values of neighboring pixels within the threshold percentage do not cause anti-aliasing to be used. Setting this number to lower values will force more anti-aliasing, a smoother appearance, and longer render times.

The calculation of light rays is a key part of any rendered image. When Radiosity is enabled, the number of light rays is controlled in the Global Illumination setting. The main setting for quality control on a simple level is the number of Irradiance Rays. The number of rays in the scene defines the quality of the lighting solution. The Supersampling option adds additional rays to further refine areas of high detail at a minimal cost to render time (this option is best left enabled). Adjusting the next group of settings (involving irradiance and interpolation) can result in higher-quality renders in some cases. For most scenes, the default settings are sufficient. When noisy or distorted sections of an image appear, these settings can improve the look of the finished image. You will look at these settings in more depth Chapter 9. With traditional lights, the number of rays is controlled on a per light basis and will need to be adjusted on any light that projects from an area or a volume.

Practice: Lighting the Water Bottle

In this exercise, you will continue to work with the model created and textured in the previous chapters. Open your file from the previous chapter or use the file `Bottle_Lighting_Start.lxo` on the included DVD. Before looking at the lighting for this object, it is important to notice that there is no environment modeled with the bottle. To see shadows on the background image, a special item called a Shadow Catcher needs to be added to the scene. This item is found in the mesh presets under the Basic category. Double-clicking on the Shadow Catcher will place it at the origin and underneath the bottle. Now that the object is grounded in the scene, we will move on to the lighting.

Currently, the lighting in this scene is provided by a default Directional Light. For this exercise, you will use a combination of global illumination and an edited version of the existing Directional Light. Go to the Global Illumination setting of the renderer properties and enable Indirect Illumination. Because much of this object is transparent, the initial change in lighting will mostly have an effect on the label and the cap. The default background gradient will provide a good start for adjusting the global illumination settings. After enabling Global Illumination, you may notice that some sections of the label are overlit. The Base Shader will provide you with simple options to balance the lighting in the scene. Under the shader section of the Base Shader, there are controls for the strength of direct lighting (traditional lights), indirect lighting (global illumination), and the saturation of color projected onto the image by indirect lights. Decreasing either the direct or indirect multipliers (or both) will allow you to quickly balance the lighting. For this scene, reduce the direct illumination multiplier to 50% and the indirect multiplier to 75%. This provides a good balance for interior lighting. In an exterior scene, setting the direct multiplier to a higher value will simulate the effects of sunlight.

Now you will add an environment to the scene, move the camera into an appropriate position, and adjust the angle of the directional light to complete this scene. Go to the indoor environments and double-click on the Kitchen 01 environment.

MANEUVERING IN SPHERICAL ENVIRONMENTS

Environments are based on an image projected around the scene as a sphere infinitely far away from the center of the scene. Simply rotating the camera will cause the objects in the scene to float above the background. After some maneuvering, you will find a position that places the scene object (or objects) in a good position relative to the background image. To maintain this relative positioning, use the tripod rotation (Alt/Option+RMB). Because this method of camera rotation maintains the position of the camera, the occurrence of parallax scrolling will be eliminated and object positioning will remain constant.

To get a better idea of the environment, it is often beneficial to see it separate from the camera view. To view the environment in the perspective view, click the Advanced OpenGL option, and under GL Background choose Environment (see Figure 4.28). This will allow you to quickly assess the position of lights in the environment.

You will notice that the Directional Light in the scene does not correspond to the position of the main light (the window). Select the Directional Light and rotate it so that its angle corresponds with the window. Now the light cast from the Directional Light will help to enhance the shading produced by the environment. Because the light from the environment is coming from a relatively large area, the Spread Angle of the Directional Light will also need to be increased. A setting of about 30° should accurately mimic illumination coming from the window. With this high spread angle, the number of samples also needs to be increased. A setting of 256 should produce smooth shadows and lighting in this case. When completed, your bottle should look something like the image shown in Figure 4.29.

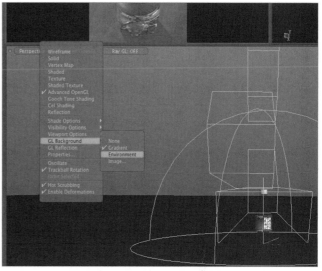

Figure 4.28

Enabling the background image in the perspective view enables you to see more than the camera view alone.

Review

Lighting is a powerful tool that can make or break an image. Proper control of lighting can be used to accentuate the form of a model and to convey many moods. In this chapter, you have looked at the various styles of lighting available in modo (and many other 3D applications). The difference between traditional 3D lights and global illumination was discussed as well as some instances where each is more appropriate. After reading this chapter and practicing the techniques presented, you should be able to do the following:

- Build a simple light rig
- Create controls to simplify the editing of a light rig
- Adjust materials for use with traditional lighting and global illumination
- Use global illumination alone or in conjunction with traditional lighting to create a completed scene

Figure 4.29

The bottle lit and rendered in a full scene

Where to Go from Here

If you want additional practice, load some additional environments and adjust the direct lighting to complement the image-based lighting. In some cases, this will require additional lights and more editing than the example from this chapter. Keep practicing. Lighting can be a powerful tool when used correctly, but can also turn a viewer (or client) off very quickly if it is not wielded carefully.

CHAPTER 5

Subdivision Surface Modeling

Creation of 3D models goes well beyond the realm of simple primitive objects. Polygons, though a mainstay of computer modeling and animation, are ineffective when re-creating realistic and organic forms. Using subdivision surfaces (SubDs) enables you to create models without the blocky edges that detract from the image and the realism of your scene. Proper use of SubDs opens the doors to a tremendous variety of models that would be difficult or impossible to create with simple polygons.

This chapter covers the following:

- ■ **Using subdivision surface modeling**

- ■ **Modeling organic objects**

- ■ **Modeling semi-organic objects**

- ■ **Modeling hard-surface objects**

Using Subdivision Surface Modeling

In subdivision surface modeling, polygons cease to define the geometry. Instead, polygonal data is used to direct the flow of smoothly contoured surfaces. To illustrate this easily, take the example of a simple cube. Eight points define the surface of a cube. When connected by straight edges to create polygons, the primitive shape takes form. With subdivision surfaces (or in this case PSubs) activated by pressing Shift+Tab, the cube turns into a kind of lumpy sphere. The facets that we see in the surface of the sphere are caused by a low subdivision level. By increasing the subdivision level to 3 or 4 (in the Mesh Properties panel), the lumpiness disappears and the spherical shape becomes properly defined. This type of rounding and curved surface creation is typical of all subdivision surface models. The addition of extra edges, weighted points (or edges), and shifts in polygonal flow (all of which are covered later in this chapter) add definition, sharpness, and detail to the surfaces of an object. Figure 5.1 shows an example of a subdivision surface model.

Figure 5.1

Subdivision surface models can combine smooth curves with sharp creases to form complex shapes.

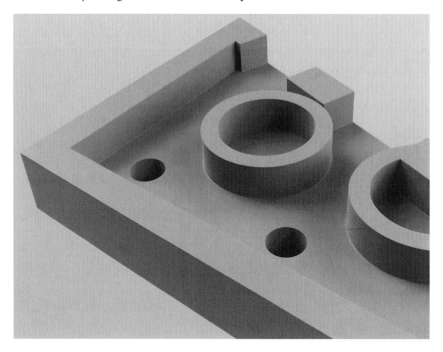

Adding Edges to Control Surfaces

One of the simplest ways to control subdivision surfaces is to add extra edges where a corner is required instead of a smooth surface. In the example of the cube that was turned into a sphere, adding a pair of edges running around the circumference of the model will change the sphere into a cylinder. After beveling in the top and bottom polygons, the final shape is defined (see Figure 5.2).

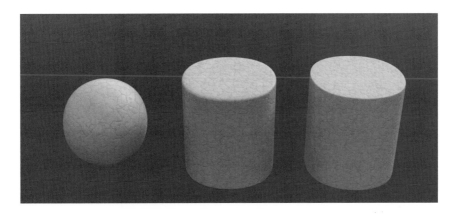

Figure 5.2

A sphere is turned into a rounded cylinder and then into a sharper form by adding edges to define the form.

This serves to illustrate an important point about SubD modeling: To define an edge with geometry, edges must be added to define the incoming and outgoing curve shape. When edges are created close to a corner, the result is a sharp crease. The farther these edges lie from the corner, the more rounded the corner will become. There are several methods for adding these *control* edges.

The Loop Slice tool is excellent for adding edges around strips of adjacent polygons or directly perpendicular edges. To use this tool, select two adjacent polygons (or perpendicular edges), activate the tool located in the Mesh Edit tab, and click in the viewport. The tool updates live so you can increase the number of edges and their positions while viewing the updates to the model in real time. Setting the tool mode to Symmetry and using two edges will enable you to add creases to the two sides of the polygon loop at once.

When dealing with individual edges that require sharpening that is the same incoming and outgoing, the Edge Extrude and Edge Bevel tools (accessed by clicking the Extrude or Bevel buttons in the Edge tab of the modo Tools toolbar) are particularly useful. Despite their similarities, these two tools work in very different ways. The Edge Bevel tool creates a chamfered edge around the selected edge or edges. This can be used in polygonal modeling to round corners, but in SubD modeling it sharpens them. This tool should be used carefully, however, because the resulting *polygonal structure* is actually rounded and not a sharp, thus making it more difficult to achieve a sharp crease. The Edge Extrude tool, however, creates new edges that slide along the polygonal surface and away from the selected edge(s) because no rounding is occurring. This tool is preferable for creating very sharp creases in geometry.

Figure 5.3 shows a staircase with extruded edges that gradually move away from the corners. The Extrude setting of the Edge Extrude tool moves the original edge away from the surface when positive values are used, or indents the edge when negative values are entered. This can be useful for creating sweeping additions to the model surface. The effect of the Edge Extrude tool along with examples of outward and inward extrusion are shown in Figure 5.4.

Figure 5.3

A subdivided stair-
case and its unsub-
divided counterpart
are shown with
sharpening edges
moving away from
the corners.

Figure 5.4

Variations on the
Edge Extrude tool:
no extrusion (left),
outward extru-
sion (middle), and
inward extrusion
(right)

Moving existing edges is another method for creating creases in geometry. Edges can be selected and moved directly, or the Slide tool can be used to move an edge along the surface of the model. Edges can be moved either individually, as loops, or in other groupings. Scaling multiple edges either toward or away from each other can also help to define geometry.

All of the tools for adding and moving edges can be used in conjunction with different action centers and falloffs. By using these tool modifiers, complex changes to edges and surface detail can be made extremely quickly. Taking some time to practice these methods on simple geometry (such as a cube) will enable you to become comfortable with the tools and begin to see the manner in which much more detailed and complex forms can be created.

Adding Edge Weights to Control Surfaces

Edge weights can be an extremely powerful way to edit geometry. Edge weights work best with models utilizing PSubs (Shift+Tab). To gain control over the weight of individual vertices and edges, do the following:

1. In the Lists tab, open the Weight Maps section.

2. Click the Subdivision Weight option to activate it.

3. Activate the Vertex Map Weight tool by pressing Shift+W.

4. Click and drag in the viewport to set the weight percentage.

Each edge can be weighted up to the given maximum, which is shown onscreen when using the Edge Weight tool. Using the maximum setting results in a completely sharp edge, whereas amounts that are near the maximum value will provide soft rounding at the corners. It is worthwhile to note that this method works better for sharply creased corners (maximum settings) because softly rounded corners tend to pull on the adjacent surfaces. Using extra loop slices or a combination of loops and weighting will usually provide the best results.

Figure 5.5 shows a model created by using edge weights for the creased sections. The model started out as a simple subdivided cube with the addition of edges and bevels to create the basic form. Then, the Vertex Map Weight tool was used to add definition.

Because the weight value transitions smoothly between vertices, it is easy to get smooth blends between creased and rounded geometry. As with other edge-editing techniques, the use of falloffs and Action Centers will enable you to see complex results very quickly. The example shown in Figure 5.6 gives a good demonstration of using edge weights to quickly visualize concept designs. Once again, this form began as a simple cube with a few subdivisions. The complex forms were created by adding additional subdivisions, moving polygons into generalized areas to create the basic form, and then adding edge weights. The rendered images show the flow of the finished form, and the weight map images show how these forms were created.

Figure 5.5

Edge weights are used here to crease sections in the object.

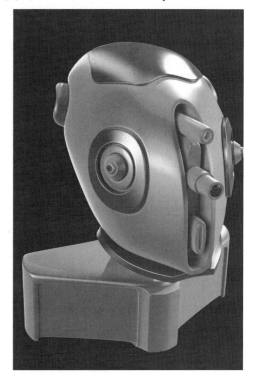

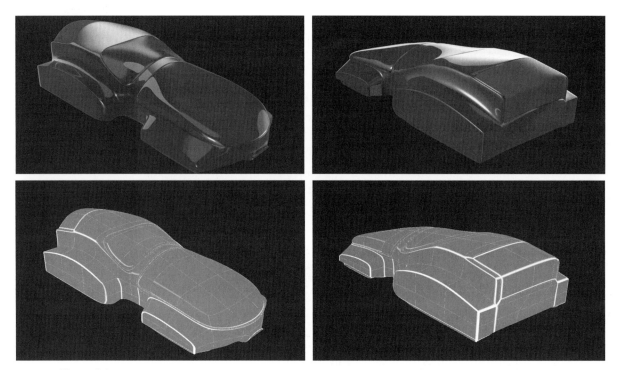

Figure 5.6

A simple example of edge weighting. The rendered images (top) show the curved surfaces, and the weight-mapped images (bottom) show the weighting used to achieve the effect.

Modeling Organic Objects

In this section, you will model smooth and organic forms by using subdivision surfaces. In completing these models, you will learn about the following:

- Traditional modeling (based on moving points and polygons)

- Edge sharpening

- The use of falloffs to create flowing models

- The use of digital sculpting

Through the combined use of these techniques, you will be able to create the models for a convincing studio scene. Figure 5.7 shows the projects you will model in this section, and then texture and render in the following chapters.

Modeling the Scene

When presenting an object, the surrounding objects in the scene can be important to convey mood, accentuate color, or enhance the form of the product being visualized. You will start by creating a pedestal covered in cloth for our object to sit on. Modeling cloth manually can be challenging and time-consuming, and may yield results that are less than convincing. Merely pushing and pulling points, edges, and polygons will typically yield a rather mechanical look for the finished model. Setting up the general parameters for the cloth and then sculpting in the details will yield better results.

Figure 5.7

**The models you will
create in this section**

Creating the Pedestal

The actual form of the pedestal, which will sit underneath the cloth, is relatively unimportant and can actually be deleted after the cloth model is completed. Because some portion of the underlying model may need to be visible and the cloth should be as believable as possible, you will start with some solid geometry and place the cloth on top of it.

In this example, you will begin with one of the preset columns that ships with the modo content (specifically, Column 01). Because the 3 m (10′) tall column is a bit excessive for a small table, it needs to be scaled down. Simply using the Scale tool here results in a tiny replica of the large pillar, so just move the top section downward and adjust the bottom section. If you look closely, you will see that the entire midsection of the pillar is made up of a single loop of very tall polygons. This type of construction makes it easy to adjust the height of the object while keeping the desired proportions in place. To scale the column down to size, do the following:

1. Right-click at a point in the middle but off to one side of the column.

2. Drag over the top and down to the opposite side before releasing the right mouse button. The resulting selection will contain the top section to the point where it meets with the main body of the column.

3. Use the Move tool to drag this selection down 2.5 m on the *y*-axis.

4. Invert the selection by pressing the [key.

5. Decrease the selection by using the Shift+down-arrow command to remove the midsection of the column from the selection.

6. Use the Scale tool perpendicular to the ground plane to adjust the size of the bottom of the column (a scale of 82.5% will keep the pillar itself straight).

After these adjustments are made, this simple piece of stock content becomes an excellent basis for the scene. This object is at relatively low resolution, and the rounded sections will show some faceting (visible polygons), so you will need to convert some sections to subdivision surfaces. Start by double-clicking the rounded section directly underneath the top of the pedestal. Pressing Shift+Tab will put this section into PSub mode.

Note that there are a few sections that become problematic, as shown in Figure 5.8. The first area of concern is the straight area between the rounded ends. Select two vertical polygons that run around this section and run the Loop Slice tool (Alt/Option+C). Set the Count to 2 and the mode to Symmetry. Click in the viewport and drag until the new edges are as far away from the center as they can get (0.5% and 99.5%). This will add some needed sharpness to this section without causing a heavy crease.

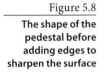

Figure 5.8
The shape of the pedestal before adding edges to sharpen the surface

The remainder of the sharpening for the pedestal will be done with edge weights. The ribbed edges that run around the model are looking a little rounded and lumpy. Increasing the weighting on some of the peaks and troughs will detail the surface more properly:

1. Select the edge pairs at the top of each ridge as well as those at the bottom, as shown in Figure 5.9.
2. Press the L key to select the entire edge loops associated with these edges.

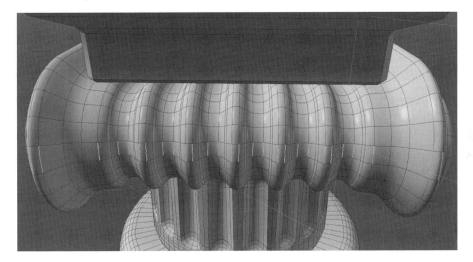

Figure 5.9

Select these edges to sharpen by using the Vertex Map Weight tool.

3. To sharpen these edges, first select the Subdivision Weight map under Weight Maps in the Lists tab (the right side of the screen in the middle).
4. Press Shift+W to engage the Vertex Map Weight tool.
5. Click and drag in the viewport to set the weight map value. The example in Figure 5.10 shows the value set to 19%.

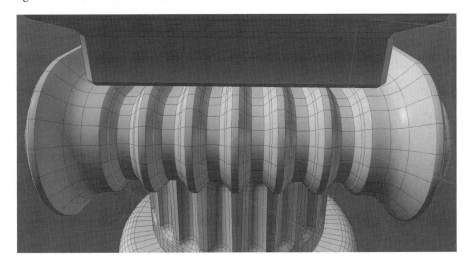

Figure 5.10

Edges weighted to 19%

> **TOOL MEMORY**
>
> Many tools in modo will remember the previous settings that were used during a work session. When enabling the tool again, a simple click in the viewport will apply your last settings without the need to adjust the actual values.

Next come the end caps. In Polygon mode, double-click one of the end caps to select and press Shift+Tab to convert the geometry into subdivision surfaces. Right away you should notice one big problem: The round end is heavily distorted. The circular n-gon has been converted to triangles. Because the triangles are created in an interlocking zipper fashion, there is an uneven pull on the surrounding geometry. This creates the elliptical shape and causes distortion on the flat surface. When n-gons exist on uneven surfaces in a model, there are several ways to deal with them. This is not really one of those ways.

Fortunately, there is a simple way to fix this problem. Select all of the edges that divide the circle (see Figure 5.11) and press Delete to remove the edges from the surface. With all of these edges deleted, your model should look something like Figure 5.12. If you continue to have distortion in this area, you likely will need to remove an additional edge or edges.

After the first piece of geometry is repaired, repeat the process on the other three pieces. With all of these circular pieces repaired, the edges will need to be sharpened to complete this section of the model. Follow these steps:

1. Select two edges at the peak of the outer rim as well as the two edges at the peak of the inner rim.

Figure 5.11

Select these edges and delete them to fix the round end of this piece.

Figure 5.12

After the edges are deleted, the shape will become round.

2. With these four edges selected, press the L key to select the loops completely.

3. Once again, make sure that the Subdivision Weight map is selected and then press Shift+W to activate the Vertex Map Weight tool. Figure 5.13 shows these edges weighted at 18%.

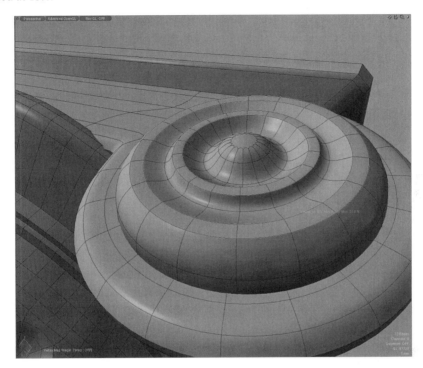

Figure 5.13

Rounded edges sharpened

Creating the Cloth

Now that the faceted sections of the pedestal are properly smoothed, you're ready to create the cloth that will sit on top of the pedestal. Before moving onto the cloth, you need to make one simple adjustment that will facilitate the creation of the cloth object. To use snapping tools to constrain the cloth to the pedestal, you'll want more points on the surface to aid the snapping tools.

Double-click on the square top of the pedestal and press Shift+D to bring up the options for subdividing the surface. In this case, you simply need to add more points to the surface of this section. The Faceted mode will subdivide the selected polygons without smoothing them. Each four-sided polygon will now be divided into four smaller polygons. Repeat this one or two more times to add surface complexity to aid in the next section.

The shape of the cloth needs to be created so that the polygons will be "shrink-wrapped" to the surface of the pedestal. If you create a flat polygon over the top, it will be very difficult to wrap the geometry around the object that exists in the scene. Because you will use background constraints and the snapping tools to create the shape of the cloth, the initial polygonal form needs to have some direction that will facilitate the creation of the form-fitted geometry of the cloth. Much of the work done in creating 3D models has to do with knowing what forms can be simply manipulated to create the desired shape.

STARTING MODELS

It is important when beginning a model to figure out what primitive shapes can be used to create rough sections of the model. Look for sections of a model that can be described by a primitive object (or a section of primitive object). This is especially useful with rounded shapes that can be described with a section of a sphere, cylinder, capsule, or a torus. Using the polygons from a simple mesh can help you to more quickly and accurately create complex forms.

In this case, a Quadball sphere will give you a great starting point because that shape is already based on a cube and the polygons are all facing away from a central point. After the sphere is created, you can cut out everything but the top panel of polygons and have a rounded square shape to snap to the geometry of the pedestal. To get the proper setup, do the following:

1. Create a new sphere with the mode set to Quadball.
2. Set the Subdivision Level relatively high (around 9).
3. Create a sphere so that the top panel is centered around the top of the pedestal.
4. Set the Radius so that the top panel overlaps all of the geometry of the pedestal from the top viewport.
5. After the spheres are created, select the four polygons on the top of the sphere and use the Shift+up-arrow command to expand the selection of polygons out to the corners of the top panel.
6. Invert the selection by using the [key and cut out the selected polygons.

You'll be left with a rounded square (see Figure 5.14) that can be used for the next phase.

With this panel of geometry in place, you are ready to use the snapping tools. Before engaging the snapping tools, there is one last step to take. This form should be changed from regular subdivision surfaces to Pixar subdivisions, or PSubs. This can be done simply by pressing the Tab key to change the selection to regular polygons and then pressing Shift+Tab to enter PSubs. The only visual cue indicating the two different subdivision types at this level will be the corners of the geometry. Notice that in regular subdivision services, the corners are rounded, but in PSubs, the corners come to a sharp point.

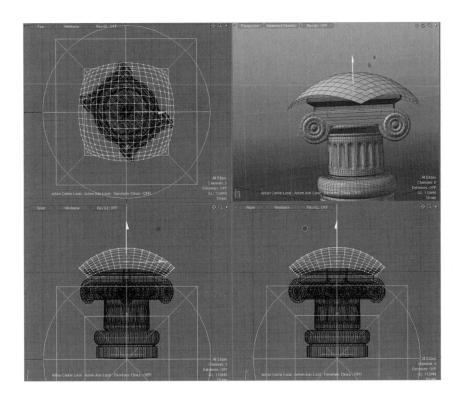

Figure 5.14

The initial cloth shape before conforming it to the table

BOUNDARY RULES

The creation of sharp creases within Pixar subdivision surfaces is governed by the boundary rules on a mesh item. By default, this is set to Crease All. This can be changed to affect the rounding level of these subdivision surfaces and the edges. On occasion, other boundary rules will be useful, but for many operations, the default setting is preferred.

To conform the cloth piece to your existing geometry, Snapping must be enabled and set up properly for your scene. Press F11 to bring up the Snapping menu. From here, clicking the Snapping button (also located at the top of the viewports) will enable the function, but further steps need to be taken to make this work properly for this scene. The Snapping menu without any features enabled offers a section for modifying the Snapping and Constraint modes as well as some fine-tuning settings that you will leave at the defaults for now. Figure 5.15 shows the Snapping menu with just snapping enabled and no features engaged.

Figure 5.15

The Snapping menu

First, you will need to set the Snapping mode. There are several choices here, but really only three categories (Grid Snap, Snapping To Pivots, and Geometry Snapping)—and only two of those are relevant to the work that will be created in this book: Grid Snap and Geometry Snapping. Grid Snap enables you to constrain your object creation and modification to the grids. This is useful for architectural modeling but not for the current case. Snapping To Pivots enables you to utilize the pivot point for the visible layer. This one is more useful in setting up complex animation hierarchies. Geometry Snapping is what you will need in this case because it enables you to snap the cloth to the model of the pedestal.

On the Snapping menu, you will recognize the lower three options as types of geometry. If you know that you will need to snap specifically to a vertex, edge, or polygon, then you can select those elements directly. However, for many functions, snapping to geometry as a whole is more desirable. After you choose Geometry, you will be presented with additional menu options in the form of an entire section labeled Geometry Snap. Within this new section, you will be able to identify the specific mode of geometry that you would like to use for snapping. As previously mentioned, you can specify snapping the vertices, edges, or polygons. In addition, you can choose to snap to the center of edges. Often, setting the mode to Auto (or Auto Center) is preferable, as this will allow modo to snap to any geometry available. In addition, the Geometry Snap heading enables you to choose the layer or layers that will be used by the snapping tool. The Background option snaps to any unselected but visible mesh items. Active snaps to any visible and selected mesh items. And the Both option snaps to any visible mesh items (selected or unselected). To simplify things in this case, set the mode to Background and make sure that there is only one mesh item visible in the background.

SNAPPING DEMO

The enclosed DVD contains a video demonstrating snapping modes and their uses in various situations.

If you try the snapping functionality at this point by moving the geometry in the active layer, you will notice that the Move tool simply stops at intervals, when elements in the foreground layer are within snapping range of elements in the background layer. The geometry does not, however, deform based on the background geometry.

To achieve the kind of deformation necessary for this purpose, you need to engage a constraint. Unlike simple snapping, a constraint (in this case, a background constraint) physically restricts the movements of geometric data on a vertex basis. As a result, when a background constraint is enabled, you can deform foreground geometry based on the geometry in the background layer. As with the Snapping mode, when a constraint is enabled, additional options appear. The Constrain To Background section enables you to set an offset (the distance between snapped geometry and existing background geometry), to constrain handles of curve objects to the geometry (Handle Constraint), and to snap to both sides of single-sided polygons (Double Sided).

With the background constraint enabled, you can now use the Push tool to constrain the rounded square to the background pedestal. There is, however, one main difficulty when using this type of tool to create a clothlike effect—and that is topology. Because the

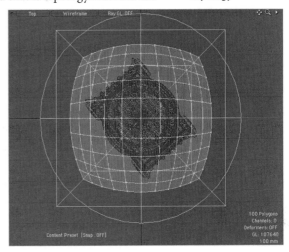

Figure 5.16

The misalignment of foreground and background topology

polygons are flowing up and down and left and right on the cloth mesh, and diagonally on the pedestal, it will be difficult to get good corners and edges when wrapping the cloth around the background geometry (see Figure 5.16). To deal with this issue, you can take two steps for a more natural appearance: first, rearrange the topology of the cloth, and second, create a closely adhering top panel by using existing geometry.

Realigning the topology is a simple process as long as you utilize the persistent nature of selections when moving between Vertex, Edge, and Polygon modes. In essence, you will need to divide all of the existing polygons diagonally (by connecting each quarter to its diagonally adjacent corner with an edge) and then delete the preexisting edges. To do this, follow these steps:

1. Enter Edge mode.

2. Lasso-select all of the existing edges in the cloth object.

3. Move to Polygons mode.

4. Select and activate the Spikey tool found in the Polygon tab of the modo Tools toolbar.

5. Return to Edges mode (note that the original edges are still selected).

6. Press Delete to eliminate the previous edge selection.

You may notice that there are some triangles along the border of the objects. Now, however, these are less of an issue than the surface abnormalities created when attempting to hold quad polygons diagonally. This type of workflow (using persistent selections) can be extremely useful in many cases when working with topology. The one place where these triangles may be a problem is at the corners. This, however, is an easy correction to make. Simply select the individual edges that run into the corners and delete those four edges (by pressing the Delete key). This creates quad polygons at the corners. To achieve a greater level of density in detail in the cloth, you now need to add one more level of subdivision to the polygons. Press the D key to physically subdivide the polygons and also create quad polygons at the edges of the object. This basic model is now ready to be wrapped around the pedestal:

1. Enable snapping and turn on a background constraint.

2. Use the Scale tool with the action Center set to origin, and scale the object uniformly toward the origin (by using the cyan-colored scale handle at the center of the tool).

3. After all of the polygons in the object have reached a collision point with the pedestal, scale up on the y-axis to decrease the amount of stretching on the lower part of the cloth.

When this is completed, your object should look something like Figure 5.17.

Figure 5.17

Rough initial cloth placement

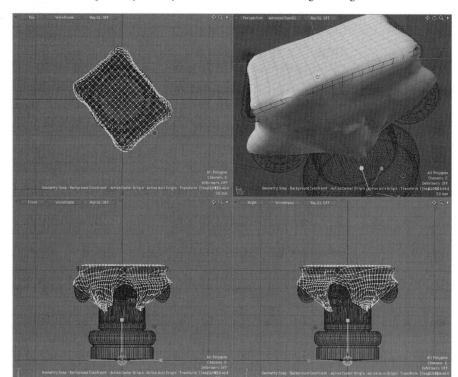

With this initial placement created, you're now ready to place a more accurate top section and then move on to sculpting:

1. Start by selecting a group of polygons in the middle of the cloth (see Figure 5.18).

2. Use the Shift+up-arrow key combo to increase the selection so that it includes the entire top of the cloth (see Figure 5.19).

3. Now cut out this section of geometry. You will replace this with a more form-fitting version.

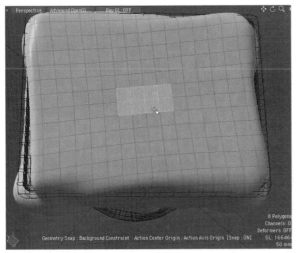

Figure 5.18

The initial selection for the top section of the cloth

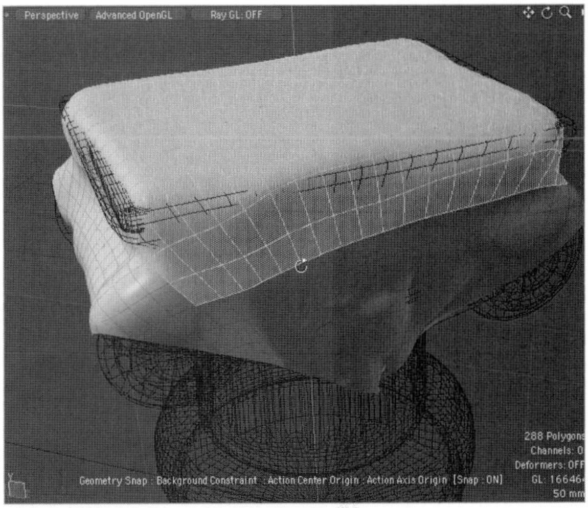

Figure 5.19

The complete top section of polygons selected

4. To create the new top section, move back to the pedestal layer, select the main top group of polygons (a grid over four-by-four polygons), copy them, and paste them into the cloth layer.

5. Double-click these new polygons and press Shift+Tab to put them into PSub mode (since the rest of the polygons in this layer are already in PSub mode).

6. If the top edge of the existing cloth section is very uneven, you may wish to use the scale tools (with the Action Center set to selection) to align the edges individually and to align them on the y-axis (to flatten them out).

Selecting this entire open ring of edges should result in a total of 38 edges selected. This is noted in the bottom-right corner of any viewport when in Edges mode. Furthermore, you will notice that the short sides each have 16 edges, while the long sides have 18. You will need to subdivide the new top in order to match these parameters. There are several ways to do this, but using the Loop Slice tool is probably the easiest and most efficient:

1. Select the interior edges that run perpendicular to the long axis.

2. Delete these edges to create a single row perpendicular to the long axis.

3. Select two polygons and run Loop Slice.

4. Set the count to 17 and click the Uniform button.

5. After you've created the proper number of rows on the long axis, repeat the process to create 16 rows on the short axis.

6. Select and scale this top section so it slightly overlaps the underlying pedestal.

7. Select the outer edge of the top section as well as the open edge from the existing cloth and run the Bridge tool. Setting several subdivisions on the Bridge tool will enable you to further manipulate the transition between the snaps geometry and the pasted geometry.

8. After spending a few moments adjusting the edges, your model should look something like the one shown in Figure 5.20. At this point, you will move on to sculpting, to create the finished look of the cloth.

Figure 5.20

The cloth, after initial modeling functions, is ready for sculpting in details

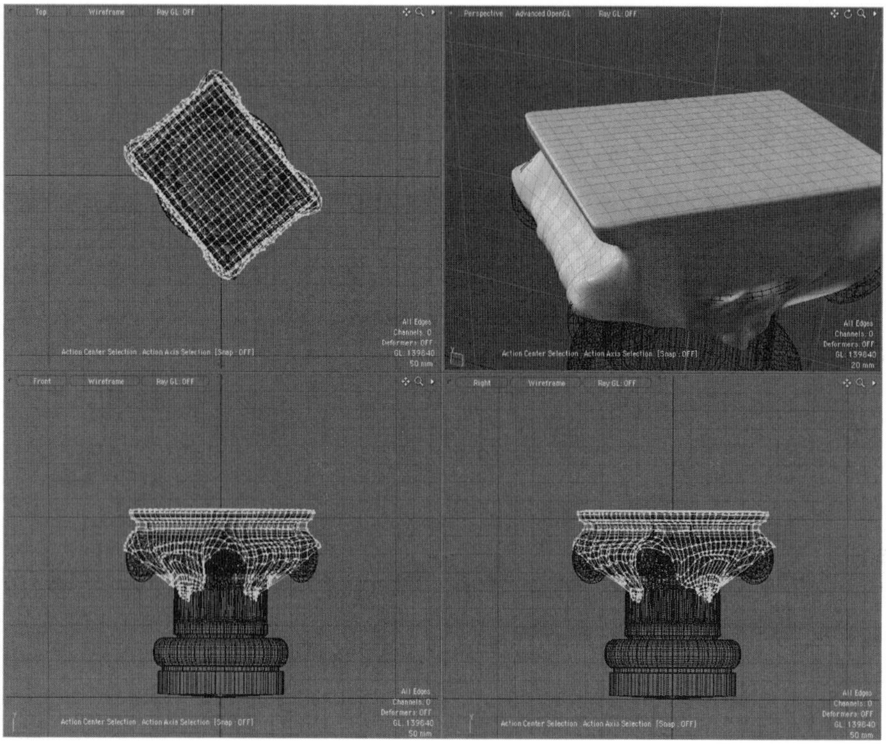

Understanding Sculpting

Before venturing into the specific job of sculpting the cloth in the scene, let's have a more generalized look at sculpting in modo. Although modo does not offer all of the options and flexibility of a dedicated sculpting application, the implementation of PSubs and multi-resolution meshes, along with improved sculpting tools, will allow you to do a great deal of sculpting directly in the application. For most common sculpting activities, modo can handle the task easily.

To start, create a Quadball sphere with a subdivision level of 6. By default, the sphere will be created in regular subdivision surfaces, so press Tab to exit SubDs and then press

Shift+Tab to put the mesh into PSub mode. Now you will be able to sculpt the model in multiple resolutions. Click the Multiresolution check box in the Mesh properties. Notice that the field marked Current Level becomes active. The current subdivision level can be anything between 1 (where the polygons are divided into four polygons) and the level set in the Subdivision Level field. Changes made in lower subdivision levels will propagate to higher levels so, for example, if you create some skin detail on a character and then decide to change the bridge of the nose, the change can be made in a lower subdivision level without harming the fine details previously created.

CHOOSING THE PROPER SUBDIVISION LEVEL

When sculpting a model, it is important to know how to properly use the subdivision level. Choosing a level depends on a few factors: the amount of detail needed, the complexity of the base mesh, and your hardware capabilities. Obviously, the last criterion is rather static unless you upgrade hardware. As a good baseline, most modern high-grade laptops or low- to mid-range desktops can generally handle around 3–4 million polygons relatively easily and 5–6 million if treated carefully. Keeping meshes hidden (or at a lower subdivision level) when not in use will allow you to work with more complexity on most systems. Higher-end desktops can handle more polygons, and with increased RAM and video cards, a higher level will be attainable. It is usually best to test your system with simple but highly subdivided meshes to get a good grasp of your capabilities. When you know the limits of your hardware, use what you need for the subdivision level on a particular object, but choose wisely (remembering that each level will multiply your poly count by a factor of four) or you will tax your system, slow your workflow, and risk crashes.

Now that you have created mesh for testing sculpting, set the subdivision level to 6 (note that when you increase the Subdivision Level, the Current Level will automatically match). There are two essential pieces to every sculpting tool: the tool type and the brush type.

You use several tools in a typical sculpting session. But for the most part, the Push, Smooth, and Carve tools cover most of your sculpting needs. The Push tool pulls geometry away from the surface. The Smooth tool softens the details on a surface (much like blurring pixels in a Photoshop image). The Carve tool creates an indent in the surface of the mesh.

When choosing a sculpting tool, there are a few simple conventions to remember. Simply clicking and dragging (or drawing on the tablet) performs the standard operation for the given tool. Holding the Control key while sculpting inverts the effect of the tool. Holding the Shift key converts any tool into the Smooth tool.

Most of the other sculpting tools (Flatten, Smudge, Move, and Spin) work as their names suggest. The Tangent Pinch tool pulls in geometry from within the brush radius and serves to sharpen otherwise rounded and undefined details. This tool is excellent for tightening the overall look of the sculpted mesh in areas of sharp detail. The Emboss tool raises and lowers the area under the brush shape by dragging right and left, respectively. This tool can be particularly effective for creating details that can be described by a gray-scale image map (for example, buttons, rivets, or screws). Figure 5.21 shows examples of each of the sculpting tools. Take a few moments to experiment with these tools on your own and familiarize yourself with each of them before moving on.

Figure 5.21

The sculpting tools in action

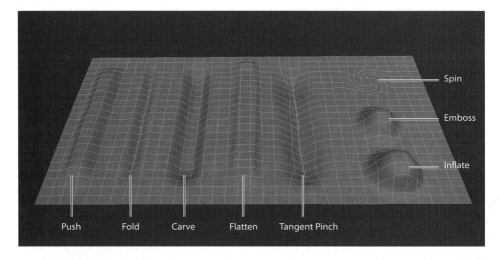

Brush types affect the shape of your sculpting tool when applied to a mesh. The Smooth Brush features a soft and adjustable falloff. The Shape Preset controls the character of the falloff (linear, smooth, sharp, and so on). In addition, the brush settings enable you to create falloff variations of your own. The Hard Brush is a simple and solid-centered brush that allows control over a simple Linear falloff via the Soft Border setting. The Procedural Brush is a randomized brush based on a Fractal Noise, a Fractal Cellular, or a Dot pattern. These patterns can be controlled in the same manner that the corresponding textures are controlled. With a small amount of customization, these procedural types can be modified to create anything from a simple skin surface to rock strata. The Image Brush uses a selected image to control the falloff shape of the brushstroke. This brush features a Stamp option (the button to the right), which enables you to click and drag out the scale and rotation of the image and then "stamp" that image onto the surface. The Stamper functionality works well with the Emboss tool. Finally, the Text Brush enables you to enter text into a field, choose a font, and stamp text onto your mesh. The controls for the text are the same as the controls for the Text tool in the modeling workflow. Again, this brush works well with the Emboss tool.

Sculpting the Cloth

Sculpting tools can be used to fix unwanted overlapping of the background objects (in this case, the column), to move large sections of the mesh with a smooth and simple fall-off, and to add organic detail objects that would be difficult to create with simple polygonal modeling. Think about using those three points to improve the look of the cloth in the scene.

Using the Push brush, pull the cloth above the background geometry and add accents where the underlying geometry contains details (such as the end caps and rounded bevels underneath the platform). Use the Move tool to fix the ends of the cloth that are clinging to the inner geometry of the column. Use the Smooth tool to keep the mesh soft and natural. Experiment with other tools to adjust the model to your liking.

As a side note, clicking and holding the Push tool reveals the Inflate and Fold tools. These tools can be helpful when sculpting cloth. With a little bit of time and effort, your cloth should look something like Figure 5.22. After you have spent some time adjusting the cloth to your liking, you will be ready to move on and create the bottle that will be on display.

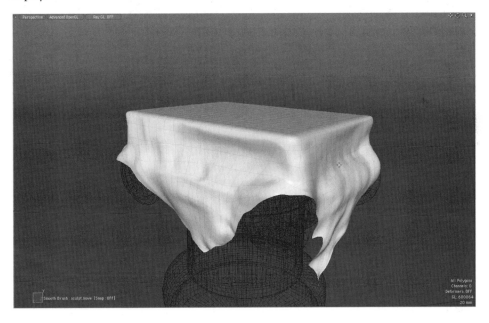

Figure 5.22

The finished cloth shape

ON THE DVD

On the enclosed DVD, you'll find a video walk-through of the creation and sculpting of the cloth object.

SCULPTING WITH FALLOFFS

Falloffs can be used with sculpting the same way that they are with other modeling functions. For example, if you want to sculpt some detail near the top of the cloth without affecting the flat surface, you can implement a small Linear falloff in which the top surface has zero effect, and the effect increases as it moves downward. This can also be an effective method for smoothly increasing the volume of folds in fabric. Set the falloff to begin where the fold should originate and end where the fold reaches full strength. That way, with one clean stroke, you can create a complex fold.

Modeling Semi-Organic Objects

The first modeling subject to consider is one that features a combination of smooth, organic curves and sharp edges. Many objects in the real world are not simply organic or hard surfaced, but contain attributes of both types of models. The first subject for this scene will be a stylized bottle that contains such elements. The bottle will have a mix of complex curves and edges that gradually sharpen. Although this subject is too rigid for sculpting tools to create, it would be very difficult to build without utilizing falloffs, action centers, and weight map-derived surface creases. The end goal is a bottle like the one shown in Figure 5.23.

Planning the Basic Structure

When you begin to create a complex object, it is important to decide where to start. This may sound like a foregone conclusion. However, making a good choice with your basic geometry can make all the difference between a successful modeling session and time wasted.

Take a moment to examine the structure of the finished bottle. Notice that the bottle goes from a square shape at the bottom to a rounded shape on top. Additionally, the shape is twisted so that the sides at the base of the model complete half a rotation and end up on the opposite side at the top. Finally, the shape roughly tapers from wide at the bottom to significantly smaller at the top, with a few variations along the way.

To successfully build this model, you need to start with a cube that fits the dimensions, and the subdivisions that enable the cube to be twisted without causing polygons to become so distorted that they will not render cleanly. The beginning cube is roughly four times the size in the y dimension as it is the x and z. Adding enough subdivisions to the y-axis will be key to manipulating this form into the desired shape.

Figure 5.23

The finished bottle exhibits attributes of both organic and hard-surface objects.

In this case, I used 40 subdivisions on the y-axis. Figure 5.24 shows the basic cage for the model. After you have created the cube, drop the Cube tool and enable a Linear falloff. This falloff will be used in the next several steps.

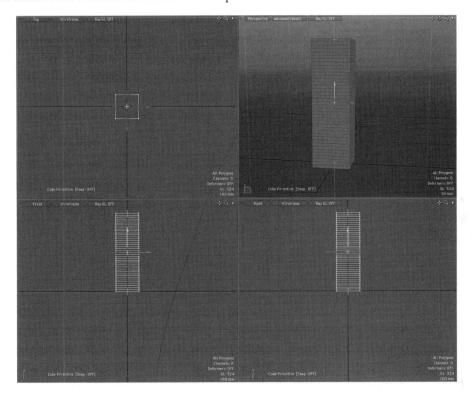

Figure 5.24

This cube will be manipulated into the finished bottle.

With the Linear falloff active, set Auto Size to the y-axis and then click Reverse so that the wide end of the falloff is at the top of the model. This same falloff can be used to twist the object and taper it. Later this falloff will be used to identify the weight map for sharpening the edges gradually. To create the twisted form, you could use the Twist tool (located in the Deform section). However, because all of these additional tools are merely combinations of simple tools, you will create the twist by hand.

1. Rotate the perspective view so that the work plane snaps to the ground plane. You will be using the Axis Rotate tool to perform the twist, and this tool bases its orientation on the work plane.

2. Activate the Axis Rotate tool (which resides underneath the rotation tool in the Basic tab, or with the hotkey Alt/Option+Shift+E).

3. Set the rotation to 180 degrees and then drop the tool. Before dropping the falloff, select the Scale tool.

4. Use the zx planar handle (the green circle) and scale down to about 20 percent.

At this point, your model should look something like the object shown in Figure 5.25.

Figure 5.25

The cube after twisting and tapering operations

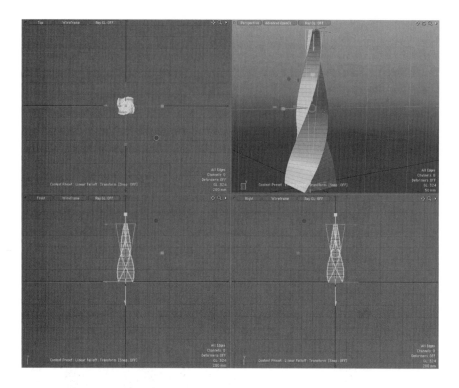

Creating the Contours of the Bottle

Now you will use different falloffs to create the bulges and other contours of the bottle.

1. Select a Cylinder falloff and, in the front view, drag it out so that it covers a section in the middle of the bottle where you want a bulge to occur.

2. Use the xz planar handle (the green circle) to scale the selection outward to create the contour.

3. While both the Scale tool and the Falloff are active, you can adjust the shape reset (for the falloff), the position of the falloff, and the amount of scaling. This enables you to place the deformations in your surface interactively and organically.

4. Repeat this process as you see fit to add interest to the shape of your bottle. In the example shown in Figure 5.26, I used three separate operations to arrive at the desired look.

As you are creating this kind of contour, it is not uncommon to get abrupt shifts in the surface, which may look unnatural. This, however, can be easily fixed. After you have completed the operations with the falloff and the Scale tool, choose the Smooth tool (under the Deform section) and then click and drag in the viewport. Drag to the right to cause more smoothing, and to the left to lessen the effect. In this way, you will be able to make the transitions between your previous modifications more subtle and flowing. Finally, take a few minutes to adjust the scale of any individual edge loops to fine-tune the shape. At this point, you should have something similar to Figure 5.27.

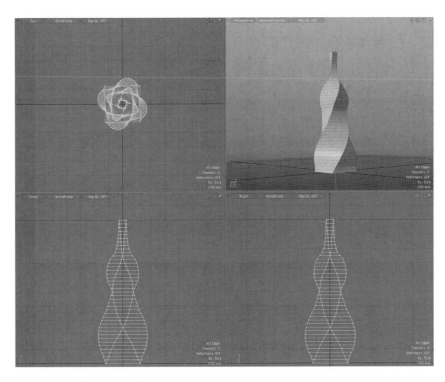

Figure 5.26

The basic bottle shape with contours added via the Scale tool and falloffs.

Before creating the interior of the bottle, you will convert this model into subdivision surfaces and properly weight the edges to achieve the subtle transition from sharp to rounded edges along the bottle's length. This can be achieved by using the Vertex Map Weight tool (Shift+W) in conjunction with another simple Linear falloff. To achieve this effect, do the following:

1. Place the object in PSub mode by pressing Shift+Tab.

2. Select the four vertical edge loops by double-clicking on one edge in each loop.

3. Activate a Linear falloff and set Auto Size to the y-axis.

4. In the lower-right section of the screen, choose the List tab, open the Weight Maps subheading, and select Subdivision.

5. Press Shift+W to activate the Vertex Map Weight tool.

6. Click and drag in the viewport to set the current weight map value (a setting of 19% to 20% should give the desired result).

7. If the falloff is causing the bottle to sharpen at the top, click the Reverse button to invert the direction of the falloff.

8. After you have set the edge weight, you can adjust the position of the falloff to smooth the transition between sharp and smooth edges.

With the edge weights set, your bottle should now look something like the one shown in Figure 5.28.

Figure 5.27

The contoured bottle is now smoothed to soften the transitions, and a few minor adjustments have been made at the top.

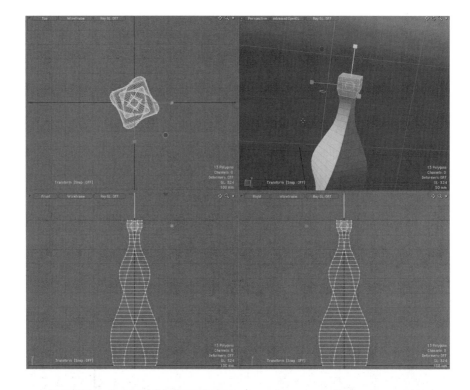

Figure 5.28

With edge weights properly set, the bottle will show a smooth transition between smooth and soft edges.

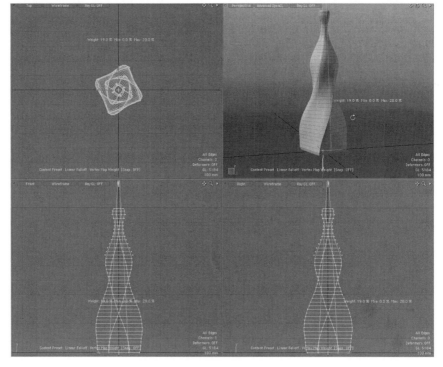

When you created the interior of the plastic bottle earlier in this book, thickening the polygons that made up the exterior made the correct interior form with very few adjustments. In this case, the interior shape of the bottle will not match the exterior shape, so this approach would not easily produce the desired results. Instead, select the top polygon and bevel it inward to create the lip of the bottle. Then create additional bevels that extend downward (by holding Shift while clicking in the viewport). You may choose to flare or taper these bevels as you go to create the finished interior. You will notice that the lip is very rounded. If you were to use edge weights to sharpen this, additional pinching could result along the vertical edges of the bottle. To avoid this, the use of additional edge loops will add rigidity without the unwanted pinching. Select two polygons running around the lip and activate the Loop Slice tool (Alt/Option+C). Set the Count to 2 and the mode to Symmetry. Click in the viewport and drag to set the sharpness, using these additional edges. You should now have the completed bottle without a cap, as shown in Figure 5.29.

Figure 5.29
The bottle without a cap

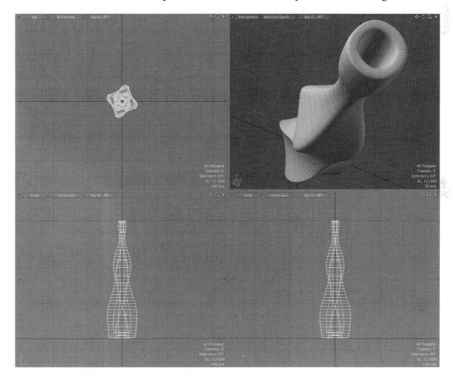

Creating the Bottle Cap

There are various ways to create a proper cap for this bottle. However, to ensure a direct match to the interior geometry, it is preferable to use existing geometry as a starting point:

1. Start by selecting two polygons that run around the outer edge of the lip.

2. Press the L key to select the entire loop. Holding Shift while pressing the left-arrow key will select more polygon loops toward the interior of the bottle. Continue until you have reached the appropriate depth for the inner section of the lid. Copy these polygons (Ctrl/Command+C), double-click the bottle to select all of the polygons, and press the H key to hide it.

3. Paste in (Ctrl/Command+V) the previously copied geometry and then press the F key to flip the polygons.

4. Use the Push tool (in the Deform section) to shrink the new geometry very slightly (this prevents overlap in the polygons).

5. Go to Edges mode and double-click the outer edge of the new geometry to select it. Use the Edge Extend tool (Z) to create new polygons extending upward from the existing edge. Just as with other tools (for example, the Bevel tool), holding Shift and clicking in the viewport creates a new edge extension without dropping the tool. Extend the geometry upward to the desired height and then press P to create a polygon at the top. Double-click the bottom edge of this piece and press the P key again to fill this open edge with the polygon.

6. If you want to create sharper edges at the top or bottom of this piece, simply select those polygons and bevel them very slightly in the same direction (up for the top, or down to the bottom), and then bevel them in just slightly. These two bevels will add the edges necessary for creating a sharper contour.

7. Finally, press the U key to unhide the rest of the bottle. Your finished geometry should look something like Figure 5.30.

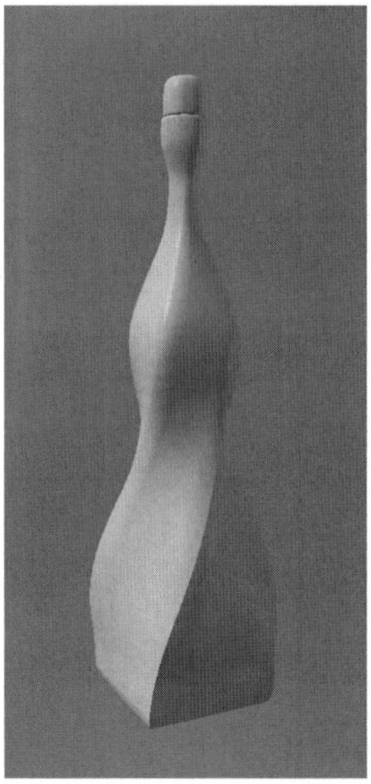

At this point, you may notice a slight stair-stepping along the vertical edges of the bottle and some awkward shading on some of the semi-sharpened edges. This is caused by insufficient vertices that define the changes in edge weights. Shifting your shaded view from Advanced OpenGL to Vertex Map will give better insight to the reason behind this issue. The vertical edges (which should be completely smoothed) show signs of edge weighting. As you will recall, the edge weights on the Subdivision weight map produce sharp edges with no smooth transition from polygon to polygon. In this case, these edges should be smooth while the vertical edges should contain the graduated shift from smooth to sharp. To achieve this effect, you will need more geometry:

1. Press the D key to subdivide the existing geometry. This fixes some issues with the structure of the mesh but requires a little adjustment to get the shape exactly right.

Figure 5.30

The finished form of the bottle

Once again, the use of falloffs will greatly expedite the work. If you are still in (or switch to) Vertex Map Weight mode, you will see that your edge weighting has been reset. You need to build this again to get the proper creasing.

2. Select two consecutive vertical edges on one corner of the model and then use the up-arrow key to continue your selection to the top of the mesh (see Figure 5.31).

3. Hold the Shift key and do the same for each of the remaining three corners.

4. After the selection is made, enable a Linear falloff, set Auto Size to the y-axis, and enable the Vertex Map Weight tool. Make sure that the falloff is weighted toward the bottom of the mesh and reset your edge weights to the value used in the previous section.

At this point, your edges will be set correctly, but the intermediate vertical edges will still be rounded on the bottom, causing the lower section of the bottle to be misshapen. To remedy this, you need to select those edges and then use the same falloff to flatten out the proper sections of the mesh:

5. Select two adjacent vertical edges that were added when subdividing the mesh (starting from the bottom of the bottle) and use the up-arrow key to select all the way to the top.

6. Once again, repeat this operation with the three remaining edges. Use the Scale tool on the xz plane until the bottom section appears flat (if your falloff is still active, the top should be untouched). At this point, your model is complete and ready for texturing and should look like Figure 5.32.

Modeling Hard-Surface Objects

Even though the majority of your modeling will be done with subdivision surfaces, often models can be created with simple polygon modeling. In this case, the scene will need lighting and photographic equipment. These objects will be used to cast light and create reflections on the surfaces of the models in the scene. Because these objects will not be the primary focus of your finished render, they do not need as much detail. Additionally, if these objects are created with simple polygon modeling tools, they will help to make the scene lighter and more easily maneuverable. For this part of the project, you will need scenes, lights, bounce cards, and a camera stand-in object.

NAMING MESH LAYERS

When you are creating several objects in their own mesh layers, it is beneficial to rename the layers as you work to keep everything organized. Right-click a mesh layer and choose Rename to enter an appropriate name for the layer.

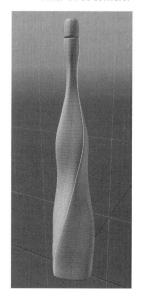

Figure 5.31

One edge is selected for edge weighting. Repeat this on each of the other three corners.

Figure 5.32

The completed bottle mesh

Light Objects

Several types of lights could be commonly used for a scene such as this. You will create a large soft box, a spotlight, and an umbrella light. You will begin with the simplest of these lights, the soft box.

The soft box is a large overhead light that behaves similarly to an Area Light in 3D. If you use an Area Light in this situation, similar effects can be achieved, but the lack of an appropriate reflection would decrease the overall realism. Also, with the optimizations of global illumination in the current release of modo, geometric lighting will resolve much more quickly and at a higher quality.

To create a softbox, follow these steps:

1. Create a simple cube over the top of the scene. An initial setting of 5 m in the x dimension by 3 m in the z should suffice. As for the y dimension, some depth is needed, but the amount is not important to the scene (I used a setting of 160 mm).

2. When you have this box created, move to Polygons mode and select the polygon on the bottom of the cube.

3. Bevel this polygon in and then upward to create the frame.

4. Next, bevel downward and in (Shift of 70 mm and Inset of 500 mm).

5. Bevel once more with Shift and Inset settings of 10 mm and 600 mm, respectively. These last two bevels create the rough shape of a rounded surface.

6. Now you can use the Edge Bevel tool to round out the shape. In Edge mode, double-click the edge that runs around the middle of the rounded section.

7. Press the B key to enable the Bevel tool (Edge Bevel in this case), set the Round level to 4, and then click and drag until the outer edges of the bevel (highlighted in orange) approach the existing edges of the mesh (about 500 mm).

8. Return to Polygons mode and select the center polygon on the bottom of the light.

9. Hold the Shift key and press the up-arrow key until the entire rounded section is selected. Press the M key and enter a name for a new material that will be assigned to this selection.

10. Press the [key to invert the selection, press the M key again, and assign a new material to the frame of the soft box

Your soft box should now look like Figure 5.33.

Creating the Spotlight

For the spotlight, start by creating a cylinder (in a new mesh layer) with a radius of 200 mm in the x and y dimensions, and 300 mm in the z. Leave the default settings for Sides and Segments (24 and 12, respectively). This cylinder will act as the main body for the light.

Figure 5.33

The completed soft box

From here, you will create a lens for the light and an attached box on the bottom. Select the front circular face of the cylinder and bevel it twice: first inset it to create the geometry for the lip and then bevel to indent the section for the lens. Now, the lens needs to be rounded (similarly to the rounded section of the soft box). The same method can be used to round the lens, but in this case, you will look at another option. To round this section by using the falloff, do the following:

1. Bevel the lens polygon with an inset of about 150 mm.
2. Select two adjacent polygons that run around the face of the lens.
3. Run the Loop Slice tool (Alt/Option+C).
4. Set the Count to 10 and click the Uniform button.
5. Enable a Cylinder falloff and to set the Axis to Z.
6. Enable the Move tool (W) and move the selection forward about 50 mm.
7. By default, the shape preset for the falloff will be set to Linear. Change this to Ease-In to create the rounded shape of the lens.

This method for creating rounded sections can be used in many instances and works well with any number of radial edges. This is also an excellent method for creating rounded sections on models using subdivision surfaces because the same effect is achieved even when using fewer edges.

At this point, it would be beneficial to create your textures. Select the lens polygons and apply a new material. Then invert the selection and apply a material to the rest of the light body. Any additional polygons attached to the body of the light will hold the new texture. Now move to the bottom of the cylinder and select six polygons on either side of the middle. Hold Shift while pressing the up-arrow key twice to create a rectangular section (as shown in Figure 5.34).

Figure 5.34

Initial selection made on the bottom of the model (left) and the end selection after expanding twice (right)

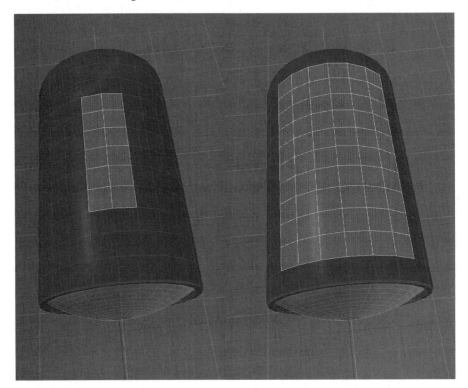

This selection will form the foundation for the attached box of electrical components.

1. Start by beveling it with a Shift of 20 mm.

2. Hold the Shift key and click to initiate a second bevel.

3. Select the Move tool (W) and drag the selection downward 150 mm (on the y axis).

4. Enable the Scale tool (R), deselect the Negative Scale option, and drag the green handle (for the y axis) until the selection has been flattened.

This model now has its basic shape. However, adding some simple rounding to soften the edges can help increase the realism of the object when seen in reflections. Select edge loops at the bottom of the box and the edge loop above that (see Figure 5.35).

With these edges selected, enable the Bevel tool, set the Round level to 4, and bevel these edges 4–5 mm. Also, select the front edges on the lip around the lens and bevel those as well. Because this same model will be used with the umbrella light, select the back circular face, and bevel it in and then out several times to add some detail, as shown in Figure 5.36.

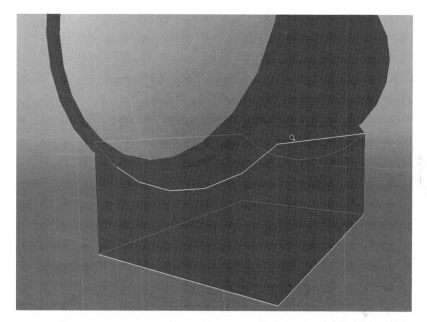

Figure 5.35

Edges selected and ready to be beveled

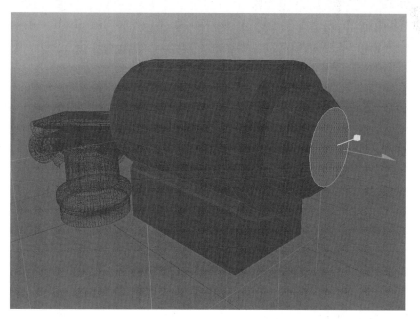

Figure 5.36

The back of the spotlight with simple details added

Creating the Umbrella Light

To begin work on the umbrella light, right-click the spotlight mesh layer and choose Duplicate. This creates a new mesh layer that contains the spotlight geometry. Now create a thin cylinder with a radius large enough to be the umbrella (800 mm to 1 m). This cylinder does not require much depth (about 15 mm), and Segments should be set to 1. Next, select the front and back faces and bevel them in together, toward the center of the umbrella, with a Shift value of 775 mm. At this point, you should have something very similar to the light lens before rounding it. Use the Loop Slice tool to add edge loops to the front and back, as you did with the light lens, and use a Cylinder falloff to pull both of these faces away from the lens. At this point, your umbrella should look like Figure 5.37.

Figure 5.37

The umbrella shape after being rounded

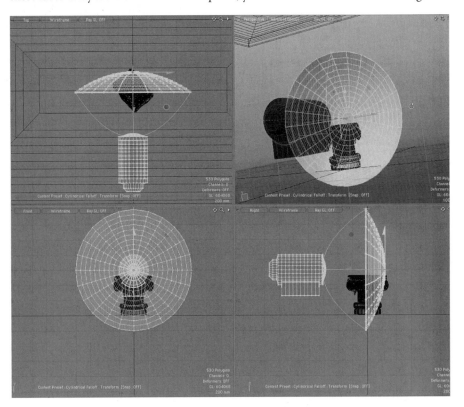

The umbrella has too many sides. Ideally, this would be a 12-sided umbrella, and the edges in between the spokes would be straight. The current mesh has 24 sides, so half of those need to be eliminated. This can be done with a simple process (which can be used in many other instances). To reduce the number of sides and eliminate the unwanted edges, do the following:

1. Select one of the edges running out from the center of the mesh.

2. Moving in a radial fashion around the object, skip one edge and then select the next. This forms the pattern for edge selection.

3. Using the up-arrow, select every other edge all the way around the object (Figure 5.38).

4. Press the L key to create loops based on all of the selected edges.

5. Press the Delete key to remove these edges but leave the existing polygonal structure (Figure 5.39).

To create spokes for the umbrella, select the remaining edges and use the Bevel tool (B) to add some thickness to these edges. Note that the Bevel tool adapts to the current geometry mode (Vertex, Edge, or Polygon). Set the value to about 5 mm, making sure that at the center of the umbrella (the circular polygon), edges are not overlapping. Now you need to select the loops' polygons, similarly to the way loops of edges were selected in the previous steps. Because polygons do not have a direction by nature, you will need to select adjacent rows, as shown in Figure 5.40.

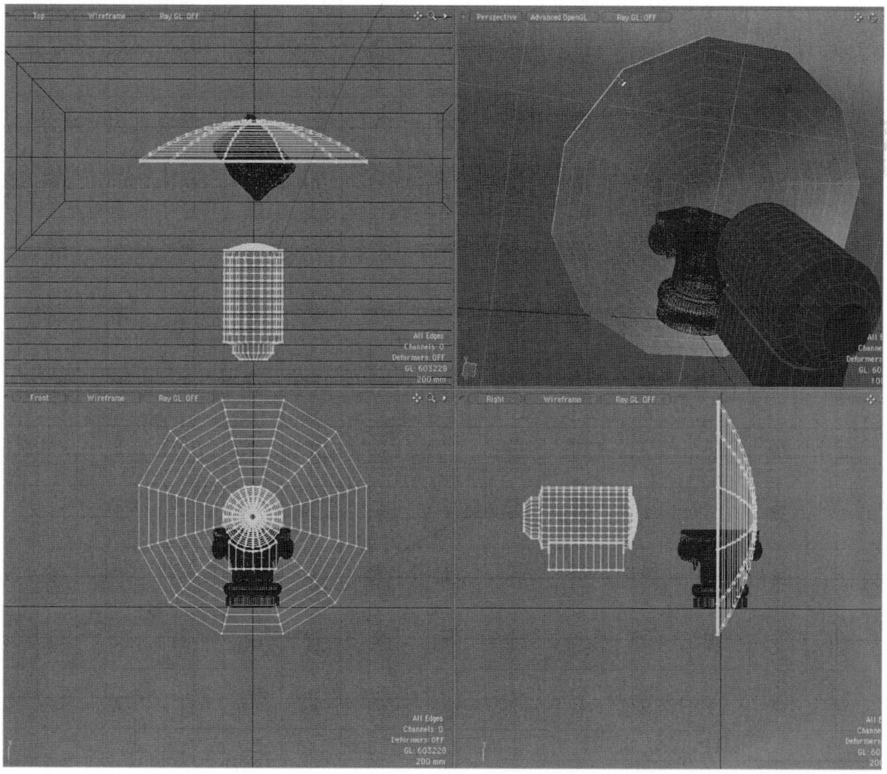

Figure 5.38

Alternating edges are selected around the umbrella.

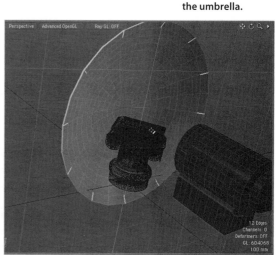

Figure 5.39

The umbrella with reduced edges

After selecting these two rows of edges, press the L key to select the loops, and use the Bevel tool to bevel these polygons outward about 5 mm. With these polygons still selected, press Shift+up-arrow once to grow the selection of polygons. With this set of polygons selected, press the M key and set a material for the spokes. Then invert the selection and deselect the spotlight. This is usually done most easily by holding the Ctrl/Control key and right-clicking a lasso selection around the spotlight in one of the orthographic views, as seen in Figure 5.41. With only the panels of the umbrella selected, press the M key to add a material.

The final piece to the umbrella is a tripod. Start by creating a tall, thin cylinder behind the umbrella object. This will be the top section of the tripod. Double-click the polygons for the cylinder and then copy, paste, and move the new cylinder behind the first cylinder. Move this leg cylinder downward so a small amount of overlapping occurs between it and the first cylinder. To rotate this leg properly, enable the Rotate tool and set the Action Center to Element. Click the vertex at the top of the leg cylinder and closest to the base cylinder. After this vertex has been selected, the rotate handles will center around it and enable you to rotate the leg to a proper position for a tripod (about 12°). The leg needs to be duplicated, but copy and paste operations will not suffice. Instead, you will re-center the world around the base cylinder and then use the Radial Array tool to duplicate the leg. Follow these steps to create the duplicates:

1. Select the polygon on the top of the base cylinder.

2. In the Work Plane menu, choose Align Work Plane To Selection.

3. Double-click the leg to select it.

4. In the Duplicate section, choose the Radial Array tool.

5. Set the Count to 3.

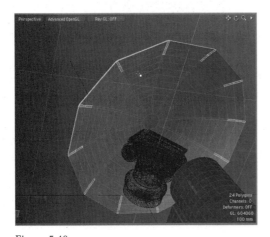

Figure 5.40

With two sets of adjacent polygons selected, pressing the L key can create loops.

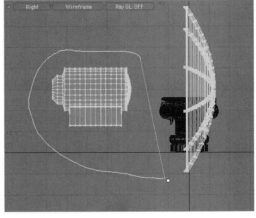

Figure 5.41

Lasso deselecting the spotlight

6. Change the Action Center to Origin.

7. Click in the viewport to create the extra legs.

8. In the Work Plane menu, choose Reset Work Plane to restore the Work Plane to its native position.

At this point, the tripod and umbrella light are adequately formed for the sake of creating reflections. If you wish to further detail these objects, the DVD contains video walk-throughs for creating the more-complex shapes shown in Figure 5.42.

Scene Objects

The final pieces of this scene can be modeled by using the same techniques as for the other simple models. To create the floor and backdrop, start with a square 12 m in the x-axis by 8 m in the z-axis. This square does not need any depth in the y-axis because the models will simply sit on top of it. In Edge mode, select the back edge (the upper one in the Top Orthographic view) and run the Edge Extend tool (Z key). Click in the viewport to activate the tool, and drag the new edge up in the y-axis about 5 m. This makes the

Figure 5.42

A more detailed model is not necessary for this application but can be helpful for practicing modeling skills.

back wall tall enough to stay in view even at low camera angles. The issue with the back wall now is that it will produce heavy shading in the corner. This is remedied by rounding the corner to soften the lighting on the backdrop. Select the edge in the corner and use the Bevel tool to round it until the flat floor extends just beyond the pedestal. Because this will be in full view and not subdivided, it is important to use a high Round level (of about 14). Your scene should now look something like Figure 5.43.

Simple models can be created for a reflector and a camera, as shown in Figure 5.44. For the reflector, you can reuse the tripod section of the umbrella along with a cube and some edge bevels. The camera is made up of a simple cylinder with a rounded front lens (like the spotlight) and a slightly modified cube. Again, you should remember that these will be visible in reflections and used to bounce/soften lighting, so a lot of detail is not necessary. If you get stuck, see the DVD for completed models (in the file 004210_Ch5_Scene.1xo) and step-by-step video guides.

Review

Good modeling techniques are crucial to the creation of believable and compelling 3D artwork. Practicing the techniques in this chapter will give you a firm starting point for many types of models. Deciding the appropriate type of modeling (polygon, subdivision surface, or sculpted) will also enable you to approach the job properly from the start. The key to many modeling tasks is identifying the basic forms and modifying them to get the finished look. After practicing the techniques in this chapter, you should be able to do the following:

- Adjust polygon models to prepare them for use as SubDs
- Create basic geometry by using PSubs
- Use multiresolution subdivision and sculpting tools to modify and detail simple models
- Model simple to complex geometry by using PSubs and edge weights
- Model simple objects with polygon creation and editing tools

Where to Go From Here

Finding other objects to model will enable you to implement these techniques without the guidance of this book. Start by identifying the type of geometry and the basic forms that make up the model. Then use the tools you are comfortable with to create the completed form. As with many other skills, practice and patience will enable you to be successful.

CHAPTER 6

Textures for Visualization

With your scene properly modeled, textures are the next order of business. Just as with other parts of a 3D workflow, texture work has the potential of creating truly inspiring art or ruining the hard work done in other areas of the design process. In this chapter, you will narrow texture work down to look at materials that are appropriate for visualization. This chapter covers the following:

- ▪ **Setting up a test environment and lighting**
- ▪ **Creating customized materials from presets**
- ▪ **Creating organic UV maps**
- ▪ **Building materials from scratch**

Setting Up a Test Environment

To properly see textures the way they will appear in final renders (with a fully custom light rig), you need to set up a proxy. Using a preset environment and some simple Global Illumination settings will allow the objects, material colors, reflections, and transparency to be seen in their best light without spending a lot of time setting up a detailed light rig and environment. Best of all, with the adjustment of a few settings, this can be customized to help you decide what the final scene will look like. For the most part, you will stay in the Render interface tab for the majority of your texturing and lighting work.

Before editing anything in a scene, lighting will appear harsh and flat. Without fill lighting, all detail in shadow areas will be lost. Additionally, the hard-edged shadows of a standard Directional Light are not suitable for simulating indoor lighting (see Figure 6.1). The existence of Ambient Intensity also washes out the scene to detract from the realism.

The first thing you will need to do is essentially eliminate any light in the scene before moving on:

1. Start by hiding (or deleting) the Directional Light. You will then be able to more clearly see the effect of the Ambient Intensity setting. Instead of a black scene, you will see a flat, dark gray.

2. In the Render viewport, select the Shader Tree tab, and select Render.

3. Click the Global Illumination tab and set Ambient Intensity to 0. The resulting render preview is a black screen. Though this may seem like a step backward, it actually gives a clean slate to work from.

4. While still on the Global Illumination tab, select Indirect Illumination. The resulting image should look something like the rendering shown in Figure 6.2.

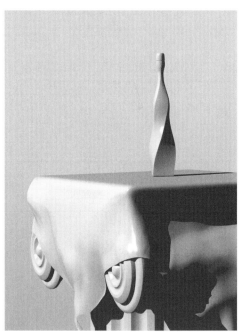

Figure 6.1
Scene with standard lighting

This is a nice start, but when the scene is lit in the next chapter, you will likely not use completely even lighting. To get an approximation that is more in touch with the finished scene, presets are very useful. In the Presets section of the Render tab (the section to the left of the camera and perspective viewports), select Environments from the drop-down menu and then open the Studio folder (shown in Figure 6.3). Here you will find a wide variety of simple studiolike environments that are excellent for approximating more-complex lighting and providing detailed reflections.

To sample these environments, simply double-click a thumbnail. This immediately loads the environment, and the render preview window will update to show the new lighting. Figure 6.4 shows several examples of lighting scenarios that are derived from these presets.

To get a good idea of the reflections caused by these environments, you may wish to temporarily enable some amount of Reflection Amount and/or Reflection Fresnel (10% - 20%) for the material of one of the objects in the scene (such as the bottle). This is a simple technique that will enable you to quickly visualize final rendered images, preview high-quality lighting, and even provide rapid feedback to clients. Even though this lighting and environment can be completely replaced by a more complex custom scene and light rig (in most cases), using a preset will give you the power to preview your materials accurately as you create them.

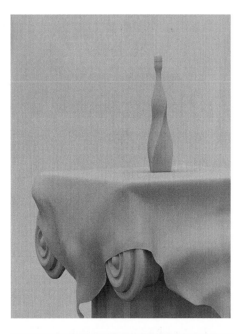

Figure 6.2

With Indirect (Global) Illumination active, the scene lighting becomes much softer and more believable.

Figure 6.3

The Studio Environments presets

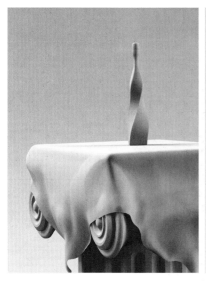 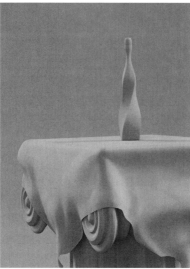 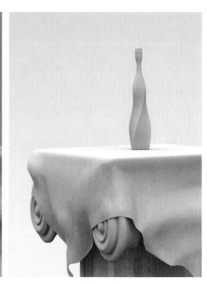

Figure 6.4

Three examples of lighting from the Studio Environments presets

Creating Customized Materials from Presets

For the first few objects in the scene, you will use preset materials. However, these materials will not remain at their default values. Instead, you will learn to modify aspects of preconstructed materials to create surfaces that fit your needs more precisely. Before editing a preset texture, you will need to make sure that it works well with your object:

1. Start by selecting the material group for the pedestal material from the Shader Tree.

2. Locate the marble material presets in the preset section of the Render tab. These are found in Materials → Stone → Architectural → Marble.

3. Double-click the Beige Marble material to apply it to your pedestal. With no alterations, your pedestal will look like Figure 6.5.

Adjusting the UV Map

In this case, you need to make some adjustments before the texture will map correctly to the mesh. The main problem is the UV map for the model. As a preset model, there is a UV, but it is not an evenly spaced one that will provide good texture placement. If you look closely at the round middle section of the mesh, you will see that the texture is being stretched significantly. This is due in part to the alterations that were made to get an appropriate scale. Also, there are a lot of sections overlapping as well. These need to be addressed to get the best quality from any placed textures. The addition of a UV Checker material (from the Miscellaneous section of the material presets) will show the distorted UV with more clarity, as illustrated in Figure 6.6.

Figure 6.5

The unaltered marble material

Figure 6.6

The distortions in the Checker pattern are evidence of a misadjusted UV map.

To clean up the UV map and remove the distortion, follow this procedure:

1. Move over to the UV interface and then, in the Lists tab, select Texture UV from the UV Maps heading. Inspection of the map will show that the majority of the mesh is laid out nicely, but the cylindrical section is heavily stretched, as shown in Figure 6.7. The easiest way to remedy this problem is to rebuild this section.

2. In Polygons mode, double-click the pedestal section of the UV map to select it.

3. Delete the UVs by choosing the Delete UVs command from the Edit UVs drop-down menu (in the middle of the tools panel on the left of the screen).

4. To make a new map for this section, use the UV Projection tool. Set the Projection Type to Cylindrical, the Axis to Y, and then click in the viewport.

5. Click the Pack UVs option and then click OK in the dialog box that comes up (default values are fine here).

    With this, your UV is almost complete. The only issues left are in areas where there are polygons on the model that are flat on the y-axis. These polygons will result in stretched image maps in that area. To get the smooth flow of textures, the edges need to be moved in the UV map.

Figure 6.7

The standard UV map that is attached to the column model, which was converted to a pedestal

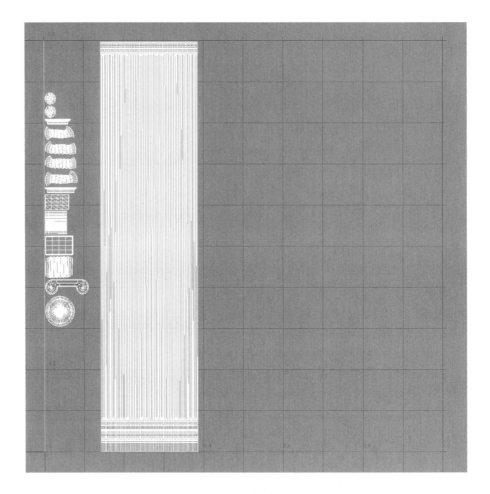

6. Double-click on an edge in the perspective view to select a loop.

7. Shift+click in the UV view to activate the view.

8. Enable the Move tool (W) and move the edge either up or down to give the polygons some UV space to occupy. Do this wherever you have an issue with stretching on the cylinder texture.

9. Spend a few minutes maximizing the spacing of the UV and adjusting the scale of some of the pieces. As you do this, keep the UV in the upper-right quadrant of the UV space (known as the *0 to 1 space*). Once completed, your UV should look something like Figure 6.8. The model with fixed UVs will look like the image in Figure 6.9.

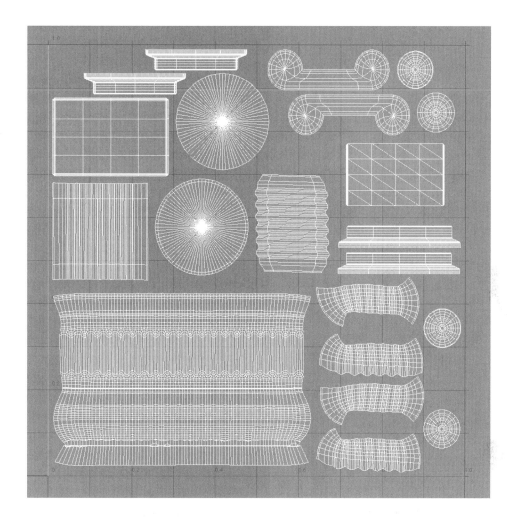

Figure 6.8

The adjusted UV allows for even distribution of image-based materials.

Altering the Preset Texture

With the UV map adjusted and textures mapping adequately, you can once again place the marble texture on the column. Because you may have unwanted layers on the Shader Tree now, it can be helpful to add a new material to the geometry:

1. Press the M key.

2. Delete the Column 01 material completely.

3. Select the newly created material group in the Shader Tree and double-click the Beige Marble material. Your model will now look like Figure 6.10.

Figure 6.9
The fixed UVs will result in clean texture mapping.

Figure 6.10
The marble material on the model with a proper UV map

Now you can look at the ways to alter this texture and create something customized. Additionally, this kind of workflow will allow you to cycle through various options in a very short period of time. There are three main ways to alter materials: adjusting the basic material settings and layers, using process layers, and using gradient layers.

Adjusting Basic Material Settings

Basic material settings can be used to massage a material into a more appropriate look. In this case, you will make the material a little more polished and vibrant. The default colors are a bit dull, the reflections are flat, and the material lacks the depth of real marble. You will need to use several material settings and the marble image map to properly adjust the material.

Let's start by looking at the reflective properties of the material (in the Material Ref section). Notice that the specular and reflective values are the same, which is good. However, as changes are made to the specular value, it would be much easier to have the reflective value update automatically, so select the Match Specular option. With a value of 60% for the Fresnel option, the material has some nice reflections at glancing angles, but it looks a bit dull on the rest of the object. Setting the Specular Amount (and the Reflective Amount) to 6% will add a lot to the reflections, but this may cause them to look a little too shiny and strong. This is where adding additional image layers can really come in handy:

1. Right-click on the marble beige image layer.

2. Choose Create Instance.

3. Right-click on Diffuse Color for the instance (the one that is italicized under the Effect heading).

4. Choose Reflection Color from the Basic Channels heading. This knocks back the reflections a bit and makes them blend a bit better. At this point, your material will look something like Figure 6.11.

    This surface is improving, but the reflections lack the depth of a polished surface such as marble. To create a multilayered look in the reflections, you will use the Clearcoat Amount setting in conjunction with Blurry Reflections.

5. Enable Blurry Reflections.

6. Set the Roughness to 50% to soften the reflections.

7. Set the Clearcoat Amount to 50%. The surface now has the effect of a soft reflection at the base of the material, with a stronger polished reflection on top that increases at angles more perpendicular to the camera (because Clearcoat Amount includes a Fresnel effect). The addition of a multilayered reflection helps to create a more realistic look, as shown in Figure 6.12.

Figure 6.11

The extra reflections help add polish to the surface.

Figure 6.12

Using Blurry Reflections in addition to Clearcoat Amount adds depth and detail to the surface reflections.

The final touch to the marble will be to add some real depth to the surface via subsurface scattering. As you may recall, subsurface scattering simulates the effect that light has on some surfaces when the light rays penetrate the surface, bounce around, and then emerge instead of simply being absorbed, emitted, or reflected.

8. In the Material Trans section, set the Subsurface Amount to 50% and the Scattering Distance to 10 mm. Note that the Scattering Distance helps define the scale of the object. Higher settings make the object look smaller, because smaller objects would have deeper light penetration. The converse is true of lower distance settings. The only problem that still appears here is the color of the scattering.

9. Create one more instance of the Diffuse Color image map and set it to Subsurface Color. With that set, the colors on the surface are now reflected in the subsurface scattering. Your finished adjusted surface will look like Figure 6.13.

These simple changes help to add additional detail and realism to the surface plus adapt the quality of it to our needs. Remember that these numbers can be adjusted to make the surface fit your needs precisely. If there are larger adjustments to be made, additional steps will need to be taken.

Using Process Layers

To make broader changes to the coloration of the surface, process layers are very powerful tools. The setup requires a few steps, but after it is in place, you can make adjustments very quickly. Follow these steps for using process layers:

1. To start, add a process layer, which is located in the Processing section (Add Layer → Processing → Process) of the Add Layer menu in the Shader Tree.

2. Right-click on the new layer and choose Create Instance.

3. Change the instance to Reflection Color.

4. Create another instance.

5. Set it to Subsurface Color.

Figure 6.13

The finished marble material

6. At first, nothing will change, but these texture layers act like adjustment layers in Photoshop. From one process layer, you can adjust the Bias and Gain settings as well as Hue, Saturation, and Value. This kind of texture layer can be used to make subtle or sweeping changes to the material. In Figure 6.14, Bias and Gain are set to 40% and 90%, respectively. Hue, Saturation, and Value are set to 450%, –75%, and –10%. As with other aspects of texturing, a little experimentation and patience will give the best results.

Making Gradient Adjustments

When it comes to more-complex adjustments to a texture, a gradient layer offers a lot of power if you are willing to take some time and experiment. At its core, this layer works much like the Gradient Map tool in Photoshop. The layer references the brightness values of an image (as if it were converted to grayscale) and applies those values to a gradient range (see Figure 6.15). Applying colors to the various points on this gradient graph applies those colors to the given brightness value. To edit a gradient, click the Edit Gradient button on the bottom of the Gradient Properties window (beneath the Shader Tree).

Figure 6.14

Process layers can be powerful tools for adjusting materials.

Figure 6.15

The Gradient Editor

GRADIENT INPUTS

For this example, you will use brightness values as the input. You could, however, choose from a wide variety of options in the Input Parameter field. Gradient input can be anything from the geometric incidence angle, to the height of an attached bump map, to the distance from a given locator.

A gradient starts with a single input at 0% that is set to white. When a gradient is inserted, it acts like a white constant, and the addition of inputs creates gradation of color. To insert inputs on the gradient graph, middle-click (or Ctrl+Alt/Control+Option+click if you do not have a three-button mouse) at the point where you want to insert a new value. Once created, these points can be edited by dragging them directly in the graph or by selecting a point and changing the Input and Value fields in the upper-left corner of the editor.

To use a gradient layer in this instance, you need to set up a control for the gradient to draw from:

1. If you are working from the previous file with the instanced image maps, start by deleting the instances and set the Diffuse Color image map to Driver A (right-click Diffuse Color and choose Driver A under the Shader Control section from the pop-up menu). Drivers are used directly as inputs for the Gradient Editor. When you do this, you will notice that the model will turn white.

2. Now, you can add a gradient layer into the Shader Tree and set Input Parameter to Driver A. This gradient will affect the Diffuse Color value.

3. Create two instances of the layer and set them to Subsurface Color and Reflection Color. Now any adjustments made to Diffuse Color will ripple through the other channels.

4. In the case of this material, you will first create some additional contrast and darken the main bulk of the material. Set the gradient as shown in Figure 6.16 to add these features to the texture.

The result will look like the image shown in Figure 6.17.

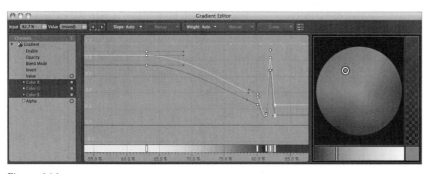

Figure 6.16

A gradient can produce much more variation than other editing types (such as process layers).

Figure 6.17

The results of the gradient from Figure 6.16 on the marble pedestal

To create another variation, new keys can be added or the existing ones can be rearranged. In Figure 6.18, you can see that the same keys from the previous example are spread out and that some of the orders have been changed.

By placing the high point of the gradient around the 75% mark (where the majority of the values in the original are located), the result is much brighter. Some tan and green islands of color also appear across the surface, as seen in Figure 6.19.

Continue to experiment with the gradients until you find an appearance that suits you. It is easy to first decide on brightness values (to define veins and islands in the texture) and then add color to the gradient to get the appropriate final look.

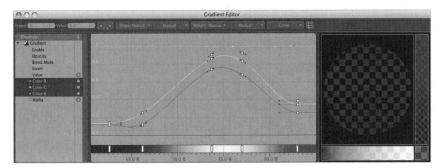

Figure 6.18

A rearranged gradient will result in significantly different coloration with minimum effort.

Figure 6.19

The result of the adjusted gradient on the model

Creating Organic UV Maps

The next section to be textured is the cloth over the pedestal. Because the mesh was created from scratch and based on two separate meshes that were attached to each other, the standing UV is not usable. Follow these steps to texture the cloth:

1. Move over to the UV interface and select the Texture UV map from the UV Maps heading in the Lists tab. Get rid of the existing UV by double-clicking on it in UV space and then choosing Delete UVs from the Edit UVs menu.

   Now that the UV space is clear, you will be able to create a new UV in its place. Because the polygons are still selected, you can move right into creating the new UV.

2. Turn on the Unwrap tool.

3. Set the Iterations to 1024, set the Initial Projection to Group Normal, and leave the other settings at their defaults. The UV will probably look a little lumpy, but that is okay because the actual geometry has a relatively uneven distribution. There is, however, a bit of pinching throughout the mesh that can be fixed by running the UV Relax tool.

4. Set the Mode to Adaptive, the iterations to 1024, and click in the viewport to activate the tool. At this point, your UV should look largely complete, as shown in Figure 6.20. You may notice that the mesh overlaps the UV space slightly, but you don't have to worry about this until the UV has been finalized.

Figure 6.20

The initial UV after unwrapping and relaxing

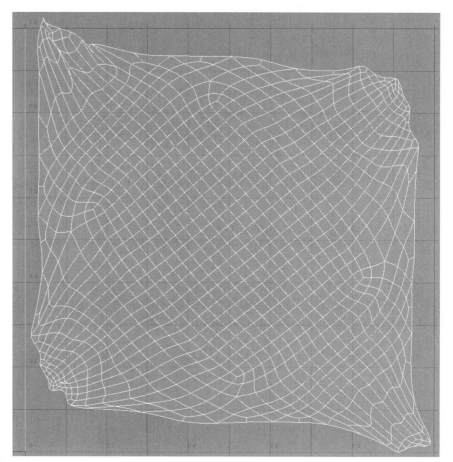

The last thing to adjust on the UV will likely be the corners of the map. There will likely be some overlapping in the corners, as seen in Figure 6.21. Overlapping UVs are shown in red in the map. To fix these errors, a little adjusting of vertices and edges is required.

5. Select an edge on either side of the red area and drag it away from the overlapped error. After a few small adjustments, your UV should look more like the one in Figure 6.22, and the overlaps will be gone. Do this on all of the corners to finish the layout of the map. To fit the map into UV space, select the Fit UVs tool (with default settings) and click OK.

Figure 6.21

Overlapping UVs will cause problems with mapping image based-textures.

Figure 6.22

Fixing the overlapped areas requires the movement of just a few pieces of geometry.

To get a better feel for the mapping created by this UV, you may wish to employ a UV Checker material like the one used on the pedestal in the previous section. Because this mesh will hold a much tighter pattern (woven cloth) than the marble texture, it is not important to have perfect mapping. A relatively even flow will do the job nicely.

Adding a preset texture will get you started with creating a finished material. Using a relatively neutral material such as Cotton Ash Gray 02 will give you something easy to edit in the same ways that the marble texture was. With this material, the fabric may be a bit too loose. To make a tighter pattern, simply increase the UV wrap to get the proper look for the fabric. With a small amount of editing, the material can look very similar to the image shown in Figure 6.23. Once again, the specific look that you are trying to achieve can be created with some simple experimentation.

Figure 6.23

The fabric material with proper UVs and an edited preset material

Building Materials from Scratch

Using and altering preset materials will enable you to quickly assemble many of the textures in your scene. You will, however, need to make your own textures at some point, so a good understanding of material construction methods is key to creating strong 3D scenes. In this case, you will look at creating three types of textures for the bottle: opaque, reflective, and transparent. You will explore several possibilities for each of these categories so you will be able to have a good general idea of how to create a wide variety of surfaces.

Opaque Materials

At face value, opaque materials seem very simple. After all, they lack transparency and reflections for the most part. Although many opaque surfaces can be easily constructed, there are a lot of things to take into account to make them look really good at render time. As you may recall from a previous chapter, all colored materials are reflective. The color of an object is determined by the color wavelengths that are reflected. Any visible object in the real world is reflective to some extent. The lack of mirrorlike reflections is simply due to the microscopic roughness of the surface. As the surface of an object becomes more perpendicular to our point of view, the reflective areas appear to get closer together because of the perspective, and the amount of reflection appears to increase. Because of this, many materials that would be typically thought of as non-reflective can benefit greatly from some amount of reflection and, specifically, Fresnel reflection.

In Figure 6.24, the bottle has a simple color applied. The look is relatively flat and basic. The material does nothing to accentuate the form of the model and really doesn't feel like it is a part of the scene.

To help this, add some Fresnel reflection and turn on Blurry Reflection. To keep the effect subtle, a lower Fresnel amount as well as a higher Roughness setting can be employed. Roughness controls the amount of blur in the reflections. Think of this as the microscopic roughness on a surface; the higher the setting, the less mirrorlike the reflections become. Another way to soften these reflections is to control the reflective color. Do this by setting the Reflection Color value (or Specular Color if you are using the Match Specular setting) to the same as the Diffuse Color value, or to a slightly lighter version of the same color. The closer the reflected color is to the diffuse, the softer the reflections will appear. Figure 6.25 shows the effect of 50% Fresnel with Blurry Reflection, Roughness set to 100%, and Specular Color (along with Reflection Color) set to the same as Diffuse Color.

In addition to reflections, the color of many objects shifts as the surface angles away from viewer. As the reflection amount increases (because of the Fresnel effect), the diffuse amount decreases. Remapped (shifted) colors can be achieved with a gradient layer (this is also called a *ramp* in some other programs). With a gradient in this case, you can alter the effect of the diffuse amount. This material has the default of 80% set for Diffuse Amount. With Fresnel set to 50%, that means you can subtract that amount from the diffuse amount as the incidence angle approaches perpendicular. To set up the gradient layer you will need to do the following:

1. Add a gradient layer, set Input Parameter to Incidence, and change the layer effect to Diffuse Amount.

Figure 6.24

A basic opaque material with no adjusted settings

Figure 6.25

Adding some tinted and blurred reflections can help add realism to the material.

2. Create two points in the gradient. Change the point at 0% (facing the viewport) to 80% and change the 100% point (equal to perpendicular to the viewport) to 30%.

3. Adjust the gradient to arc out from the left and then down to the right, as shown in Figure 6.26.

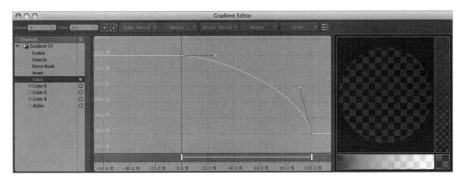

Figure 6.26

This gradient shows a falloff in diffuse amount that mirrors the increase in reflection caused by the Fresnel effect.

With this addition, the bottle will look like Figure 6.27. Note the subtle difference in shading in the areas where the Fresnel reflections come into play.

Depending on the type of material, a clear glaze is sometimes added. Increasing the Clearcoat Amount value will simulate this effect. Clearcoat adds a small amount of unblurred reflection that increases with the incidence angle (Fresnel effect). This is illustrated in Figure 6.28.

Figure 6.27

The bottle material with a gradient mapped to Diffuse Amount. Notice the slight darkening on the surfaces that are at a glancing angle.

Figure 6.28

Clearcoat adds the effect of a glaze on the surface of an object.

Another option with solid materials is to simulate a small amount of light penetration, as you saw in the marble material on the pedestal. This is common for many surfaces that are not transparent but have some level of translucency. Subsurface scattering can be used to this end. Setting the Subsurface Amount value to 25% (under the Material Trans

Figure 6.29

A small amount of subsurface scattering adds some depth to the surface through translucency.

tab in the material properties) will create a soft, translucent effect. Scattering Distance should be set relative to the scale of the object and the thickness of its surfaces. In this case, 15 mm is a good distance to help illustrate the thickness of the object. In areas where the bottle is thinner, the surface will appear to be lighter. The color setting should be similar to that of the diffuse color, but in the case of subsurface scattering, a lighter version of the color should be used. In some instances, the underlying material has a contrasting color, and in these cases, a contrasting color can achieve excellent results. These settings (without Clearcoat) can be seen in Figure 6.29.

These settings can be combined and adjusted to customize this surface to a wide variety of possible appearances. Take some time with the preview renderer and patiently adjust material settings to create the kind of opaque material that you need for your own scene.

Reflective Materials

Reflective materials offer similar challenges to opaque ones, but the increase in mirror-like reflectivity results in some additional concerns to deal with. Even a simple chrome material can be greatly improved with some careful attention to detail. As you may have noticed, when you added the Fresnel value to the previous texture, you also decreased Diffuse Amount to keep a balance of around 100% total. So when you deal with reflective materials, it is important to decrease Diffuse Amount accordingly (which may even mean turning it off). Depending on the brightness of the reflective environment, you may wish to decrease the total amount below 100% (we actually used 80% as the baseline previously). Figure 6.30 shows a basic surface with Diffuse Amount turned off completely and Reflection Amount set to 80%.

The addition of color to reflective materials comes mostly through colorizing via Reflection Color. The simple tint, however, will not produce the best look for reflective objects. In many cases, it is better to use a slight gradient to cause a falloff of Diffuse Amount. Then, Reflection Amount can be increased through the use of the Fresnel setting, as seen in Figure 6.31.

Figure 6.30
A basic chrome material

Figure 6.31
Reflective materials with a falloff of Diffuse Amount and an increase in Fresnel reflection offer some complexity to the tinted surface.

Completely clear reflections may not always be the desired look for a scene. In such cases, the Blurry Reflection setting can once again come in handy. Simply turning the blur on and setting the Roughness to a low value such as 20% will produce a simple brushed appearance, as in Figure 6.32.

Higher blur levels further soften the image and make the reflections less distinguishable. At this point, the difference between regular opaque materials and truly reflective ones becomes less obvious. Figure 6.33 demonstrates Blurry Reflections with Roughness (which controls the amount of blur in reflections) set to 100%. It should be noted that the Reflection Rays field is activated when Blurry Reflection is selected. Reflection Rays defines the render quality of blurred reflections. Low settings result in a grainy render, and higher values smooth that effect. The default of 64 rays is usually a good starting point.

BLURRY REFLECTION RAYS AND RENDER TIME

Reflection Rays defines the number of samples that are used to smooth out blurry reflections. When the sample rate is too low, blurred reflections appear to be rough and grainy. Increasing these rays smoothes out the look of the blur. Anti-aliasing also helps reduce the grain. When you prepare a final image for render, you should decide the final anti-aliasing setting before setting Reflection Rays to help optimize the render time, because extra rays can significantly increase render time.

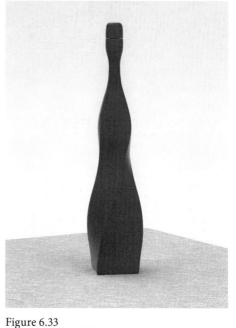

Figure 6.32

Brushed metallic effects can be achieved with Blurry Reflections.

Figure 6.33

Heavily blurred reflections soften the effect and create a look more like a kind of opaque material.

The use of textures (either image or procedural) can help add complexity and interest to reflective surfaces. The image in Figure 6.34 uses a Dirt procedural map (from Organic in the Enhance: modo Textures) for both Reflection Amount and Roughness.

To add some additional character to the material, the same dirt (with the Gain increased to 100%) is used as a bump map in Figure 6.35. Using procedural textures for this purpose can come in handy because there is no need to create a UV map for the texture to be properly applied. At times, it is valuable to view your textures out of the context of the scene. In these cases, primitive geometry (Plane, Sphere, or Teapot) can be accessed at the top of the Options drop-down in the render preview window, as shown in Figure 6.36.

Figure 6.34
Adding some randomness to reflective and roughness values can add the feel of a more complex surface.

Figure 6.35
Adding a bump map texture to the material in the previous image adds the look of physical texture to the surface of the model.

Figure 6.36
The preview render changed to the Teapot with the base material (left), the Reflection Amount layer (middle), and the fully composed texture (right)

TEXTURE PREVIEWS

Sometimes it is difficult to see what a texture will look like when placing it in a complex material (such as the dirt texture in the previous example). There is a great way to preview a texture layer or an entire material out of the context of your scene. In the Options menu at the upper left of the Preview Render window (Render → Open Preview Render), you can choose Plane, Teapot, or Sphere. These options show the selected texture layer or material in the context of a simple piece of preset geometry. In the bottom right is a scale indicator that gives the size of the object (the default is 1 m). By clicking and dragging the magnifying glass in the upper right, you can scale the object to an appropriate size.

The use of the Clearcoat Amount setting can also be useful with reflective materials. Simply using 50% Clearcoat Amount for the material with the blurred reflections produces a nice layered effect, as seen in Figure 6.37. Textures can also be used with Clearcoat Amount. The same Dirt procedural that was used as a bump map is used as the Clearcoat Amount in Figure 6.38. Notice the subtle differences in reflection across the surface of the model.

Figure 6.37
Clearcoat adds multilayered depth to reflective surfaces.

Figure 6.38
Use a procedural material to modulate the amount of clearcoat added to a material.

Transparent Materials

Transparent elements draw from the challenges faced in opaque and reflective materials. The added dimension of transparency brings a new set of challenges in both material creation and lighting. Lighting is covered in the next chapter. Here we will discuss the creation of different styles of transparency. As was the case with other material types, a balance needs to be maintained in which diffuse, reflective, and transparency levels equal about 100%. Once again, the exact balance between these elements can be adjusted to keep a desired visual appearance. More than the other types of materials, transparent materials rely heavily on reflection and diffuse values. Take the example of a basic transparent material with no diffuse or reflection values. The Transparent Amount is set to 90% with a Refractive Index of 1.517 (Zinc Crown Glass). This is shown in Figure 6.39.

Transparency tends to decrease as the incidence angle moves away from the viewer (the opposite of reflection). Because transparency does not offer a Fresnel effect this has to be done with gradients. To start, add a gradient for the Transparent Amount option, with Incidence as the Input Parameter (this should be the default when the gradient layer is created), and set two keys at 0% and 100%. The value at these two keys should be 80% and 10%, respectively. Add another gradient for Diffuse Amount and set the gradient from 5% to 40%. Then duplicate (or instance) that gradient and set it to Reflection Amount. By doing this, you will have a smooth transition between mostly transparent (when facing the viewer) and mostly opaque/reflective (when facing perpendicular). Figure 6.40 illustrates this combination.

Figure 6.39

A basic transparent material does little to define the contours of the model.

Figure 6.40

Adding gradients to Reflection, Diffuse, and Transparent Amounts can increase the realism of the transparent material and accentuate details on the model.

The Transparent Color setting is used to tint transparent objects. This, however, is not usually a simple fix for adding color, and the Absorption Distance value needs to be considered. This setting determines the amount of distance a light ray must travel through a transparent object before the transparent color is returned. When the object thickness is less than this distance, a lighter version of the color appears. When used properly, this will help add depth and the appearance of real thickness in colored, transparent objects. The distance should be set starting at the maximum thickness of the object. This allows for subtle variation in the surface color. From this point, the distance can be adjusted up or down depending on the material. Figure 6.41 shows a Depth of 60 mm.

Just as with reflection, all transparent materials are not clear. The appearance of fogged glass (or other transparent materials) can easily be created with Refraction Roughness. Because there is only a single aspect of transparency (unlike the relationship of reflectivity and specularity), the roughness setting is automatically enabled when any percentage is set. Care should be taken with the amount here, as high settings will completely obscure any transparency. Figure 6.42 shows a setting of 10%. Blurriness also increases with thickness. Higher settings require additional calculation time as well, because additional refraction rays are then required to create a smooth appearance. Figure 6.43 has the rays increased to 128 (from the default of 64). This render represents a 50% increase in render time as opposed to the previous render, and the number of rays could still be increased to achieve a result similar to that of the previous setting.

Figure 6.41

Transparent Color and Absorption Distance go hand in hand to make realistic tinted transparency.

Figure 6.42

A small amount of Refraction Roughness (10%) adds a slight fogged look to the material.

Figure 6.43

Higher roughness values require more refraction rays and increase render time significantly.

Figure 6.44

Clearcoat works well to add a fast polished touch to transparent objects.

The use of additional reflection can help make transparent materials appear shinier and more pristine. There are a couple of ways to get this effect without harming the material that has already been created. The simplest option is to turn on some amount of clearcoat (Figure 6.44 shows a setting of 50%). This can, however, leave the bulk of an object without much reflection, so there is another option. Put 10% reflectivity in the base material's Reflective Amount (or in Specular Amount if you are using Match Specular). Then change the Blend Mod for the Reflection Amount gradient layer to Add. This gives an overall increase of 10% reflectivity across the entire surface of the object, and it also keeps the relative Fresnel effect that has been custom made for the material. For an extra kick to the shine, combine the clearcoat with the 10% increase for an extra bit of sparkle, as shown in Figure 6.45.

In the case of Figure 6.46, the Dispersion level is set to 0.1. The end result is subtle but noticeable in various areas of the model. The render time, however, is increased about five times that of the previous renders (without Refraction Roughness). This is one effect that is best tested at a low resolution to get the proper setting and then left off until a final render is initiated. That way, you can walk away for a time to let the computer do the heavy lifting, while you take a break—or go home for the day!

Figure 6.45

A 10% increase in the overall reflectivity plus the Clearcoat Amount creates a clean and polished appearance.

Figure 6.46

Dispersion adds a nice touch of realism to transparent materials but can be slow to render.

Review

In this chapter, you have begun to explore the topic of material and texture creation. This is a large topic that will be touched upon often in upcoming chapters, but by now you should feel more comfortable with materials in general. Specific attention has been paid to the creation of basic opaque, reflective, and transparent textures. After reading this chapter and going through the exercises, you should be able to do the following:

- Use preset textures on your models
- Adapt presets to your specific needs
- Modify existing UV maps from preset objects
- Create and adjust UV maps from simple geometry
- Create opaque materials
- Create reflective materials
- Create transparent materials

Where to Go from Here

Using the theories and principles from this chapter, you can begin to create specific textures on your own. Find materials around you on objects that you can photograph or bring right to your desk. Take time to practice adjusting material values (for example, diffuse color, reflectivity, and transparency) to get close digital approximations of the things you find. With a little practice, you will be able to break down an object's appearance and replicate it quickly and accurately. Refer back to this chapter as a reference.

CHAPTER 7

Studio Lighting and Rendering

With models completed and textures created, lighting and render setup are the final steps for creating a finished image. Lighting can help to accentuate details in an object, glamorizing or romanticizing it. Properly setting up a lighting scenario will allow you to adapt your renders to fit the needs of your project. This chapter covers the following:

- **Creating a studio environment with simple geometry**
- **Setting up lighting based on geometry**
- **Optimizing render settings for final output**
- **Using high dynamic range (HDR) environments**

Creating a Studio Environment with Simple Geometry

In Chapter 5, "Subdivision Surface Modeling," you created models for lighting and environment setup. These will play a major factor in many aspects of the finished render. When used as lights and reflectors, real geometry can add subtlety and nuance to a lighting scenario, but can also help make reflections in objects that traditional CG lights will not. In addition, these objects can help provide visual cues that make the finished image look more realistic to the viewer. To start, each object needs to be prepared for use in lighting and reflections.

Let's start with the mesh camera model from Chapter 5, also found on the DVD. To make the camera work as you want it to, you will need to center it in the world, apply textures, and then attach it to the render camera so that the mesh camera follows the render camera around the scene. Follow these steps:

1. Select the camera and go to Polygons mode.

2. In model view, select Center Selected and choose All. This places the camera geometry in the middle of your scene.

3. The camera uses two materials: one for the body and another for the lens. For the body, enter a dark color for the diffuse material. Turn on some soft, blurry reflections if you like (shown in Figure 7.1). For the lens, choose the medium gray with 20% reflective amount and 100% Fresnel. These materials should be simple so they do not require much render time but still look good in terms of reflections and refractions in the scene.

Figure 7.1

The camera with simple materials applied

Once the camera is textured, you can attach it to the camera item in the scene.

4. Select the camera mesh item and drag it onto the rendered camera in the Items list.

5. You may notice that the camera mesh has not in fact moved. If, however, you select the mesh properties, you will see that the position and rotation values are no longer set to zero. Set the Position and Rotation X, Y, and Z values to 0.

6. The camera model will snap into alignment with the scene camera (render camera). In its current position, the camera mesh will occlude the view of the render camera. To fix this, set the Action Center to Selection, and in Items mode move the camera back slightly. You will know that the camera model is out of the way when the wireframe no longer appears in the camera view in the render (the real-time view in the upper right). When the camera is correctly placed, its relationship with the rendered camera should look something like the image shown in Figure 7.2.

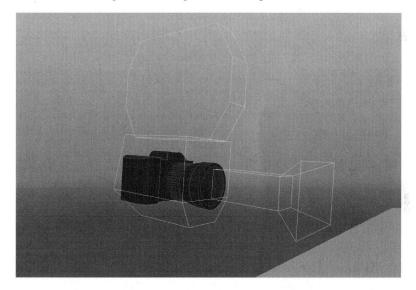

Figure 7.2

The camera mesh aligned with the render camera

SAVING PRESETS

If you have mesh items that you want to save and reuse in multiple scenes, simply select the mesh item and then choose Save Item Preset from the File menu. Store the preset in a place where it is easily accessible, such as a personal subfolder in the Content folder. This can also be done with materials by right-clicking the material group in the Shader Tree and choosing Save Preset. Do this with all of your common textures and models, and after a short time, you will have a large collection of materials and objects that are available and completely original.

Next, move on to the spotlight mesh:

1. Select the item and in Polygons mode, center it in space as you did with the camera. For my spotlight, I used the material preset from the camera body for the light housing because it is a very general, dark material.

2. For the light, use a luminous material to make the spotlight actually cast light when placed in the scene. Set the Diffuse Amount as well as the Specular Amount to 0.

3. Move to the Material Trans properties tab and set Luminous Intensity to 1. You will be able to adjust this setting later to suit the scene, but for now, this setting will suffice.

4. If you wish to do so, this is a good point to save the item as a preset. Figure 7.3 shows the scene lit by two spotlight objects.

The umbrella light is a little more difficult. It will require a simple UV map and some image-based textures to work properly. Start with the basic materials to get them out of the way. Use the dark material from the camera and the spotlight (or a similar material) on the tripod, the housing for the attached spotlight, and the wires that separate the segments of the umbrella. You can also reuse the spotlight lens material. Now let's move on to the UV map and begin work on the illuminated section of the umbrella:

Figure 7.3

Spotlight mesh items illuminate this scene.

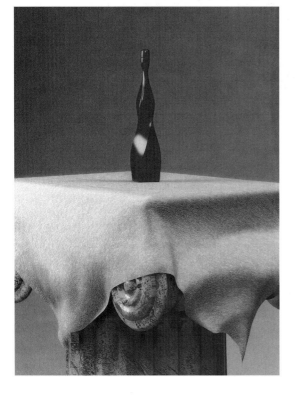

1. Select all polygons with this material attached. Go to the Lists tab and then to the Statistics portion at the bottom. click on the arrow next to Polygons to open the Polygons section and then the Material section. In this section, you will see a list of all the materials in the active mesh item.

2. Click the + icon to the left of the name of the umbrella material. This selects those polygons and nothing else.

3. With these polygons selected, open the UV Maps section of the Lists tab and click New Map.

4. Name the UV map appropriately and then select the UV Protection tool. Set the Projection Type to Planar and the Axis to Z. Click anywhere in the UV Edit viewport to create the UV. It looks something like Figure 7.4.

The UV map will serve both to create and to place an image-based texture on the model.

5. To put this UV into an image editor such as Photoshop, go to the Texture menu and choose Export UVs To EPS. The resulting EPS file can be opened in Photoshop. When opening, set the image size as 1024×1024.

In Photoshop, you will see a transparent background with thin lines where the edges lie on the UV map. Using a few layer styles and the existing pixel data, an image map like the one shown in Figure 7.5 can be created. If you have trouble creating an image like this, a short video on the DVD that is included with this book details the process. This will act as a map for both illumination and bump. Save the image as a high-quality JPEG.

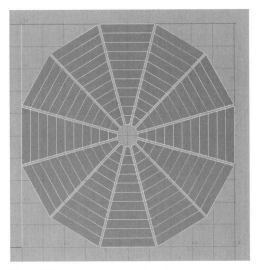

Figure 7.4

The UV map for the umbrella

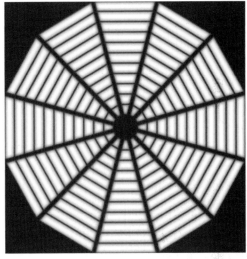

Figure 7.5

The image map created based on the UV map

Placing the image on the umbrella material in the Bump and Luminous Amount channels will result in a nice profile for both lighting and reflection. For Bump, right-click on the setting [by default set to Diffuse Color] in the Effect column and choose Surface Shading → Bump; and for Luminous Amount, right-click and choose Basic Channels → Luminous Amount. You will be able to tint this light by editing the Luminous Color setting in the Material Trans properties (click the double-arrow button under the Luminous Intensity setting). This light provides a medium (slightly diffused) source and characteristic profile in reflections with the hard-edged shape and the dark area in the middle. Figure 7.6 shows the finished light model as well as a sample of the scene lit with this model.

The overhead softbox is relatively simple. It has a frame material (for which the dark texture used on previous objects works nicely) and an illuminated material. The illumination can be handled simply by turning on the Luminous Amount setting. More detail can be added by using another image map.

Figure 7.6

The finished light model (left) and the rendered scene using the light (right)

Because this section of the mesh is based on a relatively flat surface, no UV map is necessary. Therefore, you can jump straight to the image. This texture layer requires a very simple image as well:

1. In Photoshop, create a new image with dimensions of 512 pixels square.

2. If the background is not white, fill it with white and then press Alt/Option while double-clicking the layer to unlock it and turn it into a regular layer.

3. Add an Inner Shadow layer style. Set the Distance to 0%, the Choke to 20%, and the size to 60 pixels. The resulting image will look like Figure 7.7.

Place this image on the softbox light material and then set it to the Luminous Amount channel. This will allow for a soft edge on the light in both lighting and reflections. To place the image on the object without a UV map, import the image into the material. In the Texture Locator tab, set the Projection Type to Planar, the Projection Axis to Y, and then click the Auto Size button to fit the image perfectly. Figure 7.8 shows the finished softbox and the results of its lighting on the scene.

The last item can be used as either a reflector or a small softbox light. There are two materials to this model, one is a standard dark material and the other is a reflective/luminous surface. The second material can be placed as a simple color with a high dif-

Figure 7.7

A simple image with shaded edges adds detail to the softbox mesh.

fuse amount to provide some very light spill and accent color, or it can have a luminous material mapped to the luminous amount. In this case, it is useful to employ a slightly more detailed image map that is derived from the large softbox image. By darkening the entire image, placing a set of three concentric circles (white, then light gray, then another white), and adding a heavy Gaussian Blur, the image can be made to fit this purpose, as shown in Figure 7.9.

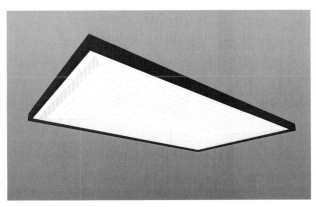

This image can also be placed by using Planar Projection and the Auto Size feature. Just make sure to use the correct Projection Axis. Remember that the Projection Axis is the one that is perpendicular to the image plane. For the example in Figure 7.10, the mesh uses the z-axis.

With these elements prepared, they can be used to light the scene entirely or to create more-complex environments. In the next section, you will look at ways to use and manipulate these scene elements to create finished studio renders such as the image shown in Figure 7.11.

Figure 7.9

The first softbox image can be changed very quickly to fill a new role.

Figure 7.10

With the image placed, the reflector makes an excellent small softbox.

Figure 7.11

A studio render based on the luminous materials on the scene objects

Setting Up Lighting Based on Geometry

Properly created and textured props will give you the necessary building blocks for a good scene. To create a scene, you will first create a completely dark room and then use the light objects to provide the illumination. Placing the lights and adjusting their intensities will suffice when using an opaque material on the bottle. For a basic setup, this will help balance the lighting. Then you can make minor adjustments for the reflective and transparent materials.

Lighting Opaque Subjects

Start by adding in the overhead softbox. With its default size, the illumination will probably look a little dark (see Figure 7.12).

There are two ways to increase the illumination that comes from this kind of light: Luminous Intensity and Scale. The simple fix is to increase the Luminous Intensity setting. The only problem with this is the increase in noise that is introduced as this value increases. To combat this issue, you need to increase the number of light rays used to calculate the lighting in the Global Illumination properties (Render Properties → Irradiance Caching → Irradiance Rays). However, this will result in higher render times. The other option is less obvious but works very well. When light is calculated, it is based on the area from which the light is generated. Larger area equals more light, so an increase in size will generate more light without the rendering artifacts, as shown in Figure 7.13.

Figure 7.12
The softbox will cast soft light with subtle reflections but might be too dim initially.

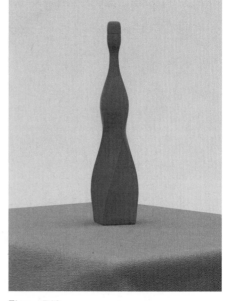

Figure 7.13
Increasing the scale of the object will cast more light into the scene without causing higher render times.

The single light will probably not provide enough illumination to properly fill out the scene. From here, it is important to remember the basics of lighting that have been discussed previously. The addition of extra lights will fill out the scene properly. Add the umbrella light to the scene and place it off to one side to fill out the lighting a bit. This is also a good place to add some coloration to change the mood of the image. With the additional fill, the image will become more dynamic but will probably have some dark areas that need to be adjusted (see Figure 7.14).

Figure 7.14

A secondary light will help fill out the scene.

In this first example, the addition of a smaller softbox or reflector helps to complete the image. The softbox adds more light. The reflector can also be useful if placed just outside the camera view to provide very subtle fill and can introduce bounced light onto the subject. For an opaque material, this lighting scenario can provide good, clean lighting and quick render times. The setup for this scene is illustrated in Figure 7.15. Placement, scale, and intensity of the lights can be altered to create different moods and to accentuate different parts of a model. The finished render is shown in Figure 7.16.

Figure 7.15

This image shows the placement of lights used to create a final render with geometric lighting objects.

Figure 7.16

The finished render based on the light setup shown in Figure 7.15

Figure 7.17

A nicely lit scene for opaque objects is far from ideal when lighting reflective ones.

Lighting Reflective Subjects

With subjects that feature mirror-like reflections, the placement of lighting entities becomes more important. With the basic lighting rig from the previous section as a starting point, you will now look at ways to fine-tune the scene to create more-dynamic reflections and a more specialized and compelling scene for this subject type. Switching to a chrome material and then rendering gives a less-than-ideal result (see Figure 7.17). The lighting rig is designed to light the subject, but the problem is that for reflective materials, the important thing to light is the scene, which will then reflect in the object.

The problem here lies in the reflections. The light objects in the scene do not reflect the bottle cleanly, so the form of the model is largely lost. To look at a better possible solution for this, you will start by simplifying the scene. Eliminate everything but the small softbox. Adjust the position of the object so it is much closer to the bottle (just out of the camera view) and scale it down significantly. This will cast some light on the backdrop and make strong reflections on the right side of the object to help define the edge of the model. There are obvious issues with the left side of the image, and those shadow areas need to be dealt with, as seen in Figure 7.18.

The next step is to define the remainder of the form. Duplicating the existing light and moving it to the other side of the scene can accomplish this task. Place the duplicate on the other side of the scene and angle it more toward the camera. This helps fill out the shape and adds illumination to the cloth without adding much more light to the backdrop, as shown in Figure 7.19.

The scene is almost complete, but an odd gap remains at the top of the bottle, which leaves the form incomplete and a bit awkward feeling. Therefore, the last step is to reintroduce the overhead light. Simply adding the overhead light will blow out the scene and make the backdrop too bright. The drama of the shot would be lost, and the work to this point would also be lost (see Figure 7.20). Instead, make the light much smaller and angle it toward the camera. Position it so that it minimally impacts the backdrop. Once completed, the scene should be arranged something like Figure 7.21.

This type of light setup will work with a variety of materials. You may wish to experiment with the scale, intensity, and position of the lights in the scene as well as color temperature to suit specific subjects. In the case of the reflective materials from the previous chapter, this lighting scenario will work nicely. As you begin to work on your own projects, you can build variations on this design that will help accentuate details and sell the shot. As you did when constructing this shot, move one piece at a time and isolate pieces while you perfect the look. Figure 7.22 shows the same light setup as the previous image, but with one of the reflective materials from the previous chapter (see Figure 6.38 in Chapter 6, "Textures for Visualization").

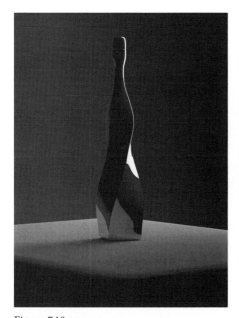

Figure 7.18

The simplification of lighting helps define the shape of the model.

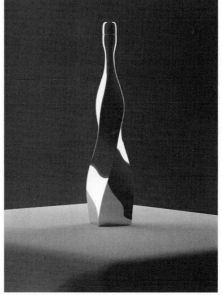

Figure 7.19

A secondary light helps to fill out the form of the subject.

Figure 7.20

The layout of the finished scene

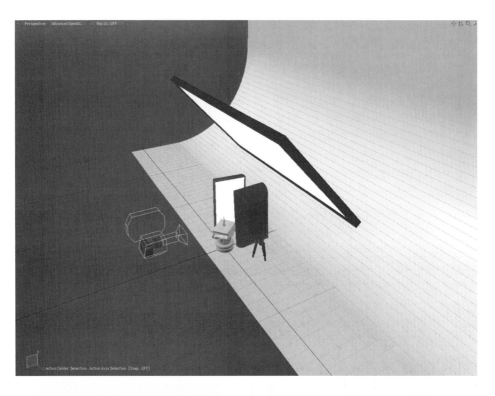

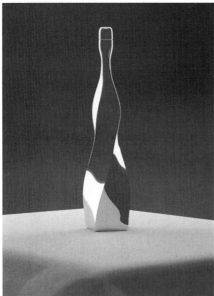

Figure 7.21

With the three lights in position, the setup is complete.

Figure 7.22

The scene works for a variety of different surfaces.

Lighting Transparent Subjects

Simply switching the bottle to a glass material will show that the previous lighting scenario is not appropriate with this object. Start with the High Gloss material from the High Gloss Glass section of the material presets. Reflections are bouncing all over in the glass, and the look becomes very chaotic (see Figure 7.23). Returning to the original lighting (the opaque version) offers an equally inappropriate result, as shown in Figure 7.24. The random reflections are reduced, but the shape of the bottle is lost in the backdrop.

Transparent objects can be significantly more finicky when it comes to setting up scenes. With the mixture of reflection and refraction and an almost complete lack of diffuse contribution, placement of scene elements takes a lot of additional tweaking to get them to look just right. A good idea to start with is simplicity. Especially when transparent objects feature complex contours like this twisting bottle, the simpler the scene is, the better the end result will be.

With that in mind, you will eliminate some of the elements in the scene. To start, scale down the backdrop and place it under the bottle. Then remove the pedestal and cloth entirely. This simple backdrop will make it easier to get good results. With this simple backdrop as the starting point, turn on (unhide) the overhead softbox. Scale down the light and position it above the scene. Figure 7.25 shows the result of the single-light setup. The reflections have improved, but the definition is still lacking (especially around the neck of the bottle).

Figure 7.23

The transparent material in the finished reflective environment

Figure 7.24

The transparent material in the finished opaque environment

With the evenly lit backdrop and flat lighting, the bottle is still getting a bit lost in the scene. Switch to the small softboxes on either side of the bottle and place them just outside the camera viewport. This will help with the definition of the object, but once again it clutters up the reflections a bit too much. Moving the lights farther out to the sides helps a bit, but not enough (see Figure 7.26).

What needs to be pinpointed now is the source of extra reflections. In this case, the background is the culprit. The best way to test this theory is to eliminate the diffuse color on the backdrop altogether. Change the diffuse color to black and render again. The result will show a marked reduction in reflections (see Figure 7.27).

At this point, the reflections may be a bit too hard. This can be fixed by adding something to diffuse the light. In a real photography studio, a piece of translucent paper can be introduced between the light and the subject. For this, you can use the geometry from the backdrop. Copy and place the polygons into a new layer and place one copy in front of each of the lights. At first, this blocks the light entirely because the material on the diffusers needs to allow light to pass through. Place a new material on this geometry. Leave all of the settings for the material at their defaults but (in the Material Trans tab) set the Subsurface Amount to 100%, the Subsurface Color to white, and the Scattering Distance to 0 (which simulates simple translucency). With these values set, the scene will be lit once again. At this point, the render will look something like Figure 7.28.

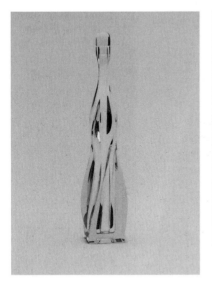

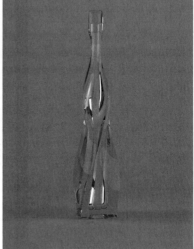

Figure 7.25

A simple scene helps reduce the clutter in object reflections.

Figure 7.26

Placing lights on the sides helps define the object at the cost of cluttered reflections. The image on the left has the lights just outside the camera view, and the shot on the right has them placed farther out.

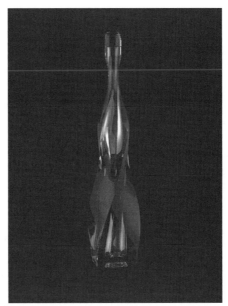

Figure 7.27

Removing the diffuse color from the backdrop reduces the unwanted reflections in the scene.

Figure 7.28

Adding diffusers softens the lighting and reflections in the scene.

This can serve as a nice point to stop and make minor adjustments to the materials in the scene. For instance, a small amount of Fresnel reflection (found on the Material Ref tab) on the floor can help ground the subject and help improve the composition of the shot. Enabling Blurry Reflection (also found on the Material Ref tab) can also provide a nice touch and help finish the shot. Figure 7.29 shows the finished setup and the render to this point.

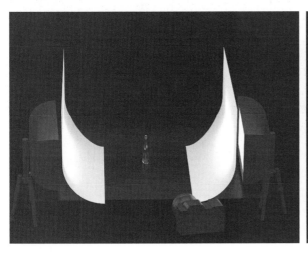

Figure 7.29

The finished scene layout (left) and the resulting render (right)

This scene can now serve as a nice starting point for further experimentation. Try adding color and varying reflective amounts to the backdrop. Colorize the diffusers and/

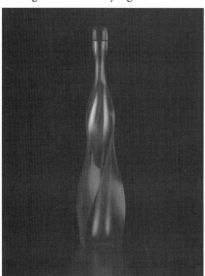

or lights as well. Depending on the object and scene, these variations can make for a great image. This scene will also work for reflective and opaque objects or for models with combinations of varying material types. With the scenes that we have designed in this section and their possible variations, you have a good start toward creating scenes for many different objects and purposes. Place the tinted transparent surface from the previous chapter on the bottle as shown in Figure 7.30. The scene holds up well with this material applied. Now you can move on to look at rendering options that will create a high-quality finished look for your renders.

Optimizing Render Settings for Final Output

You may have noticed some issues with image quality while doing your test renders throughout this chapter. In this section, you will learn ways to improve render quality and to correct some common quality issues. Simply adjusting (often increasing) a few settings will get you only so far and, in many instances, will only add to your render time and prolong your workflow without really addressing the problems. In a perfect world, we would all have massive banks of computers to do our digital bidding, and a brute-force method would get the job done, but in our world we will have to settle for being smart.

Two main issues affect the quality of a rendered image: pixel quality and lighting quality. Each of these has its own set of specific problems, but it really all boils down to those two things. Occasionally, there is overlap between the two, but more often than not, one of them is the culprit that keeps your image from looking its best.

Improving the Quality of Rendered Pixels

Often, images show jagged or oversharpened edges in areas of high contrast. The answer to this problem is *antialiasing*. When straight lines are created in digital form, they can be properly represented only horizontally or vertically, because the pixels on the screen are square. Any line angle other than that has to be represented by the stair-stepped look of jagged pixels. The addition of transitional pixels in the gaps between the stairs helps soften the look. In a 2D application, simply blending pixels does this. In 3D, there is a different approach. If an image has areas of high contrast at places where this jagged look appears, antialiasing kicks in. The offending pixels are rendered at a higher resolution; the result is then scaled down to derive an average, which is displayed as the finished pixel. This would be the equivalent of having additional resolution levels of an image or photograph and, where needed, a higher resolution could be sampled to smooth out the jagged edges and create a refined image. Anyone who has spent time rebuilding a client logo from an enlarged photocopy of a 12-year-old inkjet-printed business card can greatly appreciate this.

Fortunately, as long as the original model files are kept, 3D renders always exist independent of resolution. For this reason, you can always draw from a higher resolution or "retake" the original long after the project is completed. This is one of those amazing benefits to adding 3D into your workflow. Let's start by taking a look at a render from the previous section with no antialiasing (see Figure 7.31). As you can see from the enlarged section, there are lots of stray pixels and jagged edges.

To fix this, you need to adjust the Antialiasing settings. From the Shader Tree tab, select the Render item, and then choose the Setting tab from the Properties viewport. Let's start by adjusting the Antialiasing setting, which will control the actual number of samples in a pixel. Modo defaults to 8 Samples/Pixel. This is a decent level for test renders but will likely not give the kind of quality needed for final presentation. The same can be said for 16 Samples/Pixel, so skip up to 32 (which makes a nice baseline for finished renders). The render takes longer (about 60% longer to be exact), but it is well worth the additional time. Figure 7.32 compares the original render with one at 32 Samples/Pixel.

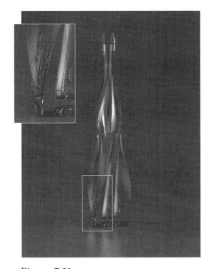

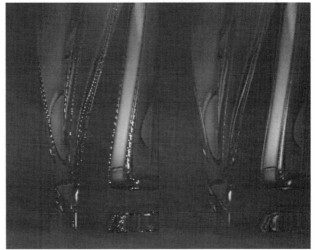

Figure 7.31

A rendered image with no antialiasing

Figure 7.32

An image without antialiasing (left) compared to one with 32 Samples/Pixel (right)

The improvement is nice, but some visible stair-stepping still exists in several areas of the image. By increasing the samples to 256, the image shows some improvement, with only about a 10% increase in render time (see Figure 7.33). The render seems remarkably quick considering the increase in quality—but there is a catch here. Close examination of the image will show little real improvement.

Figure 7.33

Setting the Antialiasing level to 256 Samples/ Pixel results in little difference to image quality.

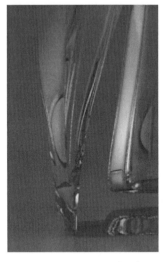

The reason for this lies in the Refinement Shading Rate setting. This controls the amount of actual pixel subdivision that can occur for any given pixel. This setting defines the fragments of pixels that can happen in each direction, so the default setting of 0.25 pixels will allow the pixel to be divided up to four times in each direction, for a total of 16 possible samples per pixel. This rate can go up to the Antialiasing level. In other words, the setting of 256 was never really reached. In fact, the level of 32 was also slight overkill. Set Refinement Shading Rate to 0.1 pixels (the lowest setting) and return Antialiasing to 32. A new render will show some real improvement because all 32 samples are now being calculated. Setting this level to 64 and 128 pixels will also show improvement, because the total possible samples can reach 100. Figure 7.34 shows a full render with 32 samples and a 0.1 Refinement Shading Rate.

Because rendering every pixel in an image multiple times (in this case, 32 times) would take a lot of time and be a waste in many parts of the image, the Refinement Threshold

Figure 7.34

32 Samples/Pixel can be an effective setting with a low Refinement Shading Rate.

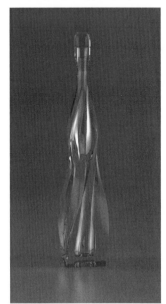

acts as a contrast check to see where the antialiasing engine will be engaged. If the brightness of two adjacent pixels falls into the percentage, the rendering engine calculates only a single pixel. Anything beyond the range is calculated based on the Refinement Shading Rate and the Antialiasing level. Lowering the percentage will cause the image to be more heavily antialiased. This can improve image quality at the cost of render time. Conversely, a higher setting will decrease render time while sacrificing image quality. This setting can help significantly if areas of an image have busy patterns of low contrast. Additionally, the Refine Bucket Borders option can help smooth areas between the rendering buckets. Because these cannot be calculated while the regular render runs, this will cause all pixels at the borders to be antialiased.

HIGH ANTIALIASING LEVELS

Because the Refinement Shading Rate essentially caps the number of samples per pixel at 100, many renders do not benefit from settings above 128 Samples/Pixel. The higher settings do, however, help provide additional smoothing when Motion Blur and Depth Of Field are enabled, because these features can benefit from the additional shading calculations.

The Antialiasing filter decides the method for smoothing. Gaussian (the default) provides a simple and reliable option. The other two settings that can be of particular use are Catmull-Rom and Mitchell-Netravali. Catmull-Rom provides a slightly more crisp result for a sharp image. Mitchell-Netravali helps improve areas where patterns or tight edges mesh and cause unwanted moiré patterns. As you will see, however, not every problem with rough areas has to do with antialiasing.

Improving Lighting Quality

Calculation of light rays can also lead to poor image quality. If you have increased and adjusted your antialiasing settings to very high levels without seeing improvement, the real issue is often in the lighting, not the image refinement. The settings you need to adjust for this are found in the Global Illumination section of the Render Properties viewport. To access these, click Render in the Shader Tree, and then in the Properties tab below the Shader Tree, click the Global Illumination tab from the set of vertical tabs. A few well-placed adjustments in this section can make the difference between a mediocre render and a pristine one.

There are essentially two types of radiosity used in modo (as well as many other applications). *Montecarlo* uses a set number of light rays and samples the entire image at that rate. This setting is found under the Indirect Illumination section. Setting the Indirect Rays will determine the number of rays when using Montecarlo (which is enabled if Irradiance Caching is not enabled). The other style is known as Irradiance Caching. This method uses more-advanced settings to determine where more rays are needed. This allows for higher image quality in less render time. A closer look at each of these will better illustrate how each one operates.

Montecarlo

This is the classic brute-force method for rendering with Global Illumination. Using the Montecarlo setting can provide amazing results but can take an extremely long time to create a finished render at high quality. At the default setting of 64 Indirect Rays, the scene will look very rough and grainy, as shown in Figure 7.35. The render time is decent, but the render is far from presentable.

Figure 7.35

Montecarlo render-
ing at the default
setting produces
rough finished
images in
most cases.

Because there is really only one setting to worry about for quality, this can be a good choice for an extremely clean look when time is not an issue, such as when leaving a computer to render overnight or over a weekend. Figure 7.36 shows increasing levels of Indirect Rays with their respective render times. For each of these, the increase in render times is very close to a multiple of the Indirect Rays. In other words, the image with 2,048 rays took twice as long as the one with 1,024 rays, and four times as long as the image with 512 rays.

The strong point of Montecarlo rendering is that it can give very clean results if you have the time to spare. Doing sample tests on a limited area can allow you to pinpoint the render quality needed, and then a final render can be launched. The resulting image will have good, even render quality and no undesirable lighting artifacts.

Irradiance Caching

Irradiance Caching provides a more elegant solution to rendering with Global Illumination, but it can be frustrating for problematic images if not approached correctly. Just like the previous render type, Irradiance Caching has a number of rays that can be set. However, this works a bit more like the example of antialiasing: a simple increase does not guarantee the best results. Irradiance Caching is on by default when Indirect Illumination is enabled. Clicking the Enable box under Irradiance Caching will toggle the mode.

Figure 7.37 shows various levels of Irradiance Rays. Notice the increase in quality around the middle of the ball. It is also important to note that the render times of all these images are less than the lowest-quality version of the Montecarlo render. In addition, the render time difference between 256 rays and 2,048 rays is only a multiple of three, whereas the same change in rays for the Montecarlo renderer was nearly eight times longer.

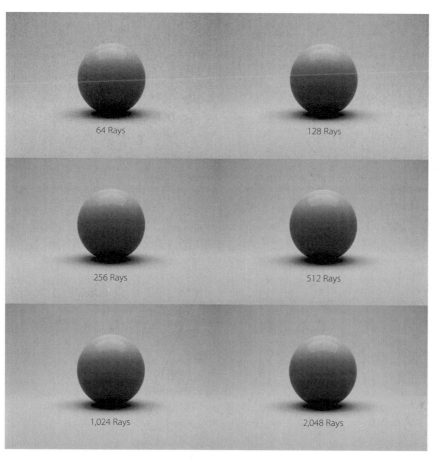

Figure 7.36
When increasing the Indirect Rays setting, the results are predictable, but render times can become excessive at high levels.

Figure 7.37
Because of the intelligent sampling methods of Irradiance Caching, the renders start off much smoother and are completed much faster.

Improvements can still be made to enhance the image quality. To do this, you will look at the next group of settings. Irradiance Rate and Irradiance Ratio work together. The *Irradiance Rate* sets the minimum value for distance between sampled pixels, and the *Irradiance Ratio* is multiplied by the Rate to get the maximum distance between sampled pixels. To understand this, a little explanation of Irradiance Cache rendering is necessary. You may notice that when a render is initiated with Irradiance Caching on, it will first launch a series of pre-passes (four in total). These passes will sample the image at full quality (based on the Irradiance Rays), and then the Rate and Ratio kick in to decide where more light samples are needed. The averaged values are used to fill in the pixels between the cached pixels. In areas where there is little detail, the pixels will be sampled from a broader area and result in faster render times. Areas of higher detail will draw from closer high-quality samples and result in good detail and slower renders. The last value for most images is the Interpolation Values field. This defines the maximum number of pixels that can be sampled to create the finished pixel. Increasing this number will smooth the render and result in slightly slower render times.

There is a balancing act between these settings that will vary from image to image. In most cases, the default settings will be a good starting point. Figure 7.38 shows the difference between the default render and the settings of 512, 0.5, 12, and 4 for Rays, Rate, Ratio, and Interpolation Values, respectively.

Figure 7.38

Default Irradiance Cache settings (left) can be greatly improved upon with a little tweaking (right).

SUPERSAMPLING

You may notice a check box labeled Supersampling. This option fires additional light rays at areas of high contrast in the image. This feature provides some improvements to quality and adds very little cost in render time. It is recommended that this setting always be left on.

A little experimentation with these settings will be necessary for the best image quality. In some cases, you can achieve smoother results with less detail (higher Irradiance Rate) if the image does not have a lot of areas of shaded detail. Other times, you might be working with a mix of sections with high detail and others with almost none. In these cases, having a wide range between the Irradiance Rate and Irradiance Ratio can be very helpful. Take Figure 7.39, which shows a render from earlier in the chapter at default settings, with double the Irradiance Rays and with the Rate, Ratio, and Interpolation Values set to 2, 12, and 4, respectively. Notice the reduction of random dark blotches in the render on the right. The render times are all fairly similar on these, with the second render representing only a 10% increase in time, and the third costing only about 2% over the second. For these kinds of improvements, these are well-spent seconds.

Figure 7.39

A render at default settings (left), with double the Irradiance Rays (middle), and with some adjusting to the other Irradiance Values (right)

Using High Dynamic Range (HDR) Environments

Sometimes, more-complex scenes are required for lighting and framing a subject. These scenes can give nice detail, complex lighting, and clean reflections to your scenes. The problem is that this can increase render time significantly. The use of HDR environments can speed your workflow and decrease render time while preserving high-quality results. These environments come in a variety of types and price ranges. A lot of free environments are available from various locations online. A simple web search for *high dynamic range environments* will provide a wealth of options both free and for sale. Figure 7.40 shows a render done with a free environment.

These environments often come in sets with images for the reflections, lighting, and backdrops. Because lighting can be simplified without loss of quality, an HDR image at low

Figure 7.40

HDR environments can provide excellent light and reflections with great render times.

resolution with a heavy blur can be used for lighting information. Because of the simplified lighting image, the Irradiance Rays can be significantly reduced without loss of render quality. The previous example was reduced to 64 rays. Then a higher-resolution HDR can be used for reflections and sometimes an even higher-resolution standard JPEG (low dynamic range) can be used as a backdrop. If you have more interest in setting up and rendering with HDR environments, a video on the enclosed DVD details their use.

Review

This chapter has detailed the creation of scenes and lighting scenarios for final rendered images as well as the optimization of render settings to maximize the speed without sacrificing quality. Lighting and rendering can make or break a project. Hours of modeling and texture work can be wasted with a poor lighting rig. Managing light, reflections, and refractions can help bring your subject to life, but it is often a balancing act. Creating a few possible lighting rigs will allow you to create related setups with minimal effort. After reading this chapter and practicing the exercises, you will be able to do the following:

- Set up model-based light rigs
- Leverage luminous materials to create soft and realistic lighting
- Create proper environments for opaque, reflective, and transparent objects
- Optimize render settings to create clean images quickly

Where to Go from Here

Watch the videos on the enclosed DVD to cover these topics in more depth. Testing these principles in your own scenes will help you gain additional understanding and become comfortable with the process of scene creation and lighting. Working with and eventually creating your own HDR environments will add depth to your options and allow you to create original and compelling scenes quickly and efficiently.

CHAPTER 8

Modeling Architectural Interiors

Looking at blueprints gives you a good idea of the layout of an interior. Seeing simple drawings of furniture in the same space gives a sense of scale, but a true 3D representation of an architectural design makes the space come alive and portrays the idea in its best light. In this chapter, you'll focus on modeling architectural interiors. This chapter covers the following:

- Modeling basic architectural geometry
- Dealing with complex sections of interior models
- Creating architectural accents and embellishments

Modeling Basic Architectural Geometry

In the previous chapters, we have dealt mainly with subdivision surface modeling. The focus in the previous chapters was on clean loops of four-sided polygons that subdivide cleanly. In addition, there was a focus on creating adequate amounts of geometry to create smooth curves and transitions. When creating models for architectural purposes, you need to consider various concerns in order to create a convincing scene. This section covers using reference images, the Pen tool, Wall mode, and Boolean operations, in addition to creating rounded corners without SubDs, and proper treatment of n-gons (polygons with more than four sides). You will also use these techniques to begin blocking an interior space that will be completely modeled in this chapter and then textured, lit, and rendered in the next chapter.

Working with Reference Images

Figure 8.1

The basic layout that will be used as a reference for your model

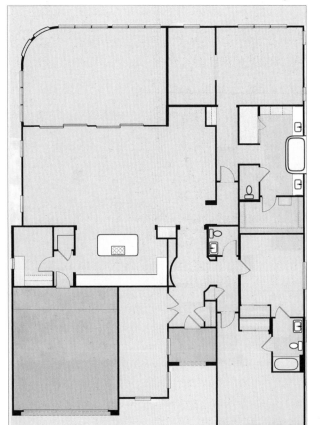

When modeling organic, creative, or free-form models, reference images are helpful and can be used to give a general idea of what will be fleshed out in 3D space. When it comes to architecture, reference images (blueprints) are indispensible and crucial to getting the project done right. The plans that you will use when working on projects like this will range from perfect vector-based digital files (for newer designs) to scans of mimeographed copies that have been on file for decades. The important thing is to be as exact as possible with the information you are given to make the end project as accurate and attractive as possible. In this case, you will be starting with a relatively simple design of decent quality. The design you will use is shown in Figure 8.1.

Take a few moments to familiarize yourself with the plans. There are a few things to notice as you begin planning. First, there are no dimensions in this design, so you will have to find a way of deriving the scale. Next, there are a couple of areas with rounded walls that will have to be treated carefully to get the best-quality results without using SubDs. Finally, wall thickness on the plan is inconsistent, so you will need to make some adjustments in the plans to get a degree of uniformity in the design. As you learn about the different methods of modeling, these facts will enable you to make a good decision about how to tackle this model.

Before modeling at all, the reference image needs to be loaded and properly scaled. To get the image into modo as a background image, do the following:

1. Locate the image on your hard drive.

2. Make the top viewport visible in modo.

3. Drag the image from the hard drive into the top viewport. (This creates a new Backdrop Item).

4. In the properties for the new Backdrop Item, enable the Invert and Blend options.

5. Set the Transparency to about 60%.

This provides you with a semi-transparent blueprint. The inversion allows you to see the walls clearly without a large amount of distraction. The Blend option antialiases the image in order to keep it smooth in the viewport and to make it easier to view the image at different levels of magnification. Figure 8.2 shows the plans in the viewport.

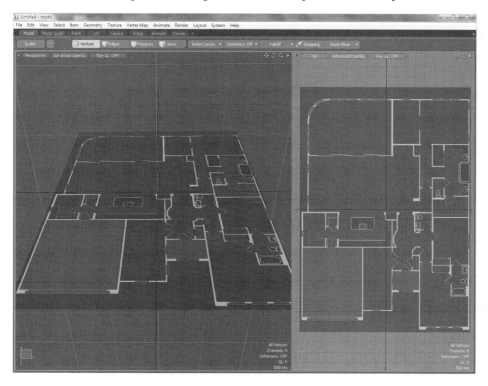

Figure 8.2

The blueprints loaded into the top viewport (right) are also visible in the perspective view (left).

Before modeling can begin, the issue of scale needs to be resolved. Because there are no actual references to specific dimensions, you will use other methods to get the proper scaling. Fortunately, modo ships with some preset mesh items that help to properly align the scale. In the Meshes section of the presets, you will find a doors section (inside the Architectural folder in the Interior category of meshes). Standard interior doors range from 0.8 m to 1.2 m in width. The Door 02 preset is about in the middle of this range (and built to scale). Add the door to the scene and then scale the background image to allow the door mesh to fit properly into one of the openings. In this case, I scaled the image up to 229.5%, and this allowed the door to fit nicely into the entrance to the master suite, as shown in Figure 8.3.

Figure 8.3

By using the mesh preset as a reference, the image can be properly scaled.

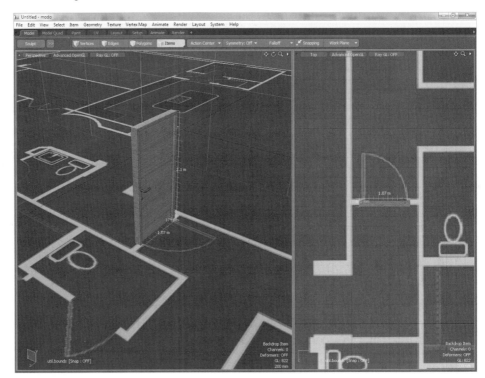

Using the Boolean Modeling Method

There are two main methods for creating this type of 3D model. In the first, you create a solid polygon and then cut out the rooms to leave walls and open spaces. This method can work well if the reference image is of high quality and has good, even wall structure. The second method is to create the outer walls and then the inner walls separately. The inner walls can be aligned with the outer walls or actually physically attached. Because the Wall mode of the Pen tool (Geometry → Draw → Pen) allows you to create walls of an exact given thickness, this method is easier when dealing with plans that have some irregularity. For the sake of practice, you will look at an example of the first method on a generic space before moving on to create the actual project by using the second method.

Boolean modeling operations are derived from Boolean logic. A simple example to demonstrate this logic can be illustrated with the example of a Venn diagram (two intersecting circles) and the resulting options of the Pathfinder tool in Adobe Illustrator, as shown in Figure 8.4.

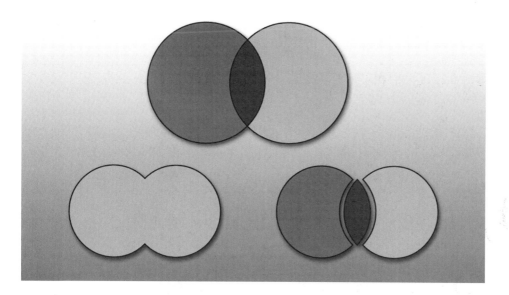

Figure 8.4

The options of the Pathfinder tool show Boolean logic. The original (top) can be used to derive various options (bottom).

Taking the illustration a step further into three dimensions, Figure 8.5 shows the same operations performed on two intersecting cubes. The resulting shapes have slightly rounded edges to make the results more clearly visible. It should be noted that rounding the edges and working with the resulting n-gons are important parts of using this technique when fine-tuning the finished model. These operations are covered in the next section of this chapter.

Figure 8.5

Boolean operations in 3D space have much of the same effect as the 2D samples from the previous example but do create specific challenges.

Most 3D programs offer a variety of Boolean operation tools. For the most part, all of these tools use a base geometric element and then a driver element that is used to perform the Boolean operation. Some, such as the Axis Drill in modo (Geometry → Boolean → Axis Drill), operate on a single axis. These tools affect everything that lies in a direct orthographic projection and, as a result, work much like the Pathfinder tool in Illustrator (see Figure 8.6). Another type of Boolean tool works on a surface level; the intersecting surfaces add edges to the surface of the base mesh. This type of tool, such as the Solid Drill in modo (Geometry → Boolean → Solid Drill), acts in three dimensions but is limited to the surfaces of the base mesh, treating it like an eggshell, as shown in Figure 8.7. Finally, the third type of Boolean works in three full dimensions, like the Boolean tool in modo (Geometry → Boolean → Boolean). The result of operations done in three dimensions takes into account the full dimensionality of both the base and the driver meshes, creating a totally new piece of geometry in the process, as shown in Figure 8.8.

Now that the basic principles of Boolean modeling operations have been discussed, you will create a simple floor plan by using simple cubes. For this example, you will create an apartment-style model. Start with an appropriate-sized cube for the outer structure:

1. Enable the Cube tool (Geometry → Primitive Tools → Cube).

2. In the top view, draw out a cube that is centered around the origin.

3. Set the X Size to 10.5 m and the Z to 6.5 m.

Figure 8.6

The Axis Drill operation places edges on a base mesh by 2D orthographic projection.

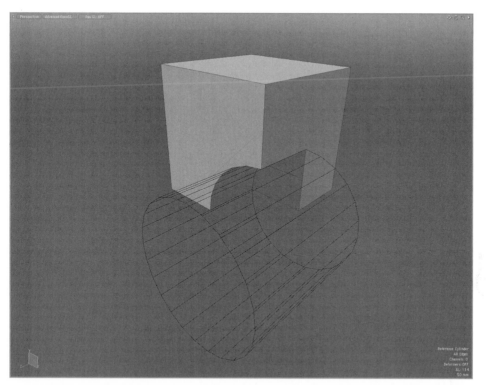

Figure 8.7

The Solid Drill operation places edges on a base mesh based on the 3D intersection of the surfaces.

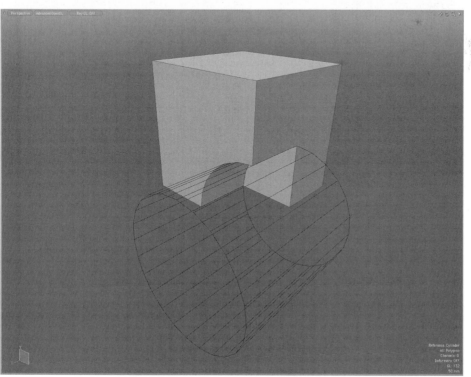

Figure 8.8

The Boolean operation takes full 3D surfaces into account to produce an entirely new piece of geometry.

4. In the side (or front) view, extend the cube up in the y-axis to a height of 3 m.

5. Extend the y from the origin down 0.2 m (this will provide space for the floor).

The cube will now look something like Figure 8.9. This will act as the basic footprint for the model. At this point, you will create geometry for the rooms. Leave doors out of the equation for now. In this space, you should be able to fit two small bedrooms, a bathroom, a kitchen, and a living room. In a new mesh layer, use the Cube tool to create the basic rooms and closets. Once those areas are in place, the Pen tool can be used to fill in open areas (or any room that is not a basic square shape). Once completed, your top view should look like Figure 8.10.

Remember that the template for the rooms does not need any depth in the y-axis. That depth will be added before the actual interior is created. To turn this 2D blueprint into actual 3D rooms, do the following:

1. Select the polygons that make up the interior space.

2. Enable the Thicken tool and drag the polygons up in the y-axis until they are above the height of the cube in the background mesh layer (see Figure 8.11).

3. Select the cube mesh layer.

4. Use the Boolean operation found in Geometry → Boolean → Boolean.

Figure 8.9

The basic shape of the apartment is created with a cube.

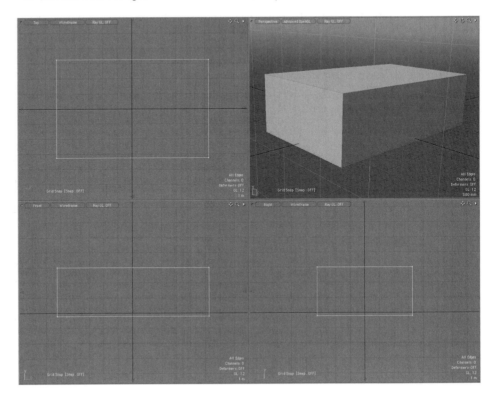

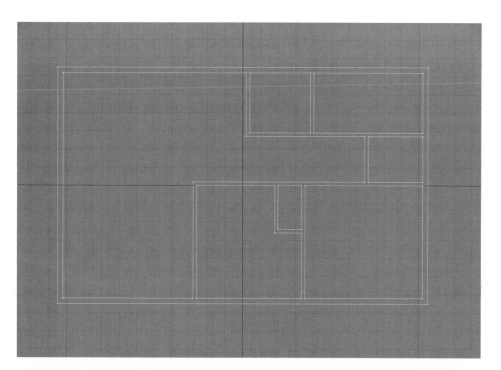

Figure 8.10

Use a combination of the Cube tool and the Pen tool to create the interior spaces.

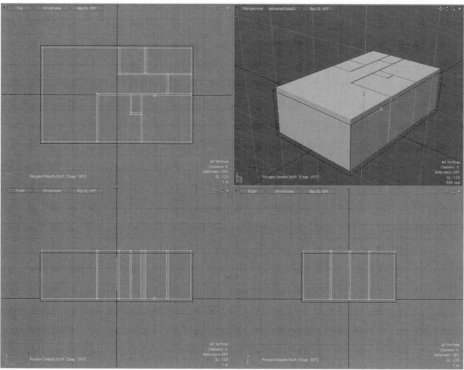

Figure 8.11

The interior space geometry is thickened to a proper height above the background layer height.

5. In the pop-up window, choose Subtract from the Operation drop-down list and choose Background from the Drive Mesh drop-down.

6. The basic rooms will now be in place and should look like Figure 8.12.

Figure 8.12

The basic interior geometry is completed.

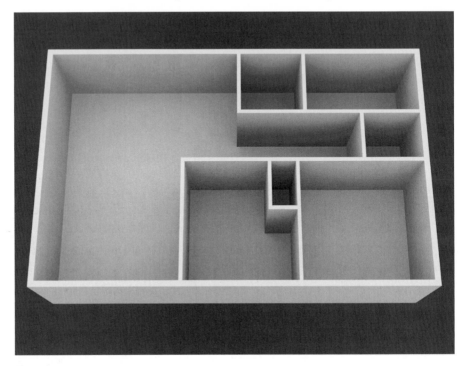

The basic model elements are now in place, but there is one thing left to adjust. The polygon on the bottom of the mesh is not needed and can actually get in the way in some of the upcoming steps.

From this point, window and door cutouts can be added quite easily by using the Slice and Bridge tools. The n-gons in this model are delicate and need to be treated carefully. The biggest problem areas are the floors. To make these easier to deal with, a similar technique to the one you used with the n-gons in SubD meshes will be employed. Surrounding n-gons with a border of co-planar polygons will help to avoid issues with shading. Select all of the floor polygons and bevel them in 100 mm. This will create a nice border around each floor space. To build the framework for windows and doors, you need to take a few steps:

1. In the front view, use the Slice tool (in Polygon mode) to create an even cut through the geometry at the height of the tops of the doors and windows (about 2 m in the y-axis).

2. Add a second slice for the bottom of the windows (about 0.6 m).

3. Select the interior floor polygons and hide them by either choosing View → Hide Selected or pressing the H key.

4. Use the Slice tool again to place cuts in the middle of each window and door space (in the top view).

5. Double-click a new edge to select the loop (make sure you are in Edges mode).

6. Use the Edge Bevel tool (B key when in Edges mode) to create the desired width for each door and window (make sure to have the Round Level set to 0).

7. Switch back to Polygons mode and select the polygon(s) on the inside and outside of an individual door (or window) and use the Bridge tool to cut the hole in the wall.

8. Repeat step 7 for each door and window to complete the openings for the doors and windows. At this point, your model will have openings like those in Figure 8.13.

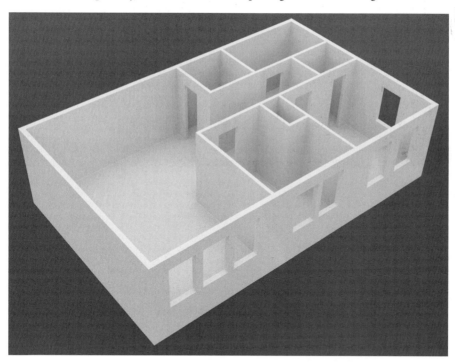

Figure 8.13

Interior with all of the door and window spaces cut

This model is relatively complete from a basic standpoint and ready for details to be added. For more-complex interiors, this method can be a bit problematic because a few highly temperamental sections (such as the wall tops and floors) do not take kindly to additions, changes, or embellishments. For more-complex interiors, the Wall mode of the Pen tool will provide a much more stable solution.

Using the Pen Tool Method

Making the structure of a more complex layout can be facilitated by the use of the Pen tool. The drawbacks of the Boolean method become quite clear because open areas, irregular walls, and rounded sections can make a mess of your geometry in a hurry. Creating the walls with the Pen tool will not only speed up the process of creating complex architectural forms but will also allow you to add greater complexity without a great deal of model cleanup later. Using the Pen tool will create clean geometry and keep the walls divided by quad polygons. To get the Pen tool properly set up for this purpose, follow these steps:

1. Enable the Pen tool (Geometry → Draw → Pen).

2. Set the Wall Mode option to Inner and then select the Close check box. This will make the walls a complete loop when in Wall mode.

3. Select the Show Angles check box. This will display the angles created at each vertex. In this case, the angles are all right angles, but this will help a lot when you have angled walls.

4. Enable Snapping (either at the top of the viewports or in the Snapping section of the tool properties).

5. Enable all of the options under the Pen Snap section of the Pen tool properties.

6. With the Wall Mode option set to Inner, you will plot the inner points, and the wall will extend outward.

7. Set the Offset to 150 mm to keep an even wall thickness throughout the model.

With these options set, the outer wall can be quickly created. Plot the inner points around the entire perimeter. Leave a hard corner in the upper left, where the finished wall will be rounded. This will also be the case in the inner walls. Rounded sections will be added in a future section. With a dozen points plotted, the main wall is complete, as shown in Figure 8.14.

There are a couple of ways to create the interior walls. The important thing is to end up with the inner walls attached to the outer walls. This

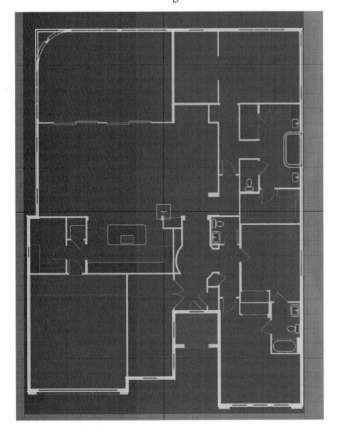

Figure 8.14

Plotting 12 points creates the main structure of the building.

will make it much easier to add details, such as floorboards, crown molding, and rounded corners. As you begin creating the interior structures, you can use a few simple techniques to make your modeling workflow efficient, accurate, and clean.

Extending Edges

One quick way to create new walls from existing ones is by using the Edge Extend tool. This will allow you to draw new walls directly from existing ones and retain good, clean polygonal flow. To use this method, you need a single edge the width of the desired wall, on the edge of the existing wall. To ensure that the edge is the proper thickness, follow these few simple steps:

1. Use the Slice tool (Shift+C) to make a cut in the center of the wall that will be created. If the wall will be attached to more than one existing wall, make the slice all the way through the wall.

2. Select the edge (or edges) and turn on the Bevel tool (B).

3. Make sure that the Round Level is set at 0 and bevel to a Value of half the width of the desired wall. Because the bevel extends in both directions, this will make an edge the correct width.

4. Select the new edge that will connect to the wall and use the Edge Extend tool (Z) to drag out the new wall.

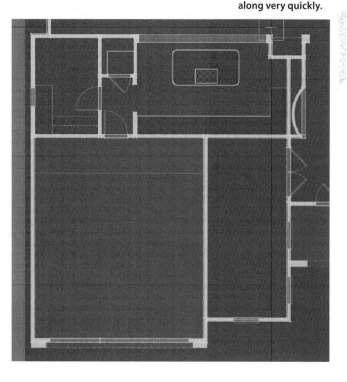

Figure 8.15

Extending new walls from existing ones can make interior creation move along very quickly.

When extending new walls from existing walls, plan ahead and include space from which you can extend doorframes and additional walls. Because the Edge Extend tool is measured when the extension is made, this tool can be used to create exact spaces for new walls by extending to the beginning of a new wall space and then to the other side of the new wall before continuing. If there is a wall that will intersect two walls that are not yet created, leave the edges out and then slice through the new walls after they are created. For this reason, it can be helpful to begin working with the parallel walls, making all of the walls in one direction first, and then adding the perpendicular walls. By using this technique, all of the interior walls in Figure 8.15 were created in just a few short minutes.

Notice that in the image, a wall is spanning the open area on one side of the kitchen (the side connected to the living room). This can be helpful for several reasons. It keeps walls that are on either side of an open space even, and it can be useful for making transitions in flooring. Remember that these walls are really only templates at this point, and when the time comes to add height to the walls, the open areas can either be excluded or removed afterward very easily. In the case of the wall in the kitchen, you want to include an archway, so you will extend this section up and treat it like a doorway when the walls are in place. Just as with the exterior walls, leave out complex sections because these can be added easily after the rest of the walls are in place.

Using the Bridge Tool

When two sides of a wall are cut into existing walls, the Bridge tool can be used to attach the open ends. In some cases, the walls created with this method will be a little crooked. When placing walls in any moderately complex floor plan, this kind of misalignment will almost inevitably occur. Spending a lot of time trying to avoid minor issues like this can be counterproductive because the solution is simple:

1. Select the crooked edge(s).
2. Set the Action Center to Element.
3. Enable the Scale tool (R).
4. Disable the Negative Scale check box.
5. Click an edge that is straight and in the correct position to align the Scale tool to it.
6. Scale the edges to 0%. (With Negative Scale disabled, this will be the lowest you will be able to go.)

This solution will allow you to quickly align walls throughout the model and should greatly increase the speed of your workflow. Using the Edge Extend, Bridge, and Scale tools with some minor Action Center adjustments (mainly using the Element Action Center), the remainder of the walls can be completed relatively quickly. The result should look something like Figure 8.16. Unlike with the Boolean method, the walls will not be given any height at this point. The curved interior walls still need to be added as well as floors.

Adding floors is the next step before moving on in the construction process. At this point, the addition of floors is quite simple. In Edges mode, double-click any edge that borders a room, and press the P key to create a polygon in that space. Many of these floors will doubtless be n-gons, but they are much easier to work with on the floor than they are in other places in the model. In addition, the n-gons here can also be sliced up into quad polygons if necessary.

Once the floors have been created, select each of the polygons and bevel them in slightly (about 25 mm) to create a ring of quad polygons around the n-gons. Before moving on, take a minute to look over the model and make sure that the corners of the floors are not crossing after the bevel operation. If this does happen, you will need to handle those sections individually and either bevel the sections less or bevel them and then scale the polygons inward instead of using the scaling built into the Bevel tool. Increase the selection (Shift+up-arrow) to select the border around the floors and assign a new material to the floors. If you wish, you can also assign a material to the walls. With the floors still selected, press the [key to invert the selection and then apply a new material to the walls. At this point, your model should look like the image shown in Figure 8.17. The base floor plan is created and ready for fine-tuning.

Just press the P key once when creating the floors. The polygons will sometimes be created facing downward. Although pressing the P key twice will create a polygon facing the right direction, it will actually create two polygons in the same space (one facing the proper direction and another facing the opposite way). If the polygon does not appear, rotate the view to the underside to check whether the polygon is actually there. If there is a polygon facing the wrong way, simply select it and then flip it by using the Flip command from the Polygon tab or by pressing the F key.

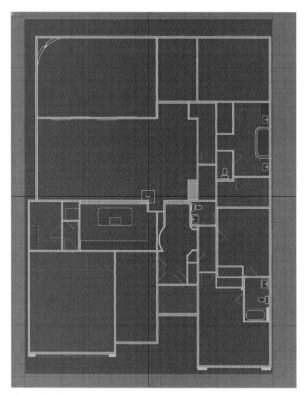

Figure 8.16

The completed wall sections are made with complex areas blocked in for the moment.

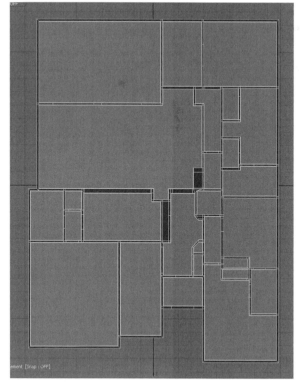

Figure 8.17

Adding in the floor polygons completes the model to this point.

Dealing with Complex Sections of Interior Models

Some models are very simple and have little need for anything beyond basic modeling. At times, however, architectural accents can produce areas that are difficult to re-create in 3D. There are several ways to handle this kind of geometric complexity.

Adding Rounded Walls

In this case, the design includes two rounded areas that need to be added to the current basic model. In addition, you will add some rounded corners and archways to add interest to the look of the interior. The first section to consider is the area at the entry. A circular section impacts three walls. Instead of trying to edit the existing geometry in this case, it will be much easier to create new walls and bridge them into the existing space. Doing this kind of modeling can be daunting at first, but learning a simple procedure can help make it much easier:

1. Make a new mesh layer (N).

2. Create a circle with the Cylinder tool at the center of the space where the mesh needs to be edited (in this case, a radius of 1.38 m will fit well). This model will not be subdivided, so a relatively large number of sides is needed. Figure 8.18 shows the circle in place with 96 sides.

3. Select a vertex near the floor border area (shown in Figure 8.19).

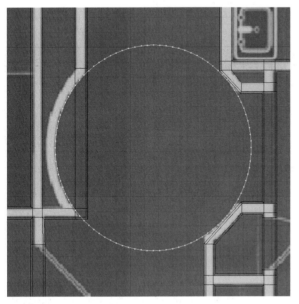

Figure 8.18

A circle will make the basis for the rounded insets in the walls.

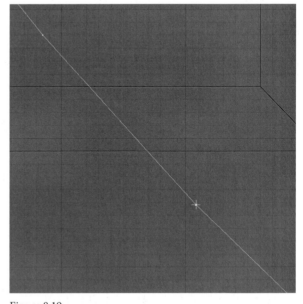

Figure 8.19

This vertex needs to be placed in alignment with the border of the floor.

4. Use the Slide tool (found under the Edge menu, or by right-clicking the vertex and choosing Slide) to move the vertex into alignment with the floor border area, as shown in Figure 8.20.

5. Select the edges that align with the wall and use the Edge Extend tool (Z) to create edges for the floor border (25 mm) and the wall (150 mm).

6. Repeat step 5 for the additional two sections.

7. Use the Slide tool to align the inner sections of the circles with the existing walls, as shown in Figure 8.21.

8. Select the unused edges of the circle (top and bottom) and extend the edges out 25 mm to create the border for the floor. Make sure to leave out the edges directly adjacent to the edges that are already in use (these will be bridged later).

9. Select all of the impacted floors and walls in the main layer and delete them.

10. Cut and paste the new circular walls into the main geometry layer.

11. Attach the new geometry to the original walls by selecting the edges on either side of the gaps in the 25 mm border area and then using the Bridge tool to close the open spaces.

12. Make floor polygons with the same technique previously used to fill the floor polygons.

The geometry is now in place to create circular walls for this section. At this point, your model should look like Figure 8.22.

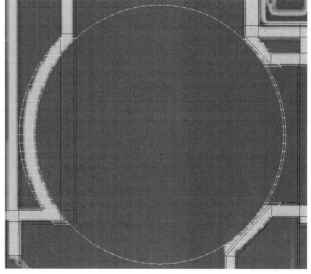

Figure 8.20
The vertex is now properly aligned.

Figure 8.21
Wall sections are extended from the circle and aligned to the existing geometry.

Some areas contain rounded sections that do not intersect with other parts of the model. The rounded exterior wall in the upper left is a good example of such an isolated case. Looking at this section, you will see two edges that create this corner, one that is in the wall and another that is at the corner of the floor border. In this case, a simple edge bevel will handle this geometry quite easily. Select the two edges at the corner and enable the Edge Bevel tool (B). Set Value to 2.5 m with a Round Level of about 24 (as shown in Figure 8.23). This will create a nicely rounded wall with plenty of edges for the windows to be placed into. The border on the floor helps to keep the n-gon in the floor cleanly placed and separated by the quad polygons created by the bevel.

Rounded corners can be added just as easily as the last rounded wall. Select the two edges that make up any corner and use the Edge Bevel. Since these are small details, a lower Round Level can be used. A setting of 5 m should suffice. Beveling these corners about 25 mm provides a good subtle detail. Repeat this on any outer corners with 90° angles. Once again, the borders on the floors will bevel into even quad polygons, and the n-gons will remain isolated in the center areas. This is a detail that is not always necessary but takes little time and adds additional polish to the model.

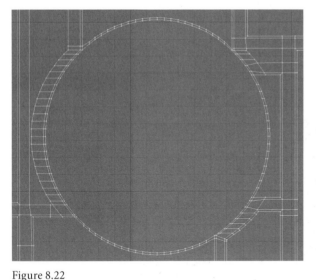

Figure 8.22
The rounded walls are now in place.

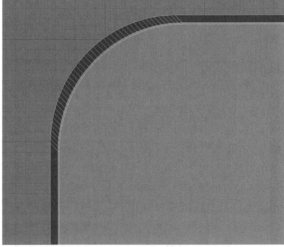

Figure 8.23
The rounded exterior wall can be created easily with an edge bevel.

Finishing the Walls

At this point, the walls can be created from the flat set of polygons, and some additional details can be added. If you added materials to the floors and walls, the walls can easily be selected by looking in the Lists tab (in the lower-right corner of the screen). You can find statistics on all of your polygons (as well as points and edges) in this section. To select all of your polygons with the Wall material, go to the Lists tab → Statistics → Polygons (open by clicking the arrow to the left of the text) → Material. In this section, you will see a listing of any materials in the active mesh layer(s) and the number of polygons that have that material assignment. Clicking the + at the left of the list will add any of those polygons to the current selection. With the walls selected, use the Bevel tool to create the walls. Eight-foot ceilings (about 2.5 m) are pretty typical.

Even though many residential interior walls extend to 9 feet, this height is not ideal for rendering 3D floor plates. Higher walls occlude more of the interior and make the view less useful. If you want to see the area above the tops of the windows and doors, a wall height of 2.5 m is a good level. At this height, upper details such as crown molding can be added. If this type of detail is not necessary, cutting off the walls at 2 m will work well. This will give a better view of the interior and simply cut off everything above the tops of the doors and windows. Creating some breakup in the solid walls and making the top side of the window glass visible can have a nice visual effect. This is an option that will probably change from project to project, but it is nice to have options available for the final look of the renders.

In this case, some architectural details, such as arches and crown molding, reside above the doors and windows, so you will bevel up to a total height of 2.5 m. It can save work later if you first bevel up to a height of 0.6 m (for the bottom of the windows), and then to 2 m (for the top of the doors/windows), and finally to a full 2.5 m for the top of the wall. This means the three bevels will be 0.6 m, 1.4 m, and 0.5 m. When these are in place, you will not need to slice the mesh to create vertical slots for doors or windows. At this point, your model will look like Figure 8.24.

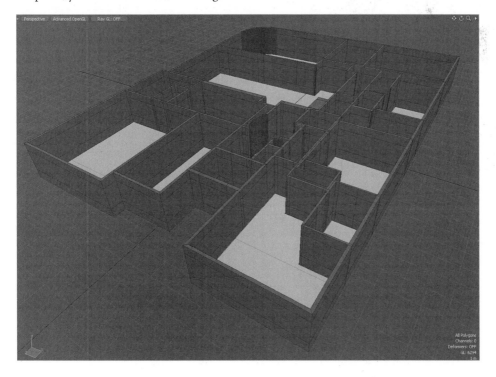

Figure 8.24

Using three successive bevels to create the walls will save time in the next phase.

Cutting Doorways and Windows

Because the doors were already included in the planning of the interior walls, they are the next order of business. To create cutouts for a door, select the two polygons on either side of the door and use the Bridge tool (found in the Basic tab or the Polygon tab). To activate the tool, click its button (with the polygons selected) and then click in the modeling viewport. Do this for all of the doors and archways. After a few minutes, the doors will be complete, and your model will look like Figure 8.25.

Figure 8.25

With all of the doors cut from the walls, the flow of the architecture becomes more evident. Simple lighting was added here to show the play of light through doorways.

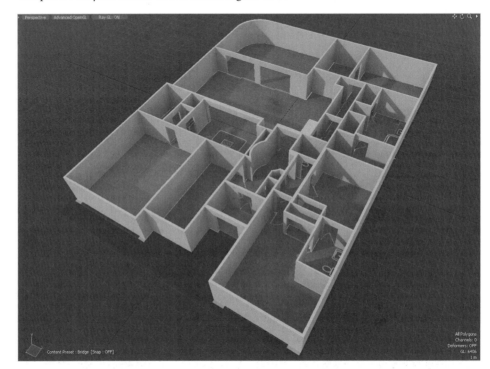

Windows require a little more effort because they do not fall as naturally into the layout. Additional edges need to be sliced in the walls and the floor borders (to keep the n-gons isolated). Then, the window slices can be made. Here are the steps:

1. Select all of the floor polygons (use material polygon statistics as you did when selecting the walls).

2. Press Shift+down-arrow to remove the borders from the selection.

3. Use the Slice tool (Shift+C) to make slices in the middle of each window.

4. Once all of the slices are made, select the edges related to the window (either one at a time or in groups of like-sized windows), and bevel the edges to create sections for each window.

5. Most of the windows in this model are 1 m wide, so beveling 500 mm makes the appropriate-size opening. There are a few windows with different sizes, so make those individually.

6. When all of the edges are created, use the Bridge tool (with Select Through enabled) to make the holes for each window.

7. At the curved wall, each window is made up of polygons that are already in place, so they do not need any slices added. However, selecting about 14 polygons on each side should make the proper hole for those windows.

After completing this task, your model should look like Figure 8.26.

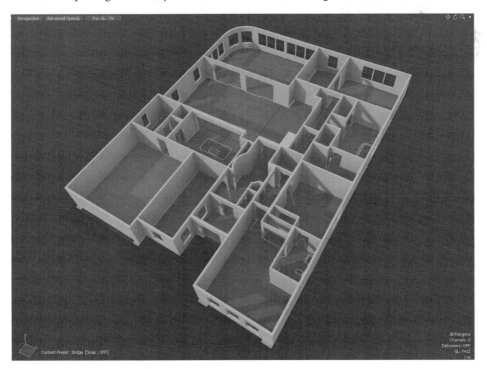

Figure 8.26

The model with all window and door openings in place

Creating Archways

The only elements left to add at this level are the archways. These can be created quickly by using falloffs. To start, you will look at the large arch between the kitchen and the living area. To make the straight section rounded, more edges are needed. Currently, a single polygon spans the entire area. Again, this is a section that will not be subdivided with SubDs, so you will need to add enough edges for a good, rounded look when this process is completed. Because this covers a fairly large amount of space, the level of subdivision will need to be high. For this purpose, the Loop Slice tool (Alt/Option+C) is perfect:

1. Select two polygons that run around the beam, where the edges are to be inserted.

2. Enable the Loop Slice tool.

3. Set the Count to 31 (this will result in 32 polygons dividing the surface).

4. Click the Uniform button to place 31 evenly spaced slices around the beam.

This sets up the geometry for the creation of the arch. A simple combination of the Move tool and a Cylinder falloff will create the curved surface. Creating the arch can now be done in a few simple steps:

1. Select all of the edges on the underside of the beam.

2. Choose the Cylinder falloff from the Falloff menu.

3. Set the falloff Axis to Y.

4. Set the Shape Preset to Ease-In.

5. Turn on the Move tool (W).

6. Move the selection up 450 mm.

7. Press the Q key to drop the tool and Esc to clear the falloff (or select None from the Falloff menu).

The arch is now completed and should look like the image shown in Figure 8.27.

Repeat this procedure in any areas where you want a similar arch. Make sure that the falloff is on the right axis (all of these will be either the z-axis or the x-axis) for each arch. With these completed, the main structure is finished and should look like Figure 8.28. Now the doors, windows, and architectural accents can be added to complete the model.

Figure 8.27
The kitchen arch completed

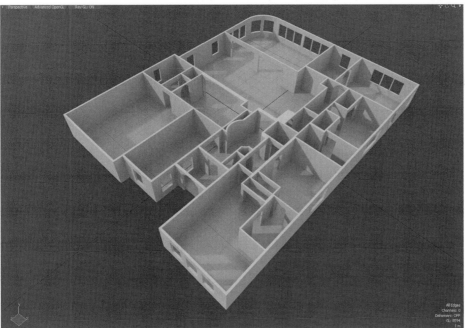

Figure 8.28
Walls and floors are completed, and the model is ready for details to be added.

Creating Architectural Accents and Embellishments

There are several details that can help to complete and polish the look of the model. Doors and windows need borders as well as geometry for the doors and windows themselves. There are also floorboards, crown molding, and chair rails that can be added to create additional interest and detail.

Adding Doors and Windows

Beveling and using profiles can help to create doorframes and windowsills in short order. To illustrate, start selecting the polygons for one doorway. Leave out the polygons on the bottom of the opening because these are not needed. Copy these polygons (there should be five for each door) and paste them into a new mesh layer. To create the geometry, a few steps can be repeated:

1. Double-click the polygons to select them all.
2. Use the Scale tool to make the polygons 25% thicker (this creates the overhang for the doorframe).
3. Flip the polygons (F).
4. Copy the polygons (Ctrl/Command+C)
5. Flip the polygons back to their original orientation (F).
6. Use the Bevel tool (B) to bevel the polygons inward (about 30 mm).
7. Select a simple profile from the Profiles section of the tool properties to add a contour to the bevel. (I chose the very first one in the list.)
8. Paste the flipped polygons back into the scene.
9. Select the Merge tool (from the Vertex tab) with a distance of 0 mm and click Apply to merge the pasted geometry to the beveled section.

This same procedure can be used on the windows. Make sure to include the entire polygon loop for the window. Find a profile that fits with the design of the building to create quick custom framing. Doors and windows themselves can be created with simple polygon primitives or by copying and pasting the polygon at the top of each frame and then thickening it to the right height. After working through the windows and doors, your model will look like Figure 8.29.

PLACING DOORS

Remember that a door is typically designed to open in only one direction. The doorframe has a thin divider down the middle that the door will push against when closed, and the door itself takes up only a little less than half of the inner space of the frame. This kind of detail may not be obvious if overhead renders are all that will be produced of the model, but if there is a possibility of creating shots from inside the rooms, this can be a good detail to add. This topic is covered in a video on the DVD if you get stuck.

Figure 8.29

Doors and windows in place

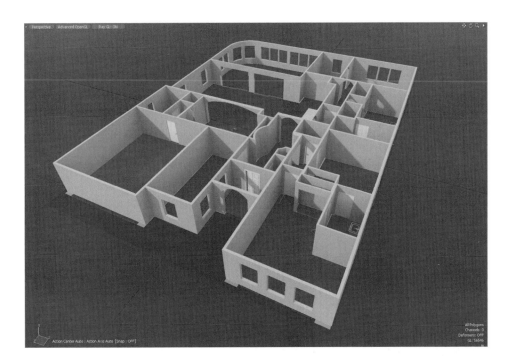

Creating Sliding Doors

Many buildings have sliding doors of some type (closets and patio doors, for example). Creating this type of door takes a little more care because the space for two individual doors needs to be created as well as the railing inside the frames. These structures start out the same way as the windows because there is a track that runs on top and bottom. As with the other frames, scale the frame out and copy the flipped geometry before beveling the frame itself. Instead of using a profile, make a few bevels to get the right shape:

1. Make a simple bevel with the Shift setting (about 30 mm).

2. Make the second bevel by using the Inset setting.

3. The third bevel will be a negative Shift to create the rail area.

4. Inset once again and leave a very thin loop of polygons in the middle.

5. One last bevel with a small Shift (about 5 mm) will complete the frame. The finished frame is shown in Figure 8.30.

Creating the doors is simple. By adding a centered loop slice through the top (or bottom) of the frame, two even sections are created for adding doors. Copying and thickening the polygons at the top makes a good start for a door. A few bevels on each side of the doors will make space for glass. The finished construction should look like Figure 8.31.

Figure 8.30

The finished frame for sliding glass doors

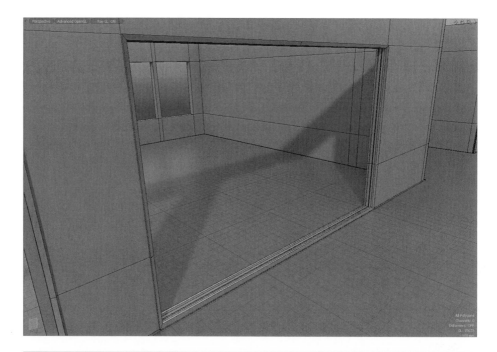

Figure 8.31

The doors created from existing geometry will fit perfectly into the sliding frame.

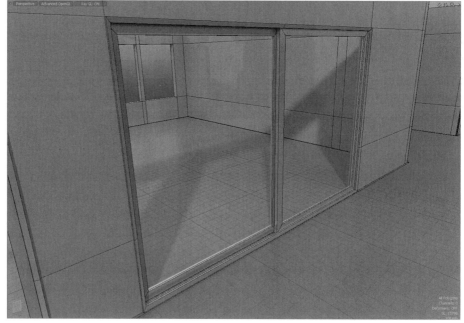

The same technique applies to other sliding doors, such as the ones in the bedrooms in this floor plan. The main difference is in the doors themselves. Because the doors are not glass, they can be simple elongated cubes or have the glass material replaced with a mirror for a change of pace.

Adding Molding

At this point, the model is essentially completed, but the addition of some detailed molding can add a high-class feel to the design as a whole. Once again, bevels and profiles will make the job easier. To make placement of these elements quick and precise, adding slices to the walls will be the next course of action. Placement of these new edges will determine what elements you will be able to place when detailing. One slice near the bottom, placed 30 mm to 50 mm from the ground will create a loop of polygons for the floorboards (which will appear in most of the interior rooms). A second pair of slices below the middle of the walls will provide space for chair rails. A final slice about 40 mm to 50 mm from the top of the walls will give you the option of adding crown molding.

Once these slices are added, the details can be created. Start with the floorboards because they appear everywhere. Select the polygons around the bottom of the interior. These polygons can be selected in large loops by clicking two adjacent polygons and then creating a looped selection by pressing the L key. Before making the beveled shapes on any of these sections, it is a good idea to add a material to the selection. This will save you a lot of time when it comes to placing textures on the model. The floorboards are simple pieces of geometry with little detail. To get the proper shape for the floorboards, follow these steps:

1. Bevel the selected polygons with a Shift of 10 mm.

2. Make a second bevel with a Shift of 10 mm and an Inset of 5 mm. This will create an angle that pulls the geometry away from the floors. This can cause some unwanted shadows, so an adjustment needs to be made.

3. With the last loop of polygons still selected, activate the Move tool and move the polygons down 5 mm to make the bottom flush with the ground.

   The crown molding and chair rails can be added wherever you see fit to complete the look of the mesh. In addition to the benefits of being able to add the molded details, these additional slices will make it easier to add different paint colors and textures without complex material editing. There are some differences between these sections and the floorboards.

4. Make the polygon selections for areas that will be beveled.

5. Bevel the polygons with a small Shift amount (starting at about 30 mm).

6. Enable a profile and check to make sure it works with the given selection. Some profiles are meant for particular-sized selections, so it is important to make sure that there is no overlapping in these areas.

7. Change the profile until you find a selection that suits your needs.

After adding molded details, your model is ready for textures, furniture, countertops, shelving, lighting, and final rendering. Completing the last steps should give you a model that looks something like Figure 8.32.

Figure 8.32

The added finishing touches complete the floor plan, which is ready for continued work on color and furnishings.

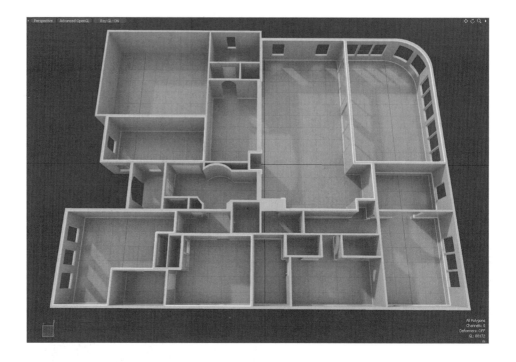

Review

This chapter has covered polygonal modeling techniques for dealing with simple to moderately complex architectural interiors. With some well-used tools, this type of visualization modeling can be completed in a relatively short time with some practice. In addition, the practices learned here can be exploited on other types of modeling jobs as well. After following along with this chapter and practicing the concepts, you should be able to do the following:

- Model simple floor plans using basic geometry and Boolean operations
- Create subtractive sections such as doors and windows in your models
- Use the Pen tool to create complex wall shapes
- Expand on existing geometry to create any type of simple interior space
- Use sections of primitive shapes and the Bridge tool to create more-complex sections of interior models
- Use the Bevel tool along with profiles to quickly create complex forms such as doorframes, crown molding, and chair rails

Where to Go from Here

Take a simple floor plan and create a 3D model of it. Simple Internet searches can provide you with a wealth of possibilities for your next practice project. Take time to add the small details that can easily be overlooked but add a lot to the finished project. At first, don't rush but keep track of your time. Since the modeling tasks here are nearly the same in most circumstances, you will be able to create quality work in a short period of time after you have mastered the essential skills.

CHAPTER 9

Texture and Lighting for Architectural Interiors

A well-built model without good textures and lighting can waste hours of modeling as far as final presentation goes. Setting up good textures and lights for this type of visualization can be done quickly with a little practice. The addition of these textures and lighting will greatly improve the look of your finished product. This chapter covers the following:

- **Creating textures for interior visualization**
- **Adding secondary models**
- **Adjusting lighting and rendering settings**

Creating Textures for Interior Visualization

As you created the interior model in the previous chapter, you assigned basic large groups of textures (floors, walls, molding, and so on). However, to get the right amount of control, you need to create some additional texture groups. This process can take a few minutes to complete, but there are some techniques that can help you make your selections faster. After creating texture groups, much of the texture work can be done very quickly.

Making Selections

Even though this model has a relatively low polygon count, it can still be time-consuming to manually select each polygon in a room to set a material for a wall or floor (especially when you are working with rounded corners). A few techniques can make your task much easier and less tedious. Making lasso selections (by using the right mouse button), using the arrow keys, and using the Polygons heading of the Statistics section (in the Lists tab) can each knock significant time off the selection task. Using all of these together will speed up your workflow even more.

Making Lasso Selections

Most 2D and 3D applications allow the use of some kind of lasso selection. In Photoshop, the Lasso tool is used to create a free-form selection. The image shown in Figure 9.1 is a simple 32-pixel square image that has been enlarged to make the individual pixels more visible.

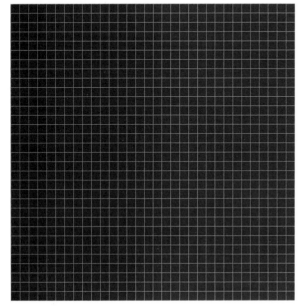

At this level, you can make a more direct comparison between pixels and polygons. In Photoshop, the lasso selection uses a percentage value to decide whether a pixel will be included in the selection. In other words, if more than half of the surface of the pixel falls into the selection region, it will be a part of the selection. In this case, making a completely straight edge can be difficult because the selection area is judged in such a qualitative way. Figure 9.2 shows the path of a quick boxlike selection, and Figure 9.3 shows the actual selection that results. Granted, a more careful selection could be made, but in a workflow that often includes repetition as a dominant feature, the need for surgical precision can really hamper creativity, productivity, and the smooth evolution of a model.

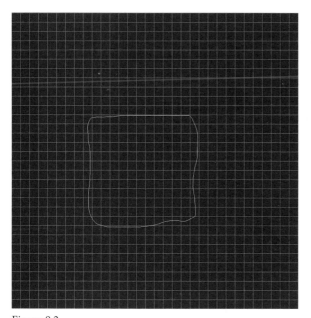

Figure 9.2

A quick squarelike selection with the Lasso tool in Photoshop

Figure 9.3

The actual selection resulting from the lasso area is anything but square.

In the course of a modeling session, quick selections will be made and dropped dozens (if not hundreds) of times. So there is a great need for quick precision. In modo, the selection of polygons (as well as other elements) is all or nothing. If the entire element is not within the area of the lasso, it will not be selected. At first glance, this may appear to be a minor differentiation, but the results can be tremendous! Consider the selection made in Figure 9.4. Even though the shape is not very different from its Photoshop counterpart in the previous example, the result (shown in Figure 9.5) is a perfect square.

In the case of pixels, the difference in what is selected would obviously be less important, but with polygons, this can be critical. One aspect of most Lasso tools is the straight line connecting the start and end points. This line allows for selections of small areas with absolute precision. Using the same grid of polygons, a single strip of polygons can be selected by drawing the selection into the open space and allowing the straight connecting line to go through the adjacent strip of polygons. The lasso area shown in Figure 9.6 results in a clean selection; the clean row is shown in Figure 9.7.

The lasso selection style can be used as the basis for a lot of the selections in your interior model. Rounded corners can be lasso-selected with a quick semicircle stroke around the thin polygons that make up the rounded areas. Using the arrow keys along with the Lasso tool allows you to quickly select a group of walls with tightly rounded corners.

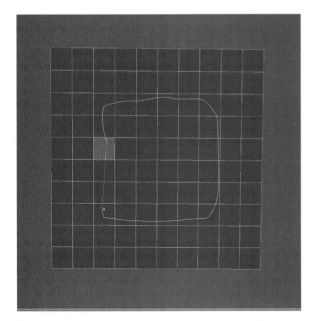

Figure 9.4

A quick square-shaped selection around a group of polygons

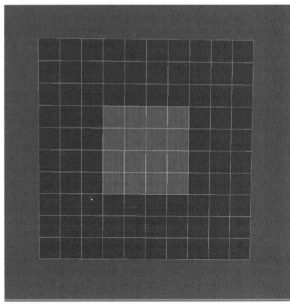

Figure 9.5

The polygons selected from the lasso form a perfect square very easily.

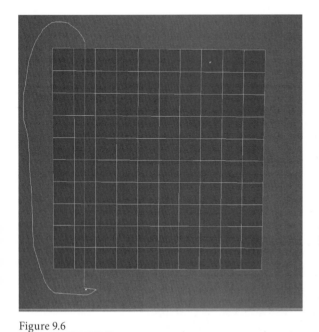

Figure 9.6

A very quick selection with a straight edge connecting the start and end points

Figure 9.7

A clean row of polygons is selected very quickly.

Using Arrow Keys with Selections

Selecting every single polygon in a section of a mesh to set a texture can be tedious at best. Even with the lasso selection, the task can waste a lot of time. Learning to use the arrow keys helps improve the speed of creating selections and applying textures. The up-arrow continues a linear selection (or pattern if a number of polygons are skipped between selected polygons). Selecting two consecutive polygons and then using the up-arrow easily selects an entire strip of polygons. You can also use the L key to select the entire loop.

However, at times the entire loop is not the goal—for example, when selecting a wall to assign an accent color. In a case such as this, selecting a partial loop with the up-arrow allows you to get just the needed polygons. If you overshoot the intended selection, using the down-arrow reverses the pattern. Figure 9.8 shows the top of a wall selected by clicking two polygons and then holding the up-arrow until the entire top section of the wall is selected.

Holding the Shift key while pressing the up-arrow adds all the polygons touching the current selection to the selection. Pressing Shift+down-arrow removes the outermost polygons from the selection. If you are aware of any small polygon borders (for example, the ones found on the floors), this operation can save you a significant amount of time. After some practice, you will learn to see distances of two, three, or more polygons from the complete desired selection. This allows you to make a much smaller initial selection. Then simply holding Shift and tapping the up-arrow a few times will select a large area without the need for carefully selecting a large number of initial polygons. In this manner, you will be able to move through your model quickly and efficiently.

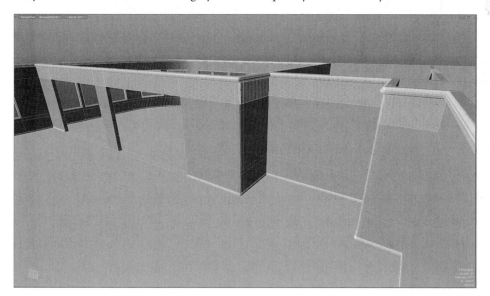

Figure 9.8

Selecting a partial loop can be done quickly with the up-arrow.

The left- and right-arrow keys can also be useful in certain situations. These keys will select the next and previous loops, respectively. The actual direction of the change in selection is based on the direction of the initial loop. To better visualize this, imagine selecting two adjacent polygons that make up a loop. The direction is set based off this initial selection. So if you place yourself on the geometry and move in the direction of the selection, the left-arrow will move you into the loop to the left, while the right-arrow will move you into the right. This is illustrated in Figure 9.9.

Figure 9.9

If two polygons are selected in the direction of the middle arrow, then the left- and right-arrow keys will select the top and bottom loops, respectively.

Holding the Shift key with either of these arrow keys will add the corresponding loop to the selection. This effect is like expanding the selection in one direction. This is useful when two adjacent loops need to be selected. Be aware that if you decide to add an additional loop on the other side of the selected loops, you will have to press the corresponding arrow key enough times to cross over any already selected loops.

Using Polygon Statistics in Selections

In addition to manually selecting (and deselecting) polygons, this task can be handled based on sets of polygons (selection sets and material tags are the most common). In the Lists tab, there is a heading labeled Statistics. From here, all elements can be accessed based on their attributes. This can be useful when polygons that need to be selected are in close proximity to other polygons with different materials or selection set assignments (selection sets are covered later in this chapter). By using the addition and subtraction functions for the elements in the Polygon heading of the Statistics, manual selections can be easily refined. This exercise illustrates the usefulness of these sets:

1. Create a new rectangle (cube) with x and z dimensions of 1 m and 20 segments in each of these axes.

2. Make a square selection in the center of the plane and assign a new material, as shown in Figure 9.10.

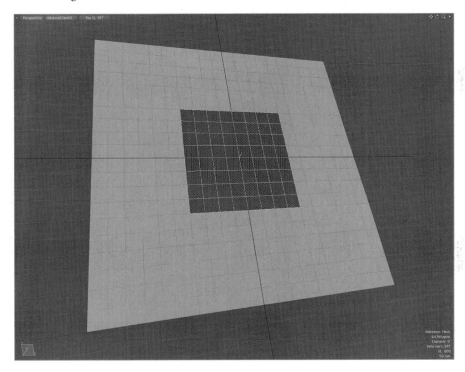

Figure 9.10

A new material is assigned to an 8×8 polygon section in the middle of the plane.

3. Use the Shift+up-arrow command twice to expand the selection.

4. Subtract the center selection by clicking the subtract (-) button next to the new material (Statistics → Polygons → Material).

5. Assign a new material to this new selection.

6. Use Shift+up-arrow twice more to expand the selection.

7. Subtract the second material from the selection by using the subtract (-) button next to the second material.

8. Assign a third material to the resulting selection. At this point, your mesh should look like Figure 9.11.

9. A fourth material can be added by increasing the selection further and subtracting materials already created or by adding just the default material polygons with nothing else selected.

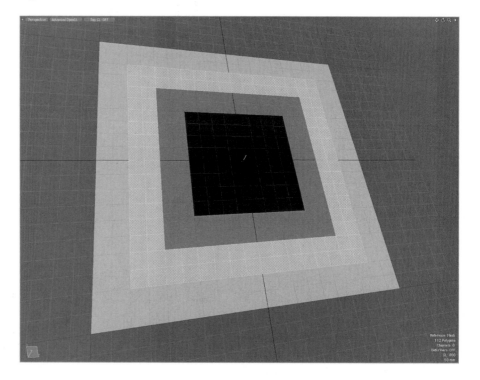

Figure 9.11

Using the Statistics settings for materials allows for quick creation of complex polygon sets.

This example is quite simple, but this type of selection as well as the others we covered will allow you to assign materials and selection sets far more quickly than merely clicking polygons alone. Moving forward, you will utilize these techniques to add material sets and selection sets to the model.

Select and create materials for general groups (walls, floors, doors, and so on). These materials should contain objects that have some similarities with each other. For example, you could place all of the doorknobs, bathroom fixtures, and anything else with a brushed metallic finish in a single material group. Once you have these materials blocked out, you can select specific parts of those materials groups that will have slight variation (diffuse color, reflective color, or bump) and assign those materials to a selection set. Perhaps the doorknobs will have a different reflective color from the other brushed metallic objects, so the creation of a selection set will allow you to make that change without changing all of the settings.

Selecting Floor Materials

The materials in the scene can be broken down into three major groups at this point: floors, walls, and details (door and window frames, molding, and so on). The detail work can usually be left white (a specific material will be added later, but it can be skipped initially). The one exception as far as details go is to apply a glass material to the windows. The walls will end up with several color variations but can also be left fairly simple, so for now simply change the color to an off-white. The simplified color scheme on walls and details will make it easier to work on the floors and see them in the context of a more completed scene. Before working on the materials, a simple light setup will help to visualize the materials more clearly:

1. In the Global Illumination tab (under Render Properties in the Shader Tree tab), set Ambient Intensity to 0.

2. Enable Indirect Illumination.

3. In the Base Shader, set the Direct Illumination Multiplier to 50% and the Indirect Illumination Multiplier to 75%.

4. Set the spread angle on the default light to 3°.

The model should look like Figure 9.12 and is now prepped and ready for work on the floors.

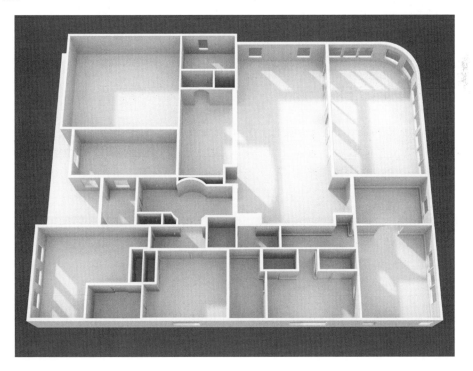

Figure 9.12

With a very basic lighting setup, the model is ready for texture.

There are two main types of flooring in this model: hard floor (tile, wood, concrete) and carpet. These categories may have subsections, but because these subsections will share many attributes, the polygons in the scene will be placed into the two main categories before continuing. All of the floors have been created with the border region (the polygons around the border that were created when beveling the floor sections inward). This not only helps from a modeling standpoint (by eliminating smoothing errors), but it also makes selecting the floors much easier. To select all of the flooring that will be given a carpet material, follow these steps:

1. Click the large polygons in the center of the floors in each room that will have some kind of carpet.

2. Press Shift+up-arrow to select the border polygons.

3. At this point, only the polygons in doorways and archways remain, so click them now to complete the selection, as shown in Figure 9.13.

Figure 9.13

In a matter of seconds, 315 polygons are selected!

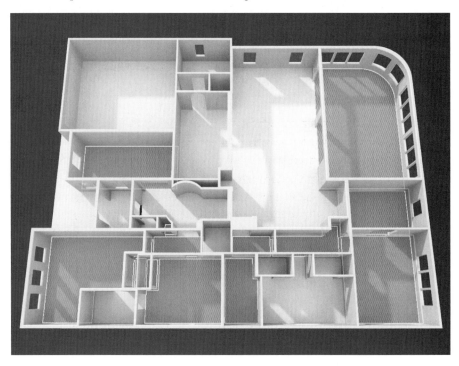

4. Assign a carpet material to the selection.

5. Repeat steps 1–4 in the areas that will have wood, tile, and concrete.

6. Use a simple basic color to represent each type of flooring.

Figure 9.14 shows the model with the floor types identified. From this point, basic attributes will be applied before specifying particular subcategories.

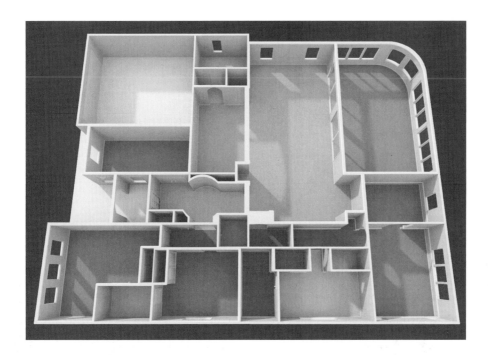

Creating Carpet

You can create carpets in a generic fashion and then customize the attributes as needed for different sections of the house. For these purposes, all carpets can share many common attributes, such as reflection/specularity, roughness, and bump. As previously mentioned, a small amount of reflection is present in many surfaces.

In this case, a small amount of Specular and Fresnel attributes can be used (settings of 1% and 10%, respectively, should be appropriate). This will help tie the materials in the scene together by allowing colors from surrounding materials to show in the carpet (it will not create recognizable reflections). Select the Match Specular check box to tie in some reflective amount. Because clear reflections are not wanted here, also enable Blurry Reflections. At this point, the reflections will likely be too clear, so turn the Roughness up to around 80%. The material will now look like Figure 9.15. Including reflections in this manner will not create visible reflections but allows for some bounced color from surrounding materials and generally helps tie the completed scene together.

Bump is an important aspect of carpet materials. Setting up a good-looking bump map adds detail to close-up or high-resolution images and helps smooth the appearance of the carpet in views where the bump itself is not visible. Finding textures to make a good bump map can be difficult, but procedurals can work well when properly designed. To get a texture that works well, follow these steps:

1. Add in a Lump procedural from the Noise section of the Enhance: modo Textures. This will be added as a Diffuse Color and look like Figure 9.16.

Figure 9.15

Soft specularity and reflectivity can be used to improve the look of carpet materials.

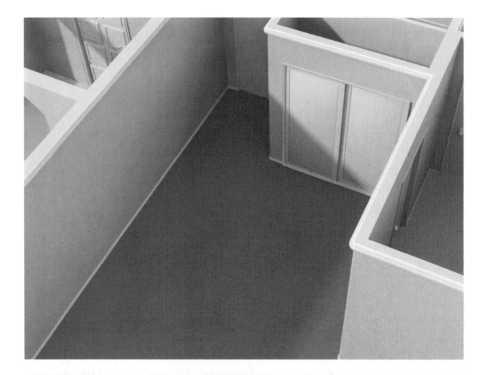

Figure 9.16

The Lump procedural texture will make a nice carpet bump with some editing.

2. The texture is obviously too large, so set the texture Size to 25 mm in all axes to reduce it.

3. The lumps are still a bit too soft, so increase the Bias to about 80% to make the light areas of the pattern more pronounced.

4. With the texture adjusted to your liking, change the Effect of the layer from Diffuse Color to Bump. This is a good start to the carpet, shown in Figure 9.17.

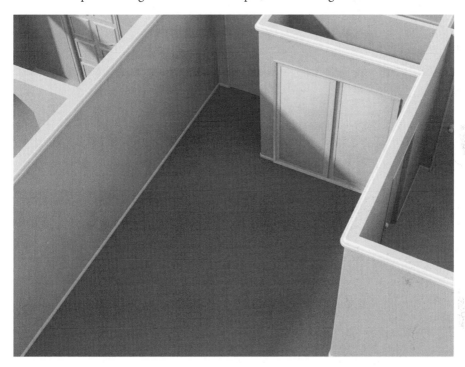

Figure 9.17

The bump map added to the carpet material

The carpet is getting close in appearance to what we want but needs a little variation to make it really work. Adding some Diffuse Amount will make the overall look of the carpet a little less flat.

1. Create an Instance of the Bump layer and set it to Diffuse Amount.

2. Adjust the values to get a result that is lighter but with less contrast than the bump layer. Set the Background Value to 40% and the Foreground Value to 90%.

3. Now add one more procedural layer finish off the basic carpet. Add a Multi-Fractal texture (also from the Enhance section under Noise).

4. Set the layer to Diffuse Amount.

5. Change the Background Value to 80% and leave the Foreground at 100%. This will be multiplied over the other diffuse amount so it can be fairly subtle.

6. Change the layer blend mode to Multiply. Now the carpet base layer is complete. The material should look like Figure 9.18.

Figure 9.18

The finished basic carpet material

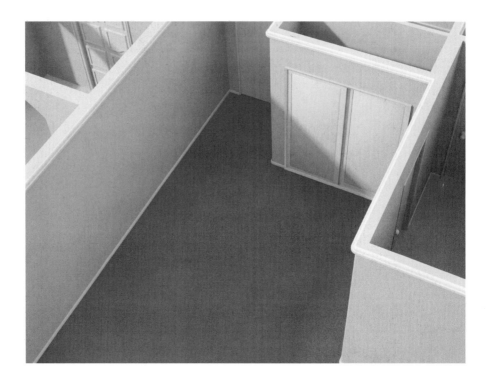

Instead of creating individual materials for each section of carpeting, you can add selection sets and then apply a simple change of color to each section. Start by selecting the polygons in the master suite. Then choose Select → Assign Selection Set. In the pop-up window, give the selection set a name (such as **Master_Carpet**). Select the Office and Sunroom and assign each to their own selection set. These selection sets can be used in conjunction with Groups in the Shader Tree to override any material settings and will be used in this instance to easily change the carpet colors while making the option to alter the materials in the future very simple. To create a group based on a selection set and assign a new color, follow these steps:

1. In the Shader Tree, choose Group from the Add Layer menu.

2. In the Group Properties tab, change the Polygon Tag Type to Selection Set.

3. Change the Polygon Tag to Master_Carpet (or whatever name you gave that area of the floor). You will see that the group has changed from the generic group name to the name of your selection set.

4. Add a Constant from the Processing section of the Add Layer menu.

5. Change the Constant Value to a color that you want to use in the selected area.

6. Repeat these steps for the other areas of the house. Figure 9.19 shows the new carpet colors.

Figure 9.19

The carpeted sections now have different colors but still share common bump, specular/ reflective, and diffuse amount settings.

Notice that there is consistency to the texture and style of the material. Any changes made to the Carpet material will appear in any carpeted section of the layout, but the colors based on the selection set will remain. If a different style of carpet is needed in any of these areas, new bump maps can also be added to the selection set groups to make the material look different in that section. If the Specular/Reflective values seem too uniform in all of the carpets, the Constant layers can be instanced in each selection set group and changed to Specular Color to make the effect less pronounced.

Creating Wood

Wood floors can be created either with procedural textures or with photo-based textures. Each of these approaches has inherent benefits and drawbacks. Procedurals can easily be edited to change the grain, colors, and other attributes, but they can lack the nuances of photographic textures. Photo-referenced textures can add subtle realism to a material, but they are more difficult to edit (beyond subtle shifts in color and brightness values). It is also possible to create a hybrid texture that uses some procedural textures and some with photographic sources.

To make the creation of a procedural wood texture easier to visualize, it is often best to create a simple test scene. By *simple*, I mean a square (roughly the size of a room) and a preset interior environment. Setting up a scene like this allows you to test material settings quickly and see the result without waiting for the rest of the model to render. With wood floors, you have two things to take into account: the wood grain and the panels that make up the individual boards. The grain is fairly easy to simulate. In the Enhance: modo Textures, there are two possible options in the Organic section. Don't be fooled by the Easy Wood texture; it is not ideal for wood floors. Skip down to the Hardwood texture; it will create the grain nicely. The scale of the wood texture can be adjusted by manipulating the Size settings in the Texture Locator. Figure 9.20 shows the texture with X and Y values of 100 mm and a Z size of 500 mm (to stretch out the texture).

The panels and wood colors now need to be created. There are a couple of decent textures that can be used for panels, but in this case, the Grid texture (in the Enhance: modo Textures → Geometric section) will do the job. When added, the texture will not appear to be a fit at all, but by selecting the Output Regions check box, the grid will be broken into panels. To get a better scale, the panels need to be elongated as the wood was earlier. Changing the X, Y, and Z Size settings to 500 m, 500 m, and 3 m, respectively, the panels begin to take form, as shown in Figure 9.21. Notice that the individual planks are evenly aligned instead of being staggered. This even distribution demonstrates one of the caveats of working with procedural textures. Procedurals are good at providing randomness and order, but are not well suited for handling something in between. To create something like the semirandom placement of wood floor panels, photographic and manually created textures work best. In some cases, however, this kind of texture (when finished) can provide the needed result when photographs are either too difficult to obtain or to implement (in cases where memory used by many large image maps is not acceptable, for instance).

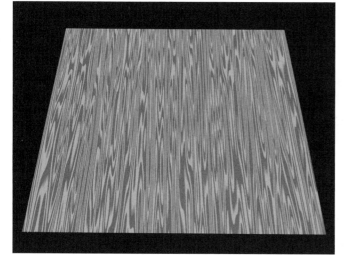

Figure 9.20

The beginning of a procedural wood floor

A few more steps will complete this wood texture. The last steps refine coloration, add bump map edges to the planks, and provide some added variation to the material.

1. Change the Background and Foreground Colors on the Grid to two shades of brown that fit in a wood texture.

2. Create an instance of the Grid layer.

3. Change the Effect to Bump.

4. Disable Output Regions (this will change the pattern back to a grid).

5. Set the Bias to 99.5%.

6. Change the layer blend mode to Add.

Figure 9.21
Grayscale planks begin to take form.

7. If the seams between the floor panels are too wide, change the X Size in the Texture Locator to 250 mm.

8. Unhide the Hardwood textures (Diffuse Amount and Bump layers).

    At this point, your floor should look like Figure 9.22. Some additional work is required to make the pattern less uniform.

9. Add a Checker texture (from the Textures section of the Add Layer menu).

10. Set the Effect to Diffuse Amount.

Figure 9.22
The wood floor begins to take form.

11. Change the blend mode to Multiply.

12. Set Values 1 and 2 to 60% and 90%, respectively.

13. In the Texture Locator, set the Size dimensions (X, Y, and Z) to 500 mm, 500 mm, and 6 m.

At this point, the basic flooring is completed and will look like Figure 9.23.

Figure 9.23

The floor material with added color variation

Adding some reflection can help to add the look of wax or polish to the surface. Adding some Specular and Fresnel amounts, turning on Match Specular (to add equal reflections), and turning on Blurry Reflection in the Material adds the reflections. If the reflections seem too bright, create an instance of the Diffuse Color layer and set the effect to Specular Color. Figure 9.24 shows the floor with reflective properties enabled. When your flooring material is complete, right-click the material group and select Save Preset. Place the preset material in the folder with your presets from previous chapters for easy access and then return to the main floor plan scene.

INVERTED MATERIAL LAYERS

In some cases, imported materials from presets will have the texture layers inverted. If the material does not show everything that appeared before making it a preset, check to make sure that the texture layers are in the correct order. This will matter only with textures that are blended (having some opacity below 100% or a blend mode that is anything besides Normal).

To apply the new wood material to the designated place in the scene, select the material group for the wood floor in the Shader Tree and then double-click the newly created preset. With the new floor in place, the scene should look like Figure 9.25.

Figure 9.24

With reflections added, the flooring is complete, ready to be saved as a preset, and applied to the floor in the scene.

Figure 9.25

The procedural wood material applied to the floor in the scene

For such a large area, this kind of wood material will probably not suffice because the tiling becomes too repetitious. If the floors are supposed to be covered with more furniture and area rugs, however, this type of material can still be useful. If you would like to keep this material for future use in the scene, it can be placed in a group. A material can have any number of groups that can be activated, deactivated, or even blended together for added layering. In Chapter 12, "Improving Final Renders," more-complex combinations of material groupings are covered, but simple groupings can be set up easily. To create a group for this material, do the following:

1. Choose Add Layer → Group.

2. Right-click the group and choose Rename.

3. Give the new material group a name to distinguish it.

4. Select all of the material components and drag them into the new material group.

5. If you will be adding an additional material now, create another new group, and you will be ready to apply the next material.

Photographic textures will add realism and variation to your materials. The next material will draw its layers from a photo source. In this case, the basic images are of a relatively unfinished wood floor. Figure 9.26 shows the diffuse color, bump, and specular image maps that will be used for the flooring. This texture, along with a sampling of other textures, is provided by Arroway Textures.

Figure 9.26

Photographic sources for diffuse, bump, and specular maps

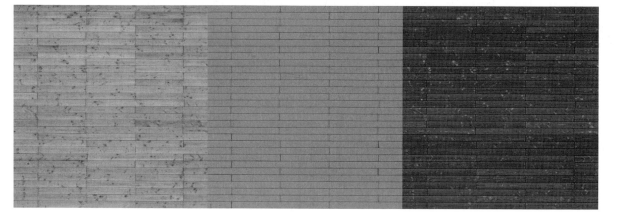

Start by placing all three of the textures (diffuse, bump, and specular) into the wood floor material. Place these images into the empty group that was created after making the previous floor material. You will need to create a new material layer. By default, all of the images will import as diffuse layers, so the diffuse map will be correct but the bump and specular layers will need to be adjusted. Change the texture with the *b* in the filename to bump. If the bump is not very apparent, increase the Bump Amplitude in the Material layer (I used 15 mm for this surface). In the case of this floor, the surface should have a fairly even sheen, so the specular (and reflective) map will not be used to give variation to the surface. Instead, this image will be used as a diffuse amount layer to increase the depth of the colors. Depending on the lighting in the scene (in the case of lower natural or artificial lighting), the low value may need to be increased for this texture to keep the floor from being too dark. Some reflective amount will also be appropriate for this type of material. Set the material Specular Amount and Fresnel to 4% and 15%, respectively. Also enable Match Specular and Blurry Reflection so the images look like Figure 9.27.

Figure 9.27

The image-based floor without any modification

In some scenes, the look of unfinished wood may seem out of place. Using an unfinished wood texture gives you the ability to adjust the colors in a simple way. Using a Constant texture with a dark saturated color, high opacity (about 95%), and the Normal Multiply blend mode can provide excellent results. This method will recolor the existing bare wood without completely blocking out the natural variance between individual wood panels. In addition to setting the Diffuse Color with this Constant, adding an instance of the layer and setting it to Specular Color will help to keep the look of the wood uniform. The only issue you may find with this method is slightly more washed-out colors than you may anticipate. If darker colors are desired, simply make a duplicate (or instance) of the Constant. Leave all of the settings the same as the original layer and decrease the Opacity to fade the effect. Figure 9.28 shows the recolored wood with a single Constant on both Diffuse Color and Specular Color channels.

Creating Tile and Concrete

Both tile and concrete can be created quickly with photographic textures. For the sake of continuity, all of the tiles in the house will be created using the same material. Several decent tile presets are included in the content that is installed with modo, but these materials have a common problem: tile size. Most of the tiled floors are made from a single tile that is repeated over and over, so the amount of variation between tiles is absolutely zero. When placed in an area where the image will repeat more than three or four times, this will not work well at all.

Instead of using the simple tiles all over the scene, another high-resolution image will be employed. In this instance, I will use another one of the Arroway textures that is included on the DVD. Look at the diffuse image shown in Figure 9.29. You will see that even though the pattern is almost perfectly even, there is definite variation in the individual tiles. There are also 12 tiles in each direction in the image map so, even in a larger room, an image like this one can be placed and have to be tiled only two or three times— so the repetition problem is solved without any further adjustment.

The three texture images (diffuse, bump, and specular) can be placed directly into the material group. Assign the texture layers to their corresponding channels. Create an instance of the diffuse layer and assign it to Specular Color (which like the Specular Amount will also affect the reflective attributes as long as the Match Specular option is selected in the material). Another option to consider here is whether you would like blurred reflections and, if so, how blurry (Roughness setting). When using photos like this, the high and low values for each layer need to be considered because they will correspond to a range of values for the assigned channel. This is most important for noncolor layers (Specular/Reflection Amount, Diffuse Amount, and so on). The default High and Low Values for the Specular Amount layer in this material have too much contrast and will result in reflections that are very strong. Reduce the High Value to around 25% and increase the Low Value slightly (about 3%). This completes the material, which will now look like Figure 9.30. Remember that the Bump Amplitude in the material layer can be adjusted to increase or decrease the illusion of depth on the surface.

Figure 9.29

The diffuse map for the tile floor texture. The amount of variation between tiles helps create a more natural-looking material.

Figure 9.30

The tile floor in context shows no real signs of repetition.

To adjust this material, a slightly different approach needs to be taken compared to the wood material. The color can be changed with an added Constant layer, but the result will not be as clean as it was with the wood. In this case, it is much easier to adjust the Hue, Saturation, and Brightness of the material. This is accomplished by adding a Process layer (Add Layer → Processing → Process) to the material. Once added, the Process layer can be used to edit Bias, Gain, Hue, Saturation, and Value settings. A small change in each of these settings can make the material fit into your color scheme quickly.

The concrete floor (in the garage) is fairly simple and can be completed by using a preset with some minor adjustments to the placement of the images and the diffuse amount. To set up the concrete floor:

1. Select the Concrete material group in the Shader Tree.

2. In the Preset tab, choose Materials → Stone → Concrete and double-click a clean concrete material (for example, Concrete 12) to apply it to the material group.

3. By default, the images in the material will be assigned to a UV for their mapping coordinates. Select the main Concrete 12 texture (the one that is not in italics) and, in the Texture Locator, change the Projection Type to Cubic and the Size to 3 m on all axes.

4. There will still be some tiling at this point, so a little additional variation in the Diffuse Amount can be used to avoid the visible repetition. Add a Concrete procedural to the material group (Add Layer → Enhance: modo Textures → Organic → Concrete).

5. Set the Size to 3 m on all axes in the Texture Locator.

6. Change the Effect to Diffuse Amount.

7. Set the blend mode to Multiply.

8. At this setting, the material will get very dark, so increase the Background Value to 75%.

At this point, the added layer will be more blended and will cause only a gradual shift in the diffuse amount over the surface, as shown in Figure 9.31.

Creating Walls

The principle behind creating the walls is much like the technique used to create the carpets. You can design a basic wall material and then use selection sets to add variation in color, texture, or other attributes. For the basic material on the walls, leave a simple color (in the material). Adding a small variation in the Diffuse Amount settings allows you to add different colors to the individual rooms or accent walls without setting up any additional properties besides a simple Constant color layer. To add a textured finish to the walls, two procedural layers need to be added and adjusted slightly. Here is the way to set up the texture:

1. Add a Dirt procedural layer (Add Layer → Enhance: modo Textures → Organic → Dirt).

Figure 9.31

The concrete floor material is created and given some modulation to break up the pattern by using a subtle procedural layer.

2. Set the Size to 250 mm on all axes.

3. Change the layer to Diffuse Amount.

4. Increase the Background Value to 40% (if the walls are too dark, this value can be increased as needed).

5. Duplicate the Dirt layer.

6. Change the duplicate to Specular Amount.

7. Change the Background Value to 3% and the Foreground Value to 12%.

8. Enable Match Specular and Blurry Reflection in the material.

9. Set the Roughness to 60%.

This completes the base layer. It will have some soft reflections that will help tie the materials together throughout the scene. At this point, the walls will look something like Figure 9.32.

Use the selection techniques from earlier in this chapter to select walls for which alternate colors are needed. After selecting each section, assign the polygons to a new selection set (choose Select → Assign Selection Set). Repeat the steps used to assign alternate carpet colors to the walls. If there is a room that needs a different textured finish (or none at all), add layers within the groups and assign them to Diffuse and Specular Amount. Adding a Constant will effectively remove the finish and adding another type of texture will replace the base layers.

Figure 9.32

The base wall material

Cleaning Up

After you create the main wall and floor materials, a few elements will still need materials. You can use preset or simple materials settings and colors to complete objects such as doorknobs, window frames, and doors. Figure 9.33 shows the model with completed materials. The scene is now ready for some additional details and furniture before the lighting and final renders are set up.

Adding Secondary Models

Although this section may appear to belong with the modeling chapter, I have included it here for two reasons: the remaining modeling is extremely simple, and the scene floor plan could easily be considered complete without these details. This finishing work does, however, add life to the scene in much the same way textures do. There are two types of models that will be added to the scene: custom models and preset models. Each of these will make a scene that helps the viewer visualize the architectural space as a real and tangible place.

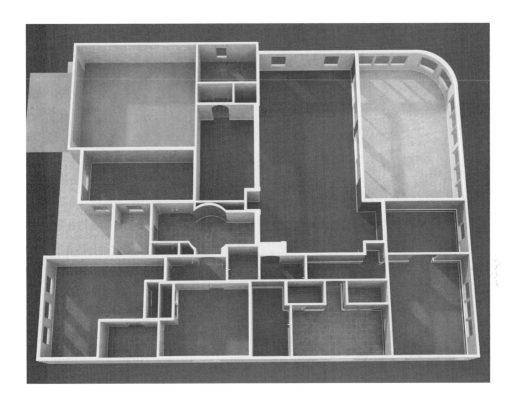

Figure 9.33

With materials completed, the house is ready for furnishings and other detail models.

Creating Custom Models

The models that will fit specifically to the geometry of the layout need to be created from scratch. Fortunately, the geometry already in place can be used to derive such elements as cupboards, countertops, shelving, and bath fixtures. Many of these objects can be created by using a few simple procedures. By learning to create a select number of items, you will be able to make the other needed items in very little time. There are two types of initial creation that can be used to make almost any shelf, counter, or cabinet: one is based on opposing wall polygons that define the boundary, and the other is based on a strip of connected wall polygons that can be thickened to create the new geometry. Both of these methods are covered in the following pages. Once the basic geometry is created, the details can be added with a few well-placed bevels.

Start with the linen nook in the master retreat. A few steps will be used over and over in custom modeling, so creating the shelves in this space will give you practice in the techniques for finishing any closet in the entire scene as well as anywhere else that a shelf or counter would exist.

1. Select a polygon on each side of the area where the first shelf will appear. Don't worry if the polygons aren't exactly aligned or are too thick to make a shelf. These details will be adjusted shortly.

2. Copy the polygons and paste them into a new mesh layer.

3. Use the Scale tool to make the polygons the height of a single shelf.

4. Select the two pasted polygons and press the F key to flip the polygons so they face outward.

5. Activate the Bridge tool.

6. Disable Remove Polygons and click the Apply button to create the bridge (this will leave the two pasted polygons and create a closed structure).

7. Press the Q key to drop the tool.

This creates a basic cube that fits precisely to the existing geometry. There are a couple minor issues with the shape, and there is still only one shelf. A little cleanup and duplication will complete the section;

1. If the front of the shelf is a little uneven, select the front polygon and use the Scale tool to flatten it.

2. Use the Move tool on the same polygon to place the front of the shelf so it is not too close to the front of the space.

3. Select the two edges on the front of the shelf and use the Bevel tool to bevel the edges a small amount (about 5 mm).

4. In Polygons mode, double-click the shelf to select it.

5. Use the Move tool to place this shelf where the bottom shelf will be located.

6. With the shelf still selected, enable the Clone tool (from the Duplicate tab).

7. Click in the viewport to engage the tool (a set of movement handles appears).

8. Use the y-axis handle (which shows as green) to drag a duplicate upward to the height where a second shelf should be located.

9. Increase the Number Of Clones field to create as many additional shelves as the space requires.

This completes the shelves for this space. You can make small adjustments as you see fit. Figure 9.34 shows five shelves in place with the front of the top two shelves pushed back slightly. Use this method wherever you want to create shelves or other elements that are attached to two opposing walls.

Sometimes elements are attached to a single wall or wrapped around two or more walls. A prime example of this type of element is the cabinets in the kitchen. They have an L shape and are attached to the back and side walls. This method will create the basic form in a few simple steps.

1. Select the polygons where the cabinet will be attached.

2. If one edge does not line up with the reference, select the edge and use the Move tool to get it in the right place.

Figure 9.34

The finished shelves

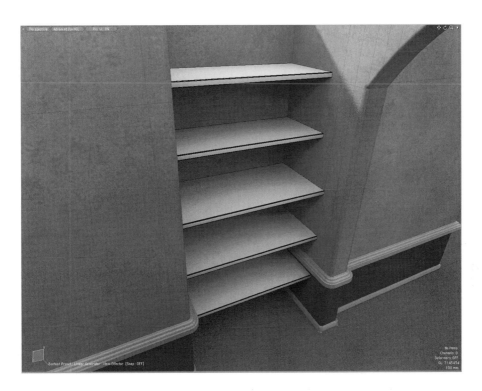

3. If there are additional edges running through the polygons, select the edges and delete them (by pressing the Delete key). This should leave only two polygons.

4. Use the Bevel tool to add depth to the counters and pull them away from the wall.

5. Select the top two faces and move them up to just below the desired top surface of the counter.

6. With the two top polygons still selected, use the Bevel tool and bevel the surface straight up to create the countertop of the cabinet.

7. Select the thin polygons that will make the front overhang edge of the countertop.

8. Bevel these polygons outward to create the lip on the countertop.

9. Select the edges running around the top and bottom of the lip.

10. Bevel these edges slightly (about 5 mm) with a small Round Level (3–4).

Your finished cabinet and countertop can be divided into individual sections (for doors) by running some loop slices through the front faces of the object The individual front faces can be beveled to create the doors. Remember that using the set of Profiles with the Bevel tool can create complex contours very quickly. Figure 9.35 shows the completed counters with spaces for a sink and an appliance such as an oven or dishwasher that will be added later.

Figure 9.35

Kitchen cabinets and countertop in two to three minutes!

The last piece of custom modeling that this scene needs can be created from primitive objects with some minor editing. Use cubes, cylinders, and spheres to get the starting geometry in place, and then use bevels (on both edges and polygons) to create detail, rounded edges, and other additions to the basic forms. Falloffs can also be used to add more-complex contours to the models. Primitive models can be used to create a large portion of the remaining geometry, including the kitchen island, bathtubs, shower enclosures, and many other elements. For more-complex shapes, the stock content can be used (or edited slightly) to complete the scene. Figure 9.36 shows the scene with custom objects added.

Using Stock Content

Often, a project calls for detail models that are not directly related to the project but that are used to help fill out the scene. In cases like this, using preset content saves a huge amount of time. This preset content might ship with a 3D application, be downloaded from online sources (such as the Share section of the Luxology website), or be objects that you have already created that can be fit into many scenes. In this case, the standard modo content gives us enough to create an interesting scene with a minimal amount of work. Using this content allows you to move through the creative process very quickly so you can spend more time on lighting and final render tasks.

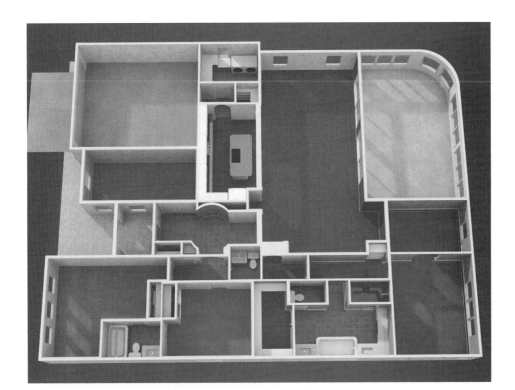

Figure 9.36

Basic objects can be used to fill out much of the scene.

When using stock content, there are a couple of things to keep in mind that will make your workflow easier. Regarding the models, it is easy to let them add up quickly and have your polygon count skyrocket. If left unchecked, even the basic components of a scene like this one can have polygon counts over 10 million and will cause memory problems and crashes unless your computer has massive amounts of RAM. To combat this, make sure that any content in subdivision surfaces has the mesh Subdivision Level set to 1. Because most of these items will be very small onscreen, higher subdivision levels are not needed. Also, if an item will be duplicated several times, consider creating instances instead of direct copies. Instances have a much lower memory footprint and will keep your render times manageable.

Textures have a few additional considerations that need to be accounted for when using them. With each added preset, some texture locators will be placed in your Items list. Once in a while, it is a good idea to place the stray texture locators in a group. If you do not have a folder for your locators in the Items list, one can be added either by choosing Group Locator from the Locators section of the Add Item menu or by selecting multiple texture locators, right-clicking them, and choosing Parent To Group Locator. This can also be done to organize mesh layers, cameras, lights, and background images. After adding a preset mesh into the scene, look at the Shader Tree. You will see a material group that corresponds to the piece of content that was added to the scene. These material groups are set to apply only to the item preset. If the polygons within the preset mesh layer are duplicated, they will retain the materials that are within the group. If the mesh item is duplicated or instanced, the materials will not be attached to anything but the original unless the Item tag (found in the Texture Layers tab in the Properties for the material group) is changed. To enable the materials in this group for all duplicates and instances, change the Item from the preset mesh name (`ItemName.1x1`) to All. With this done, materials will once again appear on the duplicated items. By using preset items, you can quickly complete your scene, as shown in Figure 9.37. With all items in place, lighting and render settings will finish this project.

Figure 9.37

Simple models and preset meshes can quickly fill a scene and help to give a better sense of the space.

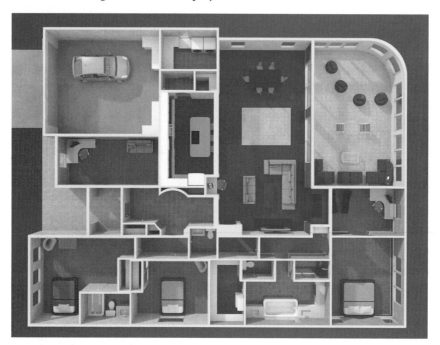

Adjusting Lighting and Render Settings

You can implement various possible lighting scenarios in an architectural scene like this. For illustration purposes, just a few will be presented in the following pages. With a little ingenuity, however, many more options will be open to you.

Using Simulated Lighting

The current lighting in the scene is essentially imaginary and mimics the lighting of a small tabletop architectural model with no roof. If the directional light provides lighting that is too distracting, a simple solution is available:

1. Hide the Directional Light.

2. In the Shader Tree, set the Indirect Illumination Multiplier (in the Base Shader) to 100%.

3. Use an Outdoor environment (for example, Outdoor 08) to change the default gradient used to illuminate the scene.

This provides some natural-colored lighting and additional environmental detail for reflective objects in the scene. This will not provide realistic lighting but gives a nice representation of the interior space. The rendered result is shown in Figure 9.38. The background may be a bit more distracting than the simple gradient, but the attached alpha channel allows you to easily replace the background after the render is completed.

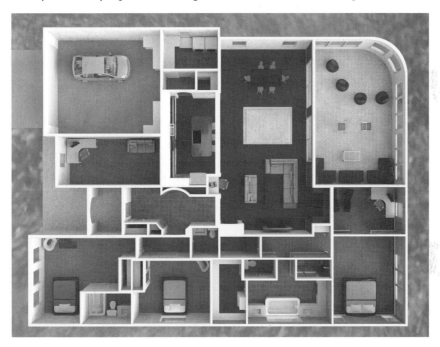

Figure 9.38

Outdoor environment presets can provide good lighting for visualization.

Lighting in this style can easily be augmented by adding some lamps or point lights (as built-in lighting). While these are not specifically necessary to display the model, they can be very useful for adding finishing touches to the scene when lighting in this style.

Using Real-World Lighting

Using environment lighting on a roofless model provides even lighting and makes it easier to get a sense of the interior space. At times, however, a more realistic lighting solution is needed. Much of the decision depends on the needs of the project or personal taste. Creating a mix between environment lighting and standard CG lights (Point Lights, Spot Lights, and Directional Lights) is key to successfully lighting a scene in this manner.

Setting up daytime and evening renders shows good contrast between possible lighting setups and allows you to make variations that incorporate some elements of both scenes.

The first step before creating the lighting for a closed structure is to actually create a closed structure. Adding a roof to the building can be done very easily because of the way the structure was built. At the top of the structure, a solid loop of edges runs around the entire exterior of the building. Double-click any edge that runs around the exterior wall at the top of the model. With the entire edge loop selected, press the P key to create a polygon in that space. The new polygon acts as the ceiling. If it is visible from the top side of the model, it is actually facing the wrong direction. In such a case, select the polygon and press the F key to flip it so that it is facing down toward the interior of the building. Finally, apply a new material to the polygon. Make it white with a high Diffuse Amount (about 90%). Because a lot of light in the scene will actually be bounced off the ceiling, it is important to make the ceiling light colored. After making the ceiling, the lighting process can begin.

Creating a Daytime Scene

Lighting in the daytime scene can be created, for the most part, by implementing physical sun and sky properties. To set up the sun and sky, follow these steps:

1. Select the Directional Light in the scene and enable the Physical Sun option.

2. Set the Time to sometime in the late afternoon or early evening so that sunlight comes directly into the windows.

3. Rotate the sun angle by using the North Offset option. A setting of about –12° should make the setting sun shine straight into the sunroom.

4. In the Shader Tree, open the Environment item and select the Environment Material (if there is an image above this layer, either disable or delete it).

5. In the Texture Layers (in the Properties tab), change the Environment type to Physically-based Daylight. This setting dynamically adjusts the environment coloration and brightness based on the time of day selected in the Directional Light.

6. For both the sun (Directional Light) and the sky (Environment), disable the Clamp option. This makes the exterior of the building very bright, but causes the light coming in the windows to more fully illuminate the interior of the house.

7. Because natural daytime lighting is largely caused by bounced light (secondary light), more bounces need to be turned on in the Global Illumination settings (first choose the Render item in the Shader Tree list). Under Indirect Illumination, set Indirect Bounces to 3.

This initial setup is equivalent to opening all the curtains and blinds in a building and turning off all the lights. Some areas (such as the kitchen and entry hall) will have very little light bounced into them. Other areas (such as bathrooms and closets) will be totally dark because there is no access for outside light into these spaces. To brighten these spaces, simply place a few Point Lights around the scene. Place the lights near the ceiling. After putting a few lights in the scene, you may notice bright specular reflections on some of the materials. In the case of materials that have bright specularity, select the material and turn off the Specular Amount. Also, make sure to turn on some Reflection Amount if it had been linked to the specular via the Match Specular option. Figure 9.39 shows the daytime lighting.

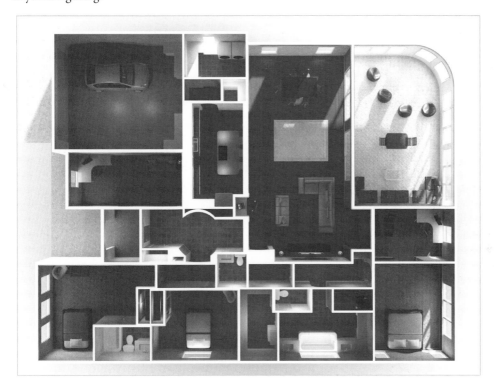

Figure 9.39

Daytime lighting offers an even mix between directional and bounced lighting.

Creating Evening Lighting

When the outdoor environment is no longer casting adequate visible light (at night), the main source of lighting needs to come from inside. Change the Environment Type to Constant and set the Zenith Color to a very dark blue. Increase the number of Point Lights to fill all of the rooms. To make control over the multiple lights easier, create instances for sections of the house or individual rooms. That way, you will be able to adjust the brightness of an entire section by changing the values on a single light. When you have finished, there should be a grid of lights covering the scene, as in Figure 9.40.

Figure 9.40

A possible light arrangement for the scene

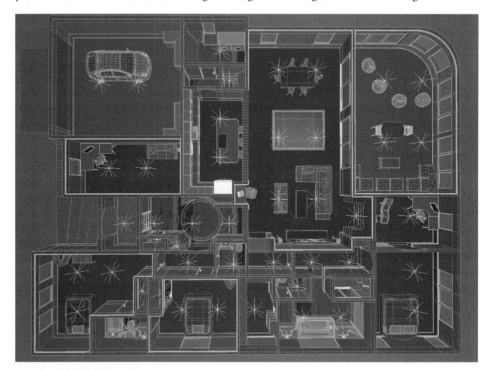

Because more of the light is now direct, the number of bounces can be decreased to 2 or even back to the default of 1. This will save render time without much loss of quality. The finished render with this light setup will look something like Figure 9.41.

These settings can be used to produce shots from many angles and can even be used for interior shots. Because the model now has a ceiling, interior renders will have a more complete and finished appearance. If the project calls for many interior shots, it is a good idea to model light fixtures in the ceiling that correspond to the Point Lights that are lighting the interior. Just like other details, these can be modeled from simple geometry such as a thin cylinder with a few small bevels and some simple materials applied. Figure 9.42 shows a finished render of an interior surface based on the evening light setup.

Adjusting Render Settings

For a scene like this, many of the render settings can be adjusted to improve the quality of the final image. These are explored in Chapter 7, "Studio Lighting and Rendering." Antialiasing (in the Settings tab of the Render Properties viewport) should be set to a good level without going too high (16–32 Samples/Pixel should easily suffice).

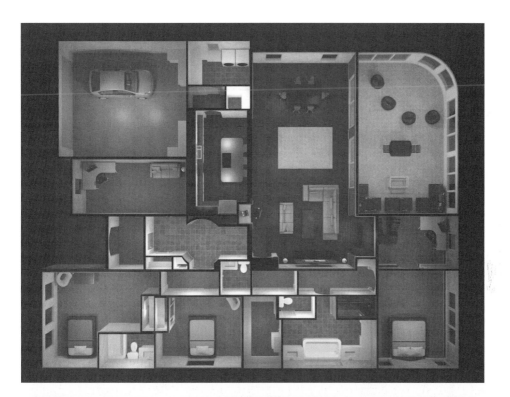

Figure 9.41

The evening render relies on interior lights.

Figure 9.42

An interior shot of the evening lighting setup

Another area of optimization is in the Irradiance Rays (in the Global Illumination tab of the Render Properties viewport) used to create the global illumination. If you have textured walls, patterns, and tiles, there is not as much need for a perfectly clean illumination. This means that the Irradiance Rays setting can be reduced. The Irradiance Rate can be increased to place some additional space between sampled rays. The main issue with the reduction of rays in a scene like this is flicker that appears in animation when the calculation between frames does not align. Enabling Walkthrough Mode creates a cache for the Irradiance Rays so that the only new rays calculated are the ones in areas outside the camera view for the previous frame. Similar to this is the ability to save a cache of Irradiance Rays to a file. These rays can then be recalled at the start of a new render to decrease the finished render time significantly. Depending on the scene, this can decrease the final render time anywhere from 20% to 75%. After the Irradiance is saved, make sure to select the Load Irradiance option and navigate to the saved cache file.

One final note on render settings: start small! Render times increase proportionally with the increase in pixels in the final rendered frame. Increasing the frame size from the default resolution (720×480) to a full high definition frame (1920×1080) can result in an increase of render time of about 9 times the lower-resolution frame size. Keep this in mind as you test lighting scenarios. Because reviewing lighting does not require absolute detail, lower the Antialiasing setting and reduce the frame size. This allows you to experiment with designs more quickly while at the same time getting a very good estimate on the time required for the final image to render.

Review

This chapter covers the fundamentals of finishing an interior scene, including textures, details, lighting, and finished render. Focusing on the needs of the scene to create simple models, building smarter materials, and using preset content allows you to complete the project quickly while spending more time adjusting the visual aesthetics of the scene. After reading this chapter and following the exercises, you should be able to do the following:

- Create textures for architectural interiors
- Use existing geometry to create customized elements such as cabinets and shelving
- Utilize preset content to populate a scene quickly
- Create multiple lighting scenarios
- Produce high-quality finished renders

Where to Go from Here

Use the techniques in this chapter to create your own interior. Read Chapter 12 to learn how to apply advanced textures to the scene and use render outputs to make sweeping changes to the final render without waiting for a new render. Chapter 13, "Animation," covers simple animation and can be used to create an animated fly-through of the interior space. As you move forward, reference this chapter to remember the fundamentals of smart scene creation.

CHAPTER 10

Modeling Architectural Exteriors

Creating the model for a building exterior can be a daunting task. Orthographic views individually offer less than the necessary amount of information for creating geometry, the complex hard surfaces can be difficult to visualize, and choosing the right type of modeling technique can be difficult. With some practice, however, this task can become quick, efficient, and fun. This chapter covers the following:

- Setting up reference images and blocking geometry

- Using blocked-in geometry to create the final structure

- Adding secondary structures

- Using subdivision surfaces in a polygonal model

- Modeling complex surfaces with displacement maps and baked geometry

Setting Up Reference Images and Blocking Geometry

When starting an exterior modeling project, your first priority should be proper setup and alignment of reference files. To start a project like this, you should have a few references on hand. Orthographic views (elevations) of the front, back, and both sides are the basic necessities. A top view and floor plans can also be useful but are not completely necessary for the creation of an exterior. If some interior space is needed for the finished render, this space can be improvised easily without creating a full interior space. The elevations that are used in this chapter are shown in Figure 10.1. These elevations are evenly spaced and require little alignment to be used as the reference for your model. Individual images are included on the DVD (`Front.jpg`, `Back.jpg`, `Right.jpg`, `Left.jpg`).

Figure 10.1

Orthographic views or elevations are used as the basis for creating exterior models.

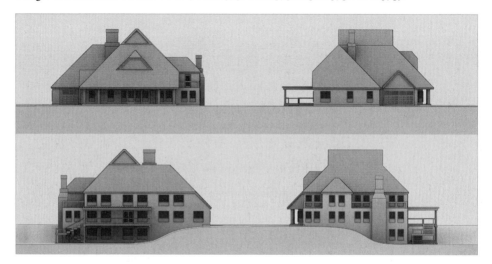

Placing Reference Images

Initial placement of the backdrop images is simple. Select an image from your hard drive and drag it into the appropriate viewport (front, back, left, and right) in modo. If the images are not labeled, you will need to use some simple deductive reasoning to place the images in the correct viewport:

- Front and back views will have profiles that are backward (the same goes for left and right images).

- Look for positions of peaks in the roof or chimneys, as these will help you separate the images into front/back and left/right.

- When looking at the front viewport, the left and right viewports are based on looking from a vantage point on the left or right side of that front view. In other words, left and right viewports are from the viewer's perspective when looking at the front.

- When placed, the images should have the same orientation they do when viewed in an image editor. If the images are reversed, you will need to use the Flip option in the image (Backdrop) Properties tab.

- If there are any measurements on the image, you can calculate the size of the individual pixels and then set the Pixel Size to give the images the exact scale.

When you have placed all four images as Backdrop Items, the viewports will display the appropriate image, as shown in Figure 10.2. Notice that the images are facing the appropriate direction. In this case, the Right and Back images were flipped.

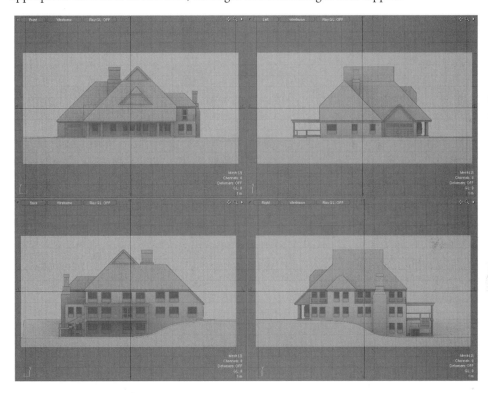

Figure 10.2

Backdrop images placed in their respective viewports. Each image has Transparency set to 65%.

Aligning Backdrop Images

After placing the backdrop images, you will need to align them. Most elevations need some slight adjustment to their positions in order to line up perfectly with each other. The quickest way to align them is to create a blocked-out version of the model by using two of the images and then align the remaining two images to the geometry. The geometry created for alignment also serves as the basis for the general blocking of the rest of the model. To align the backdrops, you will need to follow these steps:

1. Set two visible viewports to the front and left views.

2. Use the Cube tool to create a box that covers everything on the ground floor of the model (this should be a simple cube that goes from wall to wall and from the ground to the top of the first level of the structure).

3. Switch the viewports to show the back and right views.

4. Select the Back Backdrop Item and use the Move tool to align the image to the geometry.

5. Use the Move tool to align the Right Backdrop Item. When completed, your references should be aligned as shown in Figure 10.3.

Figure 10.3

A simple blocking object can be used to align backdrop items and to start the model of the structure.

Creating Blocking Geometry

The next step is to block in the individual pieces of the structure. Any piece of the structure can be defined very easily, so the real dividing line for blocking is the roof. Divide your model into different pieces of roofing. This allows you to set up a few cubes that define the basic shape of the entire building. At this point, it is not important to precisely align the individual pieces or define secondary structures (railing, pillars, and chimneys). Figure 10.4 shows the block that makes up the core of the structure. Remember to keep this process simple. Start with a cube that defines the area below the roof taper. Then bevel upward to the top of the roof and move the vertices in to create the sloped shape. If the roof has a slope that is different in one view than in another, like this piece, it is important to create the continuous taper first before adding in an edge to create the second slope. This ensures that the long, slanted section of the roof retains a constant angle.

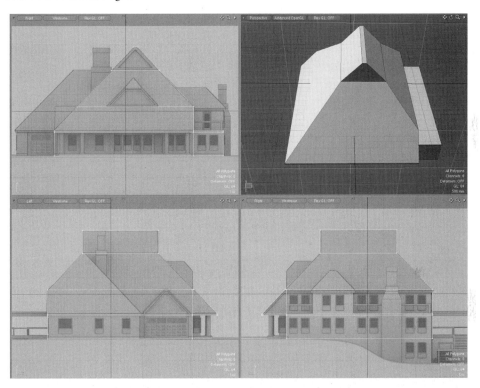

Figure 10.4

The first part of the blocked geometry. Keep this simple and just define the cube shape.

The second section of the roof was created with a large basic cube that overlaps the actual shape. Once the slope of the roof is defined on the cut-off side, a slice can be added to separate the excess geometry. Delete the extra geometry and use the Bridge tool to fill in the open section. Figure 10.5 shows the secondary section of the structure.

Fill in the remaining sections with individual chunks of simple geometry, as shown in Figure 10.6. Again, simple cubes with a bevel and a few adjusted points will create the building blocks for the full form. The assembled model is shown in Figure 10.7.

These basic geometric forms will be the basis for the finished model and will be very helpful for creating the full model in the next section.

Figure 10.5

Cutting off sections of simple geometry can produce more complex forms easily.

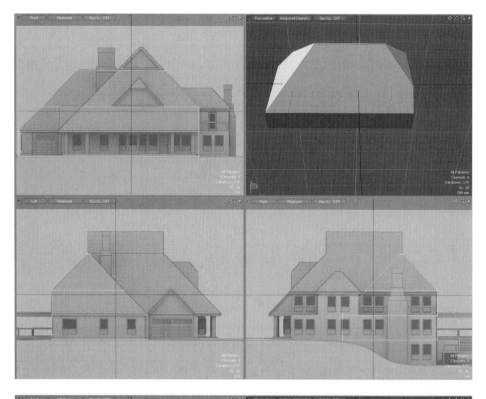

Figure 10.6

The smaller structures help define the shape of the structure.

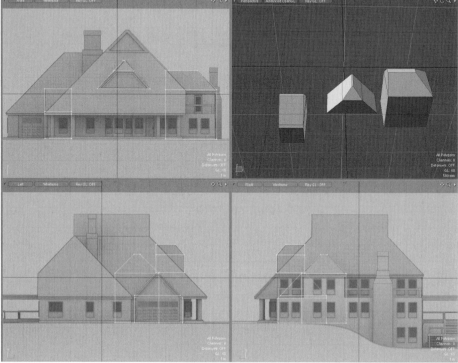

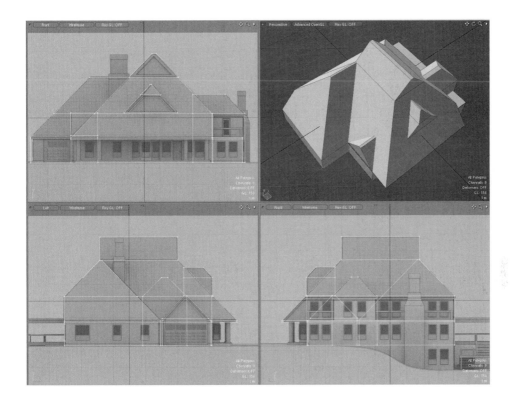

Figure 10.7

When put together, the small and simple parts give a good representation of the form.

Using Blocked-In Geometry to Create the Finished Structure

When you have completed the basic geometry, aligning the basic pieces and then joining or bridging edges together can create the solid structure. Before doing anything else, select the polygons on the bottom and delete them because they will not be needed. Then, consider the two main pieces. To attach the pieces, it is important to make sure that each part has the same number of edges. The larger part has an additional edge that was used to create the front overhang section. Using the Loop Slice tool, add an edge on the smaller piece that closely matches the existing edge on the larger piece (see Figure 10.8).

The new edge can be completely aligned by following a simple process. This procedure will be used repeatedly in the next few steps, so it is worth covering directly here:

1. Select the new edge (or edge loop in this case).

2. Enable the Scale tool (R).

3. Disable Negative Scale.

4. Set the Action Center to Element.

5. Click the existing edge (to which the new edge needs to be aligned).

6. Scale the edge down to 0% in the direction that the edge needs to be aligned (the y-axis in this case). Because the Negative Scale option is off and cannot go past 0%, drag the handle down quickly to align the edge.

Attaching the Basic Pieces

Select the interior polygons on the smaller piece and delete them. These polygons will not be needed going forward. Snapping can be very helpful to align the edges. To use snapping for this procedure, follow these steps:

1. Select the edges on the side that will be moved to attach the pieces.

2. Enable Snapping and in the Snapping Options menu, turn on Geometry.

3. Set the Geometry Snap Mode to Auto.

4. When moving in a perspective viewport, this will snap to only actual geometry. However, when moving in an orthographic view, the snap works in two dimensions so geometry can be snapped to alignment without regard to depth.

This method can be used to snap not only the edges that directly connect to the large model but also to areas that are not yet attached, as shown in Figure 10.9.

Figure 10.9

The edge shown here is aligned to the edges on the other side of the model.

Continue to attach the edge shown in Figure 10.9 to the main piece. The edges are already snapped into position, but the polygons in the main section need to be deleted. Before these polygons can be deleted, a missing edge needs to be added. Using the Edge Slice tool (C), connect the open edge through the next two polygons (terminating at the top of the roof, as shown in Figure 10.10). Once these edges are added, select the polygons where the sections will be attached and delete them. Then select the three edges on either side of the open space and use the Bridge tool to close the gap, as shown in Figure 10.11.

As you continue to attach the remaining pieces to the base model, remember to simplify the geometry as much as possible before attaching edges and vertices via the Bridge and Join tools. This allows you to create a clean, even base model before adding details. Figure 10.11 shows an example of how a selection can be simplified before attaching the piece to the rest of the model.

Be creative as you attach the geometry pieces to make the completed basic structure and remember to minimize your polygons as much as possible. A few n-gons will not cause any problems, and the roof will soon be detached, so there is no need to carry slices through the roof when adding edges to walls. Figure 10.12 shows the mesh with all of the pieces combined into a single continuous model.

Figure 10.10

Adding an edge through these polygons will set up the geometry to connect to the secondary piece.

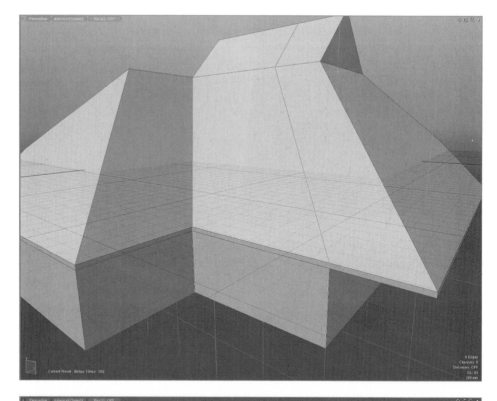

Figure 10.11

The original base mesh (left) and the modified version ready to attach to the rest of the model (right)

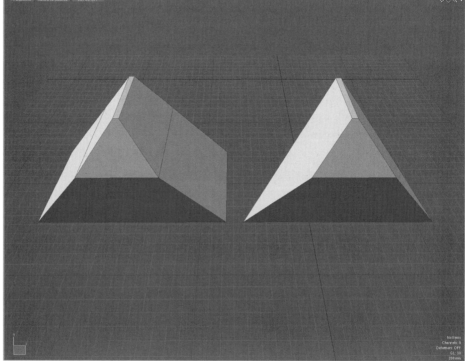

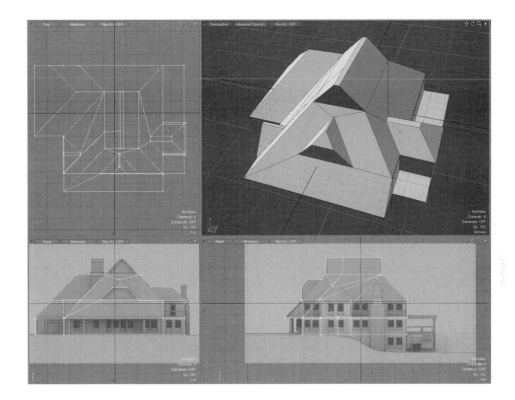

Figure 10.12

All secondary sections of the model are attached to a single continuous mesh.

Finishing the Main Structure

To create the proper structure for the walls and roof, the two elements need to be separated and completed independently. Having a roof that is separate from the walls enables you to add thickness and cutouts (for windows and doors) to the walls without affecting the clean geometry of the roof. Likewise, the roof can be finished more easily when detached from the rest of the model.

Select all of the roof polygons as well as any secondary pieces that are attached to the roof. When the entire roof is selected, cut it out and paste it into a new mesh layer. With the roof separated, hide it so that you can turn your attention to the walls. Using the Thicken tool will not produce good results with complex geometry, so using the Edge Extend tool will be useful for creating the walls. Start by making walls on one side of the building, as shown in Figure 10.13. This example shows one extension inward to make the top of the walls and then a series of extensions downward to make the inner wall and the separations for the floors.

Make your way around the model, working on a wall or two at a time. Leave at least one polygon (or edge) of space between walls as you create them so you will not have to go back and join edges that are not attached. It is much easier to work on two walls separated by a space and then fill the space by bridging the edges on either side of the gap, as shown in Figure 10.14.

Figure 10.13

Since the Thicken tool does not work well for complex geometry like this, use the Edge Extend tool to make walls in small groups.

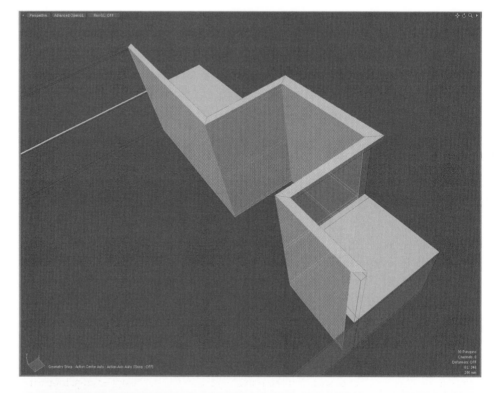

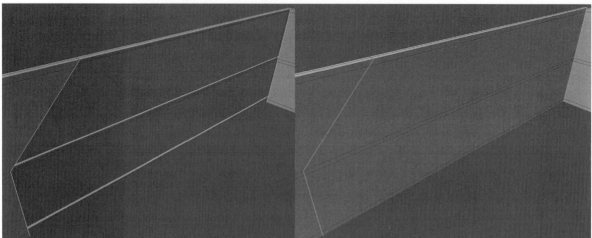

Figure 10.14

Completing all of the walls will result in something like this.

As you complete the walls in this way, some areas will not be properly formed, such as the rooms under the two balconies. To fix these areas, you will need to complete the following steps:

1. Select the walls that meet at the corner (if you have added the lower edge at the bottom of the walls, you will need to select the thin bottom polygon and the larger one above it for each of the two walls that need to be moved).

2. Cut and paste the walls. This detaches them from the rest of the structure.

3. Select the edge at the corner between the two walls. Then use the Move tool to place the edge in the opposite corner (it should align with the other walls in the structure).

4. Select the other vertical edges that were not moved. If you drag across these edges to select them, the selected edges (in the lower-right corner of the viewport) should read *2 Edges* even though only one is visible.

5. Use the Join Averaged tool in the Edge tab to merge the edges.

6. Repeat steps 4 and 5 for each edge that meets a wall in the main structure (there will be four total edges).

7. Double-click the open edge where the ceiling of this section should be located.

8. Press the P key to add a polygon in the space.

The image shown in Figure 10.15 shows the two rooms completed by following this procedure.

Floors and ceilings can be added between levels by creating n-gons from the edge loops around the interior walls. Select a loop of edges and press the P key to create a polygon that fills the area. Make sure that the polygons created with the upper edge loop are facing upward (these make up the floors) and that the polygons created from the lower edges are facing downward (to create the ceilings). If a polygon is facing the wrong direction after it is created, select it and press the F key to flip the direction of the polygon. To make sure that the floors and ceilings render correctly, select the polygons and bevel them inward slightly (just like the floors from the interior model).

Doors and windows can be added with horizontal slices to define the tops and bottoms and with vertical slices to define each window and door space. Selecting the interior section of the cutouts and beveling the polygons with a profile enabled can add frames for windows and doors. This process is nearly identical to the interior modeling process. so there is no need to cover this process in depth now. If you need a refresher on these methods, you can return to Chapter 8, "Modeling Architectural Interiors." In addition, the DVD includes videos and progressive work files that detail the processes used in this chapter for your reference. With windows and doors added, your model will look like Figure 10.16.

Figure 10.15

Opening up the spaces under the balconies can be done easily if approached correctly.

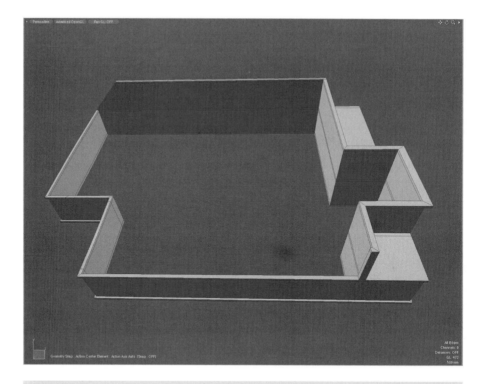

Figure 10.16

Windows and doors are added in the same way those elements were added in the interior model.

The roof can be completed in a manner similar to the floors and ceilings. Since the roof on this model is uneven, it cannot be closed with the placement of a simple n-gon. Instead, use the Bridge and Edge Extend tools to fill in the space. This geometry will almost never be seen, so it can be blocked together rather roughly. You are filling the space to create a solid structure for lighting purposes. When you have completed the underside of the roof, select the top polygons (the ones that are diagonally oriented and the flat polygons that connect them). Copy these polygons and paste them into a new layer. You will use these later for creating roofing tiles. The base structure is completed, and the rest of the elements of the scene can be added.

Adding Secondary Structures

After completing the main bulk of the model, you can turn your attention to the smaller details in the scene such as pillars, chimneys, deck, exterior stairs, driveway, and the building lot itself. Some of these items, such as the pillars, can be created with very simple geometry, while other parts are essentially groups of primitive objects. It is important to break down the objects and categorize them so that they can be created quickly and efficiently. There is no use wasting time building objects that can be created with simple models with creative materials or modeling objects that exist as preset meshes (or can be derived from presets).

Creating the Pillars and Deck

Scaling of a preset in the modo content library can create the pillars. If you are working on a project that has different needs (windows or doors), check the shared content at the Luxology website, because all of the assets there can be used for both personal and professional projects. In this case, the Column 03 preset (Meshes → Exterior → Columns → Column 03) will work perfectly for the pillars. Add the mesh to the scene, and then move, scale, and duplicate it to create the four pillars in the front of the house.

Next, move on to the deck and stairs in the back of the house. The base of the deck can be created with a simple cube. If you want a little added detail, the edges can be rounded slightly with the Edge Bevel tool to create a slightly less harsh appearance on the edges. The upper section of the deck is a little more complicated because it has an open frame and wooden beams that make up the roof. Using the base cube and editing it as follows can easily create the upper frame and slats:

1. Select the base cube.

2. Copy and paste these polygons and move them up into position for the roof.

3. Select the top polygon and copy it (this will be pasted into the scene in step 6).

4. Bevel the top and bottom polygons inward about 100 mm (this will be the width of the roof frame).

5. With the two polygons still selected, run the Bridge tool to create the frame.

6. Paste the top polygon (copied in step 3) back into the scene. This polygon can be used to create the slats.

7. Select the front edge of the polygon and enable the Loop Slice tool.

8. Set the Count to 48 and click the Uniform button to place the slices across the surface of the plane.

9. Select and delete alternating polygons from the divided surface (remember that you can select one polygon, skip one, and select the third, and then use the up-arrow to continue the pattern of selection).

10. Select the remaining polygon strips and use the Thicken tool to give them depth.

11. You can also choose to modify the front edge of these slats to create a more contoured appearance.

This type of construction is good for simple geometry, but editing these slats all together can prove challenging (if not impossible) without doing each piece one at a time. For this example, I want to put a notch in the wood where it meets the frame (to create a little overlap) and I also want to round the edges a bit. Doing this to each individual piece would take quite a while, so I make the edits on one, delete the others, and then duplicate the edited piece to fill the space. Once you have made any edits to the single remaining piece, you can create the rest by using the Clone tool:

1. Place the single piece at the far side of the open area in the frame.

2. Turn on the Clone tool (found in the Duplicate tab).

   Setting the Distance and then increasing the Number Of Clones setting can create the series of pieces, but it is difficult to fill the space completely without a large gap or overlap at the far end. This can be fixed by using the Between setting.

3. Select the Between check box.

4. Drag the placement tool handle to the far side of the open space.

5. Increase the Number Of Clones setting until the spacing is correct.

The finished section of the deck will look like Figure 10.17. Using the duplication technique, you can create the stairs, fences, and any other repeating objects in the scene.

Figure 10.17

The Clone tool can be used to create duplicated objects that require more than simple modeling.

Creating the Building Lot and Driveway

The building lot can be created with an edited plane. Start with a square in the same dimensions as the lot. Add subdivisions where the sloped areas start and stop. You will need more subdivisions later, but these will be enough to start the model of the land. Select the polygons that fall in the lowest area and move them down to the appropriate position on the y-axis. You will probably notice that the ground between the garage doors has a slope that creates a very unnatural contour in the terrain. Pulling some vertices in the area under the house will help flatten out this problem area. If you want to make the area in the basement visible through the windows, the ground in that section will need to be removed or placed below the basement floor. To make this an area that can be cut out, add in loop slices that run in the middle of the walls and then cut out the area that falls in the footprint of the house.

The last section of simple modeling is the driveway (which leads into the sidewalk and street). These elements can be derived from the geometry at the base of the garage doors. Select the polygon below the larger garage door and bevel it out, away from the house. Create a set of bevels that align somewhat with the second garage door and use the Bridge tool to attach the two sections. To create the rounded section of the driveway, do the following:

1. Cut out the polygon at the end of the straight section of the garage.

2. Paste the polygon in and rotate it 90°.

3. Move the polygon to the position where the driveway straightens out and goes to the street (make sure the polygon is facing foreword).

4. Select the edge loop around the pasted polygon and the area from where the polygon was cut.

5. Use the Bridge tool to attach the two sections.

6. Set the Mode to Curve and increase the Segments until the rounded area is adequately smooth and rounded.

7. Select the front polygon and bevel it out to the sidewalk and street.

A sidewalk and street can easily be created using a few bevels. This will allow you to position the camera a little farther from the structure without positioning it in the middle of open space. At this point, the basic structure of the entire scene is completed, as shown in Figure 10.18. Some additions will allow you to create more detail in textures and have options for creating displacement-based geometry.

Figure 10.18

The model and scene completed at a basic level

Using Subdivision Surfaces in a Polygonal Model

The majority of the models that you create for architectural visualization will be made up of simple polygons. However, subdivision surfaces will be preferable in some areas. Using SubDs can be useful in a instances such as the following:

• Detached geometry that is rounded or needs to have smooth corners

• Geometry that can benefit from sculpting to improve the shape in an organic manner

• Places where displacement maps will be used to add real depth to the surfaces

Smoothed Geometry

Several places in this scene can benefit from the use of subdivision surfaces. The pillars in the front of the house are relatively smooth, but they can be converted to SubDs so that they will never appear faceted, no matter how close the camera gets. To convert these pieces of geometry, you will need to make a few edits. To start, convert the cylindrical section to PSubs by selecting it and pressing Shift+Tab. The form will look fine, but many of the tight contours will be lost. To sharpen these edges, the weight map can be leveraged by doing the following:

1. Select the edge loops that need to be creased.

2. Select the Subdivision weight map (Lists tab → Weight Maps → Subdivision).

3. Enable the Vertex Map Weight tool (Shift+W).

4. Set the Weight to 19.5% (unless the subdivision level for the mesh layer has been altered, in which case, set the weight to about 95%–99% of the full value, as shown onscreen when adjusting the weight).

The edited weight map is shown in Figure 10.19.

The square sections at the top and bottom are not as easily adjusted with weight maps. Adding some additional edges will help solidify the form when converted to SubDs. Add mirrored loop slices in all three axes to create slight rounding on the corners while retaining an overall flat surface. Figure 10.20 shows a close-up on the top of the pillar after being converted to subdivision surfaces.

This same technique can be used to create soft corners on the chimneys, railing, steps on the deck, or on the corners of the house by adding rounded cubes (as on the top and bottom of the pillars) to add some detail and varied levels of depth.

Figure 10.19

The edited weight map results in a more appropriate form with sharp creases and smooth, rounded areas.

Figure 10.20

The pillar from the front of the house converted to SubDs

Sculpted Sections

The best example of a section of the scene that can be sculpted for added detail is the ground. Convert the polygons to subdivision surfaces so that the ground can be sculpted. You will also need to enable Multiresolution and increase the Subdivision Level setting to allow for some smooth sculpting of the terrain. Subtle variations in the roll of the surface can make the building a lot more interesting and also improve the visibility of grass when it is added in the texturing process (which you will do in Chapter 11, "Texture and Light for Architectural Exteriors"). Since the geometry is very low resolution, you will need to set the Subdivision Level to about 6 or 8 in order to have the resolution necessary for sculpting. This will add some polygons at render time, but compared to the completed scene, the added geometry will be relatively minor.

Displacement Maps

Many textures use displacement maps instead of bump maps to add roughness to the surface of the model. When applied to polygonal surfaces, seams in the geometry or UV can cause serious distortion when a displacement map is applied. Figure 10.21 shows two meshes with displacement materials; the polygonal one is broken by the displacement, but the one in SubDs (PSubs actually) holds its form and the displacement much easier.

The key to creating geometry that is prepped for adding deep displacements is rounding the corners. Softer corners create base geometry that the displacement can follow, and as a result, the shift in surfaces does not tear the polygons apart. Figure 10.22 shows the

Figure 10.21

The polygonal mesh (left) is badly damaged by a displacement texture, while the subdivided mesh (right) holds the added detail without problems.

same cubes without the displacement and other material layers. This is a very exaggerated example for the displacement, so this much rounding is not always necessary. However, keep this principle in mind when creating structures that will carry displacement maps as a part of the material. Remember, as depth of the displacement decreases, so can the roundness of the corner of the model.

Figure 10.22

The roundness required for a deep displacement is high but decreases as the depth of the displacement decreases.

Modeling Complex Surfaces with Displacement Maps and Baked Geometry

When it comes to creating the models for tiles on a roof (or other dense complex meshes), creating the individual models and aligning them to a surface can be very difficult and time-consuming. Using image-based displacement, bump, or normal maps will make this process quicker and more accurate. In essence, this process is half modeling and half texturing. The object is modeled first, and then displacement, bump, and normal maps are created from that model. The image maps are then used to create a final model in context of the structure. This can be done with any type of surface, but, for this example, a tile roof seems appropriate.

The base model for a single tile can be very simple. In this case, I created a simple tile for the basic tile, as shown in Figure 10.23. Notice that the tile is slanted a few degrees (to accommodate another tile) and that the extended piece on the left side is positioned to fit nicely underneath the adjacent tile.

Figure 10.23

A single tile for the roof displacement map. The tile has a material attached that will be created in the next chapter.

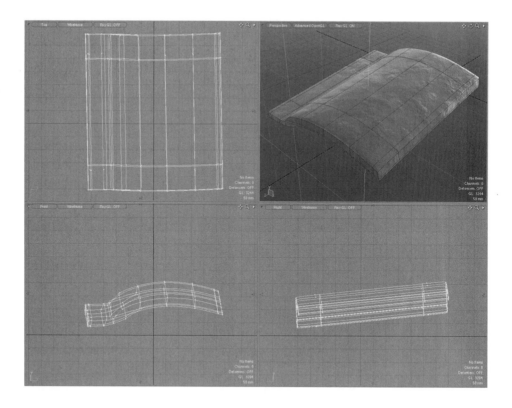

For this example, I wanted to make a group of tiles that is a square of 10 tiles in each direction. Creating the grid of exactly 10 tiles leaves odd gaps at the edges, so the best solution is to create a grid with 11 tiles and then use midpoints on the borders to make the tiled texture pattern. Use the Array tool (in the Duplicate tab) to create the grid. Make sure that the tiles overlap slightly in both directions. Center the group of tiles in the z- and x-axes (Basic tab → Center Selected → ZX). The tile group will look like Figure 10.24. Once again, this shows the tiles with a texture that will be created in Chapter 11.

With the grid of tiles created, you can easily save a preset, import it to the scene, and duplicate it as needed to create the finished roof. This solution will, however, take a lot of time and careful slicing to get the edges of the roof to align properly. Another option is to make a displacement image and apply it to any surface. In addition, material information can be baked to files that align with the displacement. You will need a piece of geometry in another layer with its own texture to create the images. To set up the baking process, follow these steps:

1. Select a 10×10 section of tiles.

2. Turn on the Dimensions tool (View → Dimensions tool).

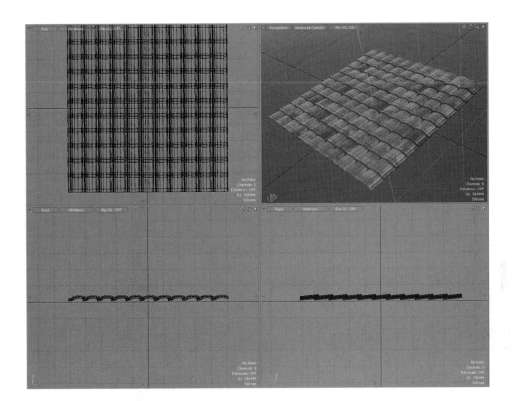

Figure 10.24

The single mesh tiled in a grid of 11x11 with the tile texture

3. Use the values for the x- and z-axes as the dimension on a plane (a cube with no y dimension) created in a new layer. When placed at the origin, the boundaries of this square will fall directly in the middle of the border tiles.

4. Apply a new material (M key) to the plane.

5. In the Shader Tree, add a new image to the plane material. Set the size to 1024×1024 pixels.

6. Change the image layer effect to Displacement (Surface Shading → Displacement).

7. Make sure that the plane mesh layer is selected and the tiles are in the background.

8. Right-click the blank image layer and choose Bake From Object To Texture.

9. The pop-up menu asks you to enter a distance. This is the maximum distance that a ray can travel to track the displacement. Look in the side view to see how far away the tiles are from the plane at their peak and enter a value slightly higher in this field. For this example, I used a distance of 275 mm.

10. After the image has baked, select it in the Shader Tree and choose Save Image from the File menu.

11. In the image texture properties, set the Low Value to –100% and High to 100%.

12. Set the Displacement Distance for the material on the plane to the same depth as the distance used to bake the displacement image itself.

13. Turn on Double Sided for the material. This will make the tiles visible from the underside.

This same process can be used to create bump and normal maps. When applied, the resulting plane will look like Figure 10.25. Please note that the displacement will not appear in real time unless the plane is in PSubs.

Figure 10.25

**The baked displace-
ment image applied
to a flat plane**

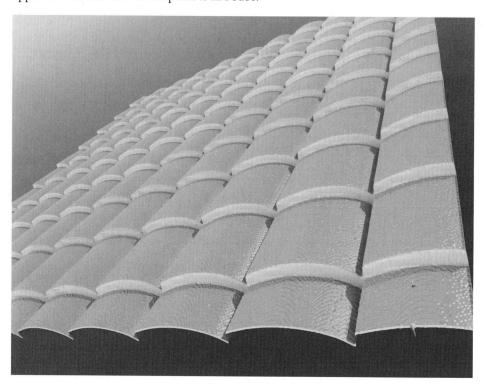

The blocky pixelation in the surface is caused by the resolution of the baked displacement. Increasing the resolution of the bake will remove this but also will result in higher polygon counts and slower renders. Since the tiles will rarely be seen up close, this resolution will usually suffice.

To bake texture images from the background, a slightly different workflow has to be employed. Baking of texture layers (Diffuse Color, Specular/Reflection Amount, and so forth) is done via the render outputs. Diffuse Coefficient and Specular Coefficient outputs can be used to get the Diffuse Color layers and the Specular Amount layers from the reference geometry into the baked image textures. With these outputs placed and enabled (it is usually best to disable other outputs to speed up rendering), you will need to set the render resolution to an appropriate scale (1024×1024 or 2048×2048). Finally, choose Render → Bake From Object To Render Outputs to bake the images all at once. These images can be saved to files and then placed in the tile material. When added, the displaced plane will look like Figure 10.26.

Figure 10.26

The plane with baked displacement and color values applied

You need to consider one thing when placing this kind of texture on a roof. The direction of application is important to keep the displacement going in the right direction. This can be done by creating a UV map with the different pieces of the roof placed evenly, with individual pieces of roofing oriented straight up and down. Alternately, the left/right-facing roof polygons can be placed in one selection set, and the front/back-facing polygons can be placed in another group, and then the image can be applied to each selection set individually, with one selection set using an x-axis planar projection and the other selection set using a z-axis projection. When applied to the roof polygons that were extracted earlier, the result will be a completed roof. The roof tiles shown in Figure 10.27 complete the finished model, are much easier to set up than individual tiles, and render faster than a model with actual tiles.

Review

This chapter builds on the modeling techniques presented in several other chapters. It implements all of the skills you have learned and adds a few techniques that help solve the visual problems presented in a modeling project. When confronted with a complex or difficult modeling task, use good references, block in basic forms, and break large tasks into small sections to tackle any task as you continue to practice and improve your skills. After reading this chapter and practicing the exercises, you should be able to do the following:

- Load and use architectural elevations as modeling references (this also applies to other types of models that require references)

- Use simple forms to block in simple geometry to break down complex forms

- Utilize basic blocking geometry to start creating complex finished structures

- Combine simple shapes (cubes, cylinders, and spheres) to create finished geometry

- Use subdivision surfaces in selected sections to add smooth curves and sculpted details

- Implement displacement maps to create highly complex pieces of geometry

Where to Go from Here

Take the model created here and add extra details, such as gutters, a mailbox, and gates in the fence. This will give you an opportunity to apply the techniques you practiced to create a complete and complex scene. When you feel comfortable, find some new elevations (there are plenty available via a simple web search that you can use for practice). Remember the basics and create something new!

CHAPTER 11

Texture and Light for Architectural Exteriors

Creating textures, scenery, and lighting solutions for exterior models presents challenges that are quite different from interior or studio renders. The complex and much more random nature of an outdoor scene necessitates the use of new techniques to create renders that display models as cleanly as possible. This chapter covers the following:

- **Creating textures for architectural exteriors**

- **Using fur and replicators to populate the scene**

- **Designing lighting scenarios for outdoor scenes**

Creating Textures for Architectural Exteriors

Most of the materials created for the interior visualization featured largely even, clean colors with very few bump or displacement maps. In a rendered floor plate, this is important to make the space easy to read. In such instances, a little texture, such as on the carpet or walls, goes a long way. When creating the exterior, material creation is different. Most real-world materials on the outside of a building are much rougher because they are created to stand up to sun, wind, and rain.

For a quick comparison, look at Figure 11.1, which shows a wood surface from the interior. The only bumps appear at the seams between floor panels. Contrast that with Figure 11.2, which shows a wood material from an exterior render. Since exterior materials are rarely polished, bump and displacement maps are much more prevalent.

In most cases, this type of contrast between interior and exterior materials is the norm. Aside from the difference in tactile quality, exterior surfaces often display greater variance in color, reflectivity, and roughness across the same surface. This is frequently seen in objects that are composites of many smaller objects, such as tile roofs and stone walkways.

The main types of materials that need to be considered for exterior applications are wood, stone, metal, and glass. The construction of these materials will play a smaller role in the completed image than texture creation did in the interior example. Scenery will take a much more prominent role in a complete exterior render, because the lack of appropriate surroundings can be a significant detriment to many aspects of a finished project. The effect will be seen in lighting, reflections, and the general tone of the scene.

Figure 11.1

Interior wood materials are polished and smooth.

Figure 11.2

Exterior wood materials have visible depth to the grain.

Using Selection Sets

When creating the materials for the interior project, selection sets were a key element to quickly designing materials with consistent attributes and minor variations (diffuse color, for example). For the exterior model, this same principle holds true. Before you begin adding materials to your model, take the time to assign selection sets in places of similar surface types, such as wood, rock, stucco, and concrete. The addition of these sets will greatly enhance your workflow moving forward. For a review of setting up selection sets, see Chapter 9, "Texture and Lighting for Architectural Interiors."

Creating Wood Materials

As previously mentioned, there is a significant difference between the composition of interior and exterior wood materials. In many cases, exterior wood materials are painted. The actual color and reflective values are governed by the paint. The visual cue to the grain of the wood is apparent only in the physical roughness (bump map) of the material. In addition, exterior wood is typically composed of large, solid pieces, as opposed to smaller segments. For this reason, the grain of the wood is consistent across a large area and is not broken up into smaller pieces.

Creating Painted Wood

To create a painted wood material, the first element that you should consider is the surface of the paint. After this is finalized, you can add a wood grain to properly break up the surface. Exterior paint is typically thick and durable. This results in a surface that features soft but noticeable reflections and rich, even color. The majority of the material attributes for painted wood can be controlled directly within the material layer. Specular/Reflective settings should range between 3%–5% with a Fresnel amount between 15%–20%. Enabling Blurry Reflection is the key to the quality of the surface. The Roughness value should be low (around 20%–25%) or can be controlled by the grain of the wood when it is added. Figure 11.3 shows an example of a painted material without an added bump map.

Unlike interior wood materials that cover large, flat surfaces, exterior woods typically do not cover uninterrupted space in two dimensions. That is to say, a tall piece of interior wood rarely has a large amount of width, and visa versa. This lack of area allows procedural materials to be used without the obvious lack of realism.

Figure 11.3

An example of a simple painted material; note the soft blurring in the reflection.

Because the wood grain is only mildly visible, its photographic textures are not as important. To create a wood bump map on the painted surface, do the following:

1. Add a Hardwood texture layer to the painted surface (Add Layer → Enhance: modo Textures → Organic → Hardwood).

2. Leave the layer set to the default Diffuse Color effect while adjusting the scale of the texture.

3. Reduce the Size values to around 50 mm (adjust as needed for your scene).

4. Change the layer effect to Bump.

5. In the material layer, adjust Bump Amplitude to around 1 mm to make the effect less pronounced.

At this point, you should see the effect of the wood grain under the surface of the paint. If the effect is too rough, the Wood Graininess value can be decreased to smooth the surface appearance. Smoother values are typically equated with thicker paint, while a rougher grain is equated with thin paints or stains. With the graininess set to 5%, the painted wood material should now look something like the image shown in Figure 11.4. This demonstrates the effect of a thick paint.

Creating Stained Wood

To create the appearance of thinner paint, the graininess needs to be increased to around 20%. However, increasing the Wood Graininess value alone will not complete the effect. The thinner the paint, the less reflectivity there will be across the surface. To achieve the look of stained wood, the Specular/Reflective values need to be decreased significantly or completely disabled. Adding a small amount of Fresnel (3%–5%) is appropriate for this type of material. The reflections also need to be spread more widely across the surface, so the Roughness should be increased to around 30%. Finally, the Bump Amplitude should be increased to show that the paint is filling in less of the fine gaps and crevices in the surface of the wood. A height of around 15 mm will suffice. Figure 11.5 shows a stained wood material that has been created by adjusting a few settings in the material and wood texture.

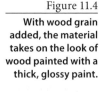

Figure 11.4

With wood grain added, the material takes on the look of wood painted with a thick, glossy paint.

As was the case with the interior walls and carpets, selection sets can be employed to vary the color of wood without the need to design completely different wood materi-

Figure 11.5

Adjusting two settings can change the look of thick paint to a thin stain.

als for each section. Within the material groups that are assigned to the various selection sets, Constant layers can be used to control color and Specular/Reflective values. In addition, duplicates of the original Hardwood texture can be added to those groups for which Wood Graininess needs to be adjusted. Because these wood materials will rarely reside in close proximity to one another, the consistency of the procedural wood pattern will be virtually unrecognizable.

Creating Natural Wood

Natural (unfinished or sealed) wood materials are much more difficult to create procedurally. Because the wood grain is visible in surface quality as well as coloration, the use of procedural woods makes it difficult to achieve the desired variation and realism of photographic textures. Photo-based textures of either solid wood or wood planks can be used to create this type of material. Figure 11.6 shows the diffuse color image from an included Arroway Textures texture set. From this type of photograph, individual wood boards can be either implied or derived geometrically.

Simply applying the diffuse, specular, and bump image maps to a flat polygon can produce an adequate look in many situations. If additional detail is needed, the photograph can be used as a template to create individual planks. To derive geometry from this pho-

Figure 11.6

Photographic textures are necessary when creating realistic natural wood materials.

tograph, complete the following steps:

1. Create a square the size of the desired final mesh. For this example, I am using a 3-meter square.

2. Apply a new material to the polygon.

3. Add the diffuse color image to the new material. This image should map perfectly by using the default UV map.

4. Select the two boundary edges that run parallel to the photographed wood planks.

5. Run the Loop Slice tool (Alt/Option+C).

6. Set the Count to 23 and click the Uniform button. This creates 24 individual polygons for the 24 planks in the photograph.

7. Select all of the polygons and activate the Bevel tool (B).

8. Disable the Group Polygons option and bevel inward slightly (to create the gap between the planks).

9. Press the [key to invert the selection and cut out the selected polygons.

10. Once again, select the existing polygons and activate the Thicken tool (from the Basic tab). Thicken the polygon slightly to add some depth.

This photo-based model can be adapted quickly to suit the needs of your scene. Individual planks can be selected and moved without altering the attached material. Planks can be duplicated and reused anywhere in the scene. Because the photo is attached by using the UV map, the location of the polygons in 3D space is irrelevant. Adding details, such as slightly rounded edges, can also be done without distorting the texture. Figure 11.7 shows a wood deck created from this type of photo-referenced geometry. In this image, the diffuse, specular, and bump map images are applied to the material. In addition, the specular map has been instanced and set to Reflection Fresnel.

Figure 11.7

In addition to being used as textures, photographs can be used to quickly derive geometry.

Creating Rock and Stone Materials

This section covers a broad spectrum of materials ranging from stone and brick, to clay and stucco. These materials share many common attributes, such as diffuse and reflective amounts, coarse surface qualities, and a general location on architectural models. Many of these materials can be used interchangeably to quickly vary the appearance of a façade. Building up a library of these materials will allow you to make quick adjustments that demonstrate sweeping changes in the appearance of the model.

As a general rule, smoother materials in this category, such as stucco, can be created by using procedural texturing methods. In contrast, rougher and more-complex materials, such as a rock wall, will usually require photographic textures. This differentiation is largely due to the scale of the surface displacement. Processed materials (for example, clay and stucco) have a fine grain, so the individual details are rarely seen. The larger scale of walls created out of bricks or rocks result in recognizable elements that are easily picked up by the viewer.

Procedural Materials

Perhaps the most commonly seen material in this category is stucco. The small, nondescript details and random patterning that result when the mixture is sprayed on make it an excellent candidate for procedural textures. In the Noise section of the Enhance: modo Textures, there is a Stucco texture. When applied, this texture will look like anything but stucco! However, with some clever adjustment, a convincing material can be produced. Figure 11.8 shows a material with the default Stucco settings mapped to the Displacement channel.

Start by identifying the issues with the texture. The scale is far too large, the details are too round and lumpy, and there is a lack of clustering, which is characteristic of stucco walls. To create a more realistic material, you will need to do the following:

1. Adjust the scale of the texture by changing the Size to 100 mm on all axes.

2. In the Stucco texture layer's properties, increase the Octaves to 6.0 (this will increase the permutations of the pattern).

3. Increase the Frequency to 4.0 to increase the random jitter of the pattern.

Figure 11.8

Don't be discouraged by the default settings. The Stucco texture will work well with a few small adjustments.

4. Change the Increment to 0.65 (this decreases the falloff of intensity between Octaves).

5. Change the Upper Clip to 35%. This will flatten off the taller bumps.

6. Change the Bias to 75% to cause some of the bumps to clump together more.

After making these adjustments, the Stucco texture will begin to live up to its name. The material should now look like the image shown in Figure 11.9. Making slight adjustments to the Output Controls (Lower and Upper Clips, Bias, and Gain) will allow you to further customize the appearance of the stucco material.

As far as the general material settings go, stucco walls use very low Specular/Reflective amounts (1%–2% is typical), as well as low Fresnel (around 5%). This very low reflectivity helps add subtle realism and ties texture into the overall scene. Variations of color can easily be utilized to add style to the material. The addition of some subtle variation to the Diffuse Amount (with any simple noise texture) keeps the surface from looking too uniform. These options were taken into account in Figure 11.9.

One possible pitfall of working with such dense displacement maps is increased render time due to the massive number of polygons created in the displacement process. In images that use the stucco material heavily, render times can become unwieldy. In such a case, a mixture of bump and displacement maps can be useful. A combination of the default stucco texture (as displacement) and the modified stucco texture (as bump) can yield a good-quality result (though less accurate) with a greatly reduced render time. The image shown in Figure 11.10 features two layers of the Stucco texture. In the Material settings, the Bump Amplitude is set to 2.5 mm, and the Displacement Distance is set to 12 mm. While the material retains many of the features of the displacement texture, the render time drops from 12 minutes to 1 minute.

Figure 11.9

Slight adjustments to the Stucco texture result in a much more natural and realistic material.

Figure 11.10

A mixture of bump and displacement maps can reduce render time without a dramatic loss of quality.

A common material used in exterior architecture (both in structural and aesthetic roles) is clay. Like stucco, clay is a material that can be quickly created by using procedural textures. The basic material of clay is similar to the base material that was created for stucco. The surface includes low Specular/Reflective amounts (3%–5%), as well as slight Fresnel (5%–10%). Because reflections are broadly spread across the surface of a clay object, the Roughness is also very high (about 80%). Unlike stucco, the tactile surface of clay is typically smooth. The variation found across this type of surface is usually present in diffuse color, reflectivity, and roughness. Subtle surface variations can easily be created with a single procedural texture duplicated (or instanced) across multiple texture channels. A sample scene is included on the DVD as a starting point for creating a clay material. Open the file Clay_Starter.1xo. It has a simple model and scene. Adjust the Clay material by doing the following:

1. Start by adding a procedural texture to the material group (I am using Dirt for this example).

2. While the procedural texture is mapped to the Diffuse Color layer, it is easy to quickly adjust the basic parameters. Adjust the size of the texture to get variation without being too busy (I chose 150 mm on all axes).

3. When the scale seems appropriate, change the layer from Diffuse Color to Diffuse Amount.

4. Duplicate the Dirt layer and change the effect to Reflection Fresnel.

5. Change the blend mode to Add. This will slightly increase some reflections along the edges of the material.

6. Adjust the Background and Foreground Values to fine-tune the effect of this texture.

7. Duplicate the Dirt layer once more and change the effect to Roughness.

8. To make the variation in the Roughness fit with the overall material, choose Background and Foreground Values near the initial Roughness setting (going from about 20% below to 20% above the initial value).

At this point, the clay material should look like Figure 11.11. This clay material can be used for a wide variety of purposes. Save this basic material as a preset so you can quickly access it from any scene. With some additions, it will make an excellent material for the tile roof.

Figure 11.11

A basic clay material can be used effectively on many objects.

Decorative accessories, such as outdoor pottery, are relatively smooth and even. Architectural elements, such as tile roofs, are rougher, more weathered, and varied in their appearance. Start by applying the basic clay material to the tile roof. Even for a newly constructed roof, this material will look too clean and uniform. A greater degree of variance will be required to make this version of the clay have the appropriate character. All of the existing texture layers will be used in the tile roof texture, and additional layers will be added to make the overall material more arbitrary in appearance. Additional texture groups within the clay material will be used to organize the new material. To create the aged clay, follow these steps:

1. Select the Clay material group and choose Group from the Add Layer menu. Repeat this to add a second group.

2. Select the Dirt texture layers associated with the basic clay and place them inside the first group.

3. Select the second group and add a procedural texture. For this example, I chose Dented from the Noise category of the Enhance: modo Textures.

4. Select the group containing the new textures and change the blend mode to Normal Multiply.

5. Set the Size values to 400 mm.

6. Set the texture to Diffuse Amount.

7. Increase the Background Value to 25%.

8. Create an Instance of the Dented texture and set the effect to Roughness.

9. Increase the Background Value to 60%.

10. Create a second instance and set the effect to Reflection Fresnel.

11. The effect of the reflection will likely be too strong for the material. To decrease the effect, the Background and Foreground Values need to be detached from the main Dented texture. To edit these values independently, click twice on the purple dots to the left of the fields (they will appear gray).

12. Set the values at 40% and 90% for Background and Foreground, respectively.

13. Create another instance of the main Dented texture.

14. Set the effect to Bump.

15. Detach the Octaves and Dentedness settings (see step 11), and then change these values to 8.0 and 6.0.

The material should now be suitable for a basic tile roof, as shown in Figure 11.12. To add variation, you can select some of the tiles and add them to a selection set. You can then make additional changes to color, diffuse amount, bump, and other channels in much the same way that you added variation to wall and carpet colors in Chapter 9. Figure 11.13 shows the same material with additional texture layers added in this manner.

Figure 11.12
With some additional texture layers, the basic clay material is altered for use on the tile roof.

Figure 11.13
Utilizing selection sets, additional variety is added to the tiles.

Photo-Based Materials

Re-creating the dense pattern of stucco, or the random weathering of clay tiles, is a task well suited for mathematical algorithms (procedural textures). Large, recognizable elements such as individual stones and bricks are more difficult to create without the use of photographic textures. After setting up an appropriate material with photographic texture layers, the actual images can be substituted, and entirely new materials can be created with very little adjustment. Consider the texture shown in Figure 11.14, which will be used as the Diffuse Color map.

Figure 11.14

The Diffuse Color image for the rock wall texture

As with the previous photographic textures, this image set includes bump and specular images. Placing the three photographs into their respective channels hints at the look of the finished material, but better allocation of the image maps is required to create the finished product. One of the main reasons for using photographic reference images is the scale of detail. Because the main details in a material such as this have a relatively large scale (individual rocks in this case), the depth created by a bump map is insufficient. A displacement map is more appropriate for this type of material creation. Simply changing the bump layer to displacement will not complete the material alone. The intensity of contrast in the bump layer will produce a displacement map that looks very rough and takes a long time to render because of the massive number of polygons created. Remember, while bump maps give the illusion of details, displacement maps actually create geometry. Left unchecked, displacement maps can exponentially increase the polygon count of your scene and your render times. At default settings, the rock displacement map greatly increases render time and results in a very noisy surface, as shown in Figure 11.15.

A number of settings can improve the visual quality and keep the polygon count within reason. Every image imported into modo has an oft-neglected setting called Minimum Spot. This can be used to effectively decrease the resolution of an image. In the case of a displacement map, this can smooth the overall appearance and decrease the number of polygons needed to describe the surface at render time. Figure 11.16 shows a comparison of two textures with the default Minimum Spot setting and another with the setting increased to 150. This is dependent on the resolution of the image, so a very large image like the one pictured requires a high value to take effect. Lower-resolution images do not require as high a setting to smooth the texture. This technique can be used to decrease render time significantly at the cost of detail in the final rendered displacement. Figure 11.17 shows the Minimum Spot on the displacement map set to 30.0.

The other option for reducing complexity of displacements is the Displacement As Bump setting, which is located in the Settings tab of the Render properties. When enabled, this option decreases the Displacement Rate (controlling the resolution of the displaced geometry) without having a serious impact on quality. Using Displacement As Bump can significantly reduce the number of polygons in the scene and also provide a bit of an increase in speed. This will prove to be more critical to memory usage than render speed. Over small areas, this setting will adequately improve the efficiency of the rendering process. Figure 11.18 shows the result.

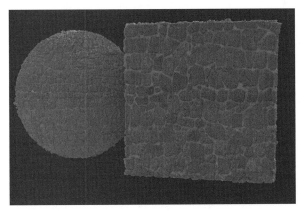

Figure 11.15
Using a bump map directly as a displacement can produce a rough and slow render.

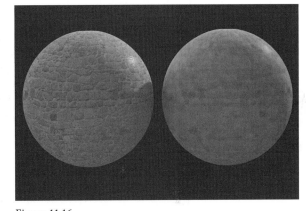

Figure 11.16
An original image applied to the Diffuse Color (left), and the same image with increased Minimum Spot (right)

Figure 11.17
Increasing the Minimum Spot setting on a displacement layer can soften the effect and reduce render time significantly, but fine details will be lost.

Figure 11.18
Displacement As Bump significantly lowers the polygon count of a scene and increases render speed slightly.

A mixture of both techniques will give the best combination of polygon reduction and speed increase. The essential goal is to re-create the Displacement As Bump option manually to save memory and increase speed. A material like this can be created by changing a few settings as follows:

1. Set Minimum Spot to 30. The rock texture is high resolution, so with a lower-resolution image, the setting can be lower.

2. Duplicate the displacement image layer and set the effect to Bump.

3. Reset the Minimum Spot setting on the bump layer to 1.0.

4. In the Render Properties tab, set the Displacement Rate to 6.0.

5. Disable Displacement As Bump (the effects are seen through the addition of the bump layer).

6. Increase the Bump Amplitude on the Material properties to 40 mm (matching the Displacement Distance).

The finished result is shown in Figure 11.19. The render represents about a 90% decrease in render time over the original Displacement rendering and an 85% decrease over the simple Displacement As Bump render.

Use the Specular image in both the Specular Amount and the Reflection Fresnel. In the case of this texture set, the values are low enough that the Low Value can be left at 0% and the High Value at 100%. When creating materials with other textures, these values (especially the High Value) may need to be adjusted. Leave Blurry Reflection disabled while fine-tuning the reflective values. After an appropriate amount of reflection is achieved, Blurry Reflection should be enabled. Because reflections on a porous material carry the same colors as the material, create two instances of the Diffuse Color layer for use in the Specular and Reflection Color channels.

The setup and adjustment of a material like this may seem a bit extensive, but there is a very bright side to this arduous process. The images that create the textures in this material can be swapped out for another set of images. Then, with a small amount of adjustment, an entirely new material can be created, complete with aligned bump and displacement layers, reflective settings, and basic material settings. Figure 11.20 shows a new surface created entirely by replacing the images that make up the texture layers. The images can be replaced by changing the Image menu in the properties for each texture layer. Changing each layer manually can be a real chore if several layers are tied to each image in the texture set. The images can be replaced globally (in every duplicate or instance in the scene) by going to the Images tab, right-clicking each image, and choosing Replace As Still.

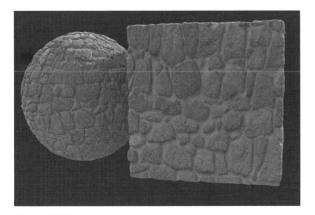

Figure 11.19

A manual version of the Displacement As Bump setting can produce excellent quality, lower polygon counts, and reduced render time.

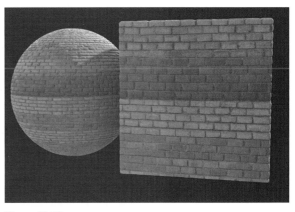

Figure 11.20

Swapping out three image files results in a completely new texture with little to no adjustment to material properties.

Spend some time creating presets for the textures that you are likely to use in your finished scene. It is useful to create materials in a simple scene instead of on your completed model because you can focus on the material creation without worrying about the rest of the scene taking up memory while you work. Because the finished materials can be saved as presets, they can be added quickly to the full scene. The important thing to keep track of when applying presets (either your own or ones that are included with the application) to a scene is the texture placement. Many presets base image placement on UV maps. Applying these materials to a scene without UVs will cause problems such as stretched textures, black areas, incorrect scale, or wrong orientation. Change the Projection Type to Cubic (or Planar) to quickly fix the problem.

Creating Glass and Metal

I include glass and metal in the same category since they are relatively simple to create (often implementing similar techniques) and they are materials that are easy to neglect. A little time spent with the glass and metal materials in a scene can make a significant difference in the quality and believability of a final render. When evaluating a scene, these are some of the details that help to separate great work from the rest of the pack.

Glass

Windows are easy objects to forget about. Increasing transparency and adding some reflection will give you a good start. You may be tempted to leave a simple material applied (with high transparency, low diffuse, and some reflection) and move on to other tasks, but by taking a few things into consideration, you can add some realism to the glass.

In real glass, the values for transparency and reflectivity are directly tied to the index of refraction. The higher the refractive value, the higher the reflectivity. As the reflectivity increases, the transparency decreases (these two values add up to 100%). An additional consideration is the Fresnel effect. As the incidence angle of the surface increases relative to the viewer, the reflectivity increases to eventually reach 100% when the surface is parallel to the viewer. Fortunately, this is not difficult to set up after the correct reflective value is derived. To avoid a lengthy explanation of the math behind this, the reflection amount for typical glass is about 4.2%, so setting up the rest is relatively simple:

1. Set the Specular Amount to 4.2% and the Fresnel option to 100%.

2. Enable Match Specular so that the reflective values will fill automatically.

3. Enable Conserve Energy. This keeps the balance between reflective and transparent values and takes the Fresnel effect into account automatically.

4. In Material Trans, set the Transparent Amount to 95.8% (100% minus the Reflective Amount).

5. Set the Absorption Distance to 5 mm.

6. Enter a Refractive Index of 1.52, which is common for glass.

Set like this, your glass material will behave mostly like real glass and should appear like the image shown in Figure 11.21.

There is some amount of dispersion on most glass (a value of about 0.01). This may add a slight touch of realism to your scene, but with the thickness of the glass in the windows, the effect will be miniscule and the increase in render time can be very high. The increase in render time can be double or more, depending on the amount of glass in the rendered view. If render time is not a consideration, set Dispersion to 0.01. Otherwise, leave the setting off. If you need the effect for a final render, wait until the rest of the scene is completed and then turn it on for the finished render, when you intend to wait for the result anyway.

Figure 11.21

The completed glass material decreases in reflectivity as the incidence angle increases.

Metal

Like glass, metal can be created with a few simple settings. Low Diffuse Amount, high Reflective Amount, and Blurry Reflection will fit for many simple metals with some adjustment to the Reflection Color. This is another case in which some minor attention to detail can make a great improvement to the completed image. By varying the reflective values (Reflection Amount, Roughness, and Reflection Color), you can add interest and realism to the look of common metallic elements. Figure 11.22 shows some examples of metal materials with some variation added in. In each of these examples, applying a single procedural texture to a combination of channels (Reflection Amount, Diffuse Amount, Specular/Reflection Color, Diffuse Color, and Roughness) creates the effect.

ON THE DVD

Videos for the creation of the metallic textures as well as other elements in this chapter are included on the DVD.

Another good type of metal to look at is a surface that features *anisotropic reflections*. These are reflections that are stretched in some way. This stretching can be either unidirectional or multidirectional. In its simplest form, the Anisotropy setting stretches reflections based on a UV map—positive values stretch reflections along the vertical (V), and negative values stretch along the horizontal (U). Figure 11.23 shows a blurred material with Anisotropy set to 0%, 100%, and –100%.

Another method of controlling anisotropic reflections is through colored image maps. Image colors control the direction. Blue stretches the reflections vertically, red stretches horizontally, and black represents no stretching. Combinations of the colors represent diagonals and various amounts of stretching. Figure 11.24 shows some examples of image maps and the resulting anisotropic surface when the image is applied to the anisotropic direction.

Figure 11.22

A little variation in texture layers makes for more interesting metallic objects.

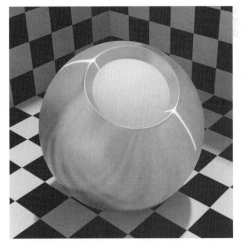

Figure 11.23

Anisotropic reflections stretch reflections based on the UV.

Figure 11.24

Examples of color image maps and the resulting anisotropic surfaces

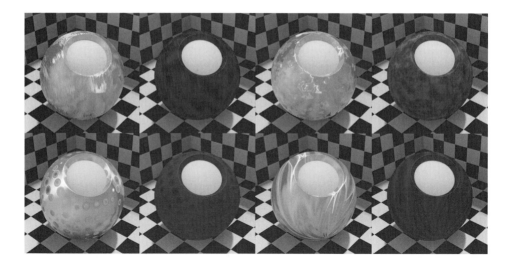

Adding Materials to the Scene

Once you have completed all of the textures needed for the scene and saved them as presets, reload your scene and begin placing the materials on the proper materials and selection sets. Remember that using presets will never give the perfect material for every model in every situation, so a few adjustments will likely be necessary in any scene. After spending a little time applying and adjusting materials, you should have a completed building that is ready to have the environment detailed. Figure 11.25 shows a textured building.

Figure 11.25

Your preset materials applied to the finished model

Using Fur and Replicators to Populate the Scene

Unlike the interior of a building, the exterior has a lot of small, random objects. Grass, rocks, trees, and other natural objects cannot always be placed manually in a scene. Random placement is key to the believability of these elements. Fur is a common feature in 3D applications and with a little adjustment can be modified to create grass. Random object instancing is also employed to make up the random selections of natural objects such as rocks and leaves. Modo uses a system called *replicators* to handle this task.

Using Fur

Hair and fur are typically complex topics. Most artists working in architectural visualization do not require complete implementation of a fur system. Therefore, this section covers the topic in a simpler manner so that you can see it as a useful tool rather than a side feature with too many options to implement without a significant amount of time dedicated to study and experimentation. Rather than spend time going over all of the possible functions of the fur material, I will show you how to use it to create grass and how to manipulate some of the settings to adapt it to suit your needs.

Fur is a version of what is known as a *particle generator*. Particles—in this case, small strips of polygons—are scattered randomly on a given surface by using a procedural pattern to mimic random placement. Individual particles can derive their color and other properties from the base material, from a texture attached to the surface, or from random values of the individual particles. Before coloring the grass (or fur, in this case), the elements need to be generated.

To add fur to an existing material, choose Fur Material from the Special section of the Add Layer drop-down menu in the Shader Tree. You will need to adjust the default settings significantly to create a proper grass material. Make the following changes to adjust the fur to make it look like grass:

1. Set the Render Density to 250%.

2. Decrease the Spacing to 3 mm. This places the grass blades 3 mm apart, but since the density is at 250%, there will be 2.5 blades in that space.

3. Set the Length to 50 mm. This makes grass blades that are about 2 inches tall.

4. Set the Width to 50%. This will create blades that are half of the Spacing distance in width (about 1.5 mm).

5. Set the Taper to 75%. This will make the tip of the blades one-quarter the width of the base.

6. Change the Type from Cylinders to Strips. This both simplifies the geometry and makes particles that are more similar to grass in appearance.

These settings on a simple terrain will look like Figure 11.26.

Figure 11.26

Grass particles with no color attached

As previously stated, the color of the fur can be controlled from the base material, in which all of the strands are a single color. However, subtle and realistic shading comes from image maps or gradients. To attach random color to the individual blades, create a gradient layer (from the Processing section in the Add Layer menu) and then make the following changes:

1. In the Input Parameter menu, choose Sample Parameters → Particle ID.
2. Click Edit Gradient.
3. Set the existing gradient key to the desired base green color.
4. Create an additional key at 1.0 along the horizontal axis and set the color to an alternate green color. (I chose a darker, more yellow color for the secondary color.)

This will randomly assign a value from somewhere in the gradient to each individual blade of grass, as shown in Figure 11.27. This method of colorizing the grass gives you exact control over the range of colors in the material but no control over the position of these colors.

To gain more control over the coloration, image maps can be useful. Any image can be applied to the Diffuse Color channel to add color to the grass. In addition, the Diffuse Amount can be altered in the same way. A photograph of grass can make an excellent start because the particles can derive their color from the color in a real-world sample. If the colors in the photo do not match exactly with your designs, a process layer can be used to alter Hue, Saturation, and Brightness of the image, and as a result, the grass blades. Figure 11.28 shows the grass with an image of grass (from the preset modo content) used as the Diffuse Color and a process layer used to add some additional saturation and darken the colors slightly.

Figure 11.27

A gradient set to Particle ID randomly controls the color of each blade.

Figure 11.28

Grass colors based on a photograph that has been slightly altered via a process layer

There is one last thing to note about using fur materials with Global Illumination. Irradiance Caching (the default Global Illumination engine) does not behave well with fur because of the way that lighting samples are calculated. The Monte Carlo method is preferred for these materials for increased render speed. To set the material to use Monte Carlo rendering, follow these steps:

1. Create a new shader (from the Special section of the Add Layer menu).

2. Place the shader inside the material group that contains the fur material.

3. Select the shader and choose Monte Carlo from the Indirect Illum Type menu.

4. Drag the entire material group above the base shader to allow the independent render type to become active.

Using Replicators

Beyond grass on a lawn, there are other random elements in an outdoor scene. Rocks on the ground and leaves on trees are the two examples demonstrated in this section. For these cases, I am using preset content, but the basic parts can easily be created manually. Rocks will provide a good starting point for working with replicators and can be used to create rocks in the grass, driveway, street, or anywhere else that detail is needed. Three items are needed to make a replicator work:

- A prototype (one or more items that are to be replicated)
- A point source (where the items will be placed)
- The replicator layer (which tells the other two items how to behave)

Start by adding a mesh that will be a rock. This can be either a preset mesh or a simple scratch-built model. Make sure that the polygons in the mesh layer are centered in space and sitting on the ground plane (the Y = 0 coordinate). Replicators are capable of utilizing multiple prototypes, but for now a single mesh will suffice. Also, in a second mesh layer, create a simple square with several subdivisions in both the x- and z-axes. The basic building blocks are in place, as shown in Figure 11.29.

Figure 11.29

A plane (divided into an 8x8 grid) and a preset rock are the necessary components of a replicated series of rocks.

With these objects in place, you are ready to begin work on the replicator. To start, follow these steps:

1. From the Items tab, choose Add Item → Duplication → Replicator.

2. In the Replicator properties, choose the rock mesh layer as the Prototype.

3. Choose the Square mesh layer as the Point Source.

4. Leaving the rest of the settings at their defaults, the rock will be placed at each vertex in the square grid. The replicated meshes will be represented as bounding boxes in the 3D viewports (as shown in Figure 11.30) but will be rendered as complete objects in finished renders.

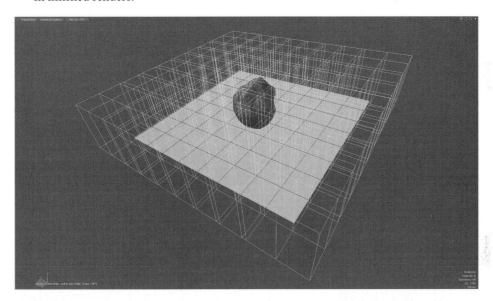

Figure 11.30

Rocks (Prototype) placed at each vertex in the grid (Point Source)

This result obviously leaves much to be desired. Reducing the Render Density setting decreases the number of vertices that have an attached object and randomly scatters the objects across the grid (see Figure 11.31). However, the position is still limited to the actual location of the vertices on the point source aside from the addition of some Random Offset values (under Variation in the Replicator properties). To break away from the grid, another method of placement must be utilized. Surface generators can be added to a material in the Shader Tree and then used as a point source. Add a material to the grid square and place a surface generator inside the material group (in the Shader Tree, choose Add Layer → Special → Surface Generator). Now that there is another element capable of acting as a point source, choose it from the menu in the Replicator properties.

At the default, the density of the placed rocks will be extremely high, and bounding boxes will quickly overwhelm the surface. Increase the Average and Minimum Spacing attributes in the Surface Generator properties and decrease the Scale Factor to about 30%. The rocks will now be neatly scattered around the scene, as shown in Figure 11.32.

Figure 11.31

A reduced Render Density value places the objects on fewer random vertices, but the rocks are still stuck on vertices.

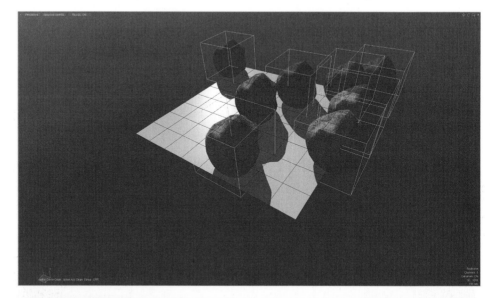

Figure 11.32

Surface generators allow for more random placement of replicated items.

Now that the placement is more random, you need to add more variation to the rotation and scale of the rocks. For this, return to the Replicator properties. Under Variation, add a large amount of y-axis Random Twist (180° works well) and a small amount on the x and z-axes (10°–15° at most). Because the rock is sitting on the Ground plane, twisting it in the Y direction will not cause problems, but high X and Z values will cause the rock to rotate under the ground. Also add Random Scale values. Figure 11.33 shows the replicated rocks with some variation added.

Finally, you can add some variation in color to the rocks by adding a gradient layer to the Rock material in the Shader Tree. With the Input Parameter set to Particle ID, different points on the gradient will be used to color each individual rock. If you set the gradient blend mode to Multiply, the existing texture will show through but be modulated by the gradient on a per item basis. Figure 11.34 shows the rocks with added diffuse variation.

Figure 11.33

Some random variation can make one rock look like many rocks.

Figure 11.34

The addition of a Particle ID gradient can help add more random variation to the rocks.

Replicators can also be used to place leaves on trees. For this example, load one of the trees without leaves from the mesh presets (Meshes → Organic → Trees). Also add a leaf from the Organic presets. By using a replicator with the leaf and the surface generator that is attached to the tree mesh preset, you can quickly create a complete tree. It is important to note that the trees also contain a weight map that has high values on the branches and no value on the rest of the tree. This weight map is used to modulate particle density. Using the rock example as a guide, you can adjust the leaves on the tree in a variety of ways. A finished example of a tree is shown in Figure 11.35.

Figure 11.35

A replicator tree with leaves attached to the weight map-driven branches.

Designing Lighting Scenarios for Outdoor Scenes

Many of the lighting principles covered up to this point apply to the lighting task at hand. The real necessity with outdoor lighting falls in the balance between direct (sunlight) and indirect (environmental) lighting. The use of an environment as the sole light source can provide a quick solution for creating a moderately effective lighting scheme using only indirect light. Physical Sun and Sky simulations are another way of making a good outdoor scene by primarily using direct lighting. As usual, a combination of the two styles can provide the best results and feature quality lighting, fast render times, good reflections, and a clean backdrop for final presentation of the scene.

HDR Environments

There are many kinds of high dynamic range environments available. Most HDRs are either spherical maps (showing a complete 360° view of the photographed scene) or light probes (chrome sphere showing the environment behind the camera). A large selection of free images is available online. A simple web search will yield a fair range of resources.

There are also commercial kits available that provide excellent quality if you are willing to pay. For the most part, excellent-quality images can be rendered by using free images and a little creativity.

For a good start, look to the Outdoor environment presets that install with modo. These images are made up of both spherical images as well as image probes and are moderate in quality. Delete the default Directional Light or hide it, and load one of these images for a good, quick light setup, as shown in Figure 11.36. Depending on the environment image, the Intensity may need to be adjusted (in the Environment properties). This example has the Intensity set to 3.0.

Figure 11.36

An HDR environment from the Outdoor environment presets

LIGHTING WITHOUT TEXTURES

When looking for a lighting solution, it is often helpful to render without visible textures. To do this, simply select the Base Material (located at the bottom of the materials in the Shader Tree) and drag it up to just under the Base Shader. Any materials that you still want to see (for example, the grass) can be placed above the Base Material (still under the Base Shader). This will allow you to see the lighting unencumbered by the visual differences between materials.

To further enhance the speed and quality of the rendering, you need to think about the way that lighting with HDRs actually works. With the environment image wrapped around the scene, light is calculated based on high and low values in the image and then directed toward the scene. If the background image is 2000×2000 pixels, there are a total of four million possible variations in lighting. For the sake of reflections or use as a backdrop, this kind of resolution is valuable, but for lighting it is definitely overkill.

The easiest solution is to create an alternate image for lighting and use the higher resolution for the reflections and, if need be, for the backdrop. You can lower the image's resolution by increasing the Minimum Spot value. Alternatively, you can create a duplicate of the image in Photoshop, reduce the resolution (256×256 pixels works well), and blur the image a bit (5–10 pixels). Either of these methods works, but using a completely separate image gives better results and faster renders. To set up the environment by using both images, you will need to follow these steps:

1. Load the desired environment (either a preset or an outside image).

2. Duplicate the environment item (choose Item → Duplicate, or right-click the environment and choose Duplicate).

3. Select the first environment and in the Properties tab, deselect Visible To Indirect Rays.

4. In the second environment, deselect all options but Visible To Indirect Rays.

5. Select the image in the second environment and replace it with the blurred, lower-resolution version.

With the illumination portion of the environment simplified, the render settings can be lowered without a reduction in quality. The Irradiance Rays value can be lowered to 256, and Irradiance Rate can be increased to 5.0. Both of these changes result in a smoother and faster render. Figure 11.37 shows the result of the altered environment. This image was rendered in just over half the time of the previous image. With this kind of increase in speed, other settings (for example, Antialiasing) can be increased while render times remain reasonable.

Figure 11.37

Blurring the illumination section of the environment can reduce render time significantly without loss in quality.

Physically Based Sun and Sky

The accuracy of time-relative coloration makes physically based daylight simulation a compelling option for exterior architectural renders. This option must be enabled in both the Directional Light that will act as the sun (providing direct illumination) and the Environment material that will simulate the sky (indirect illumination). Because time of day, global position, and date can all be adjusted, and the coloration of both sky and sun update dynamically, this is also an easy solution. The downside of this kind of lighting is that it offers almost no effect on reflection and no real background image (just a color gradient). This means that camera angles that show the environment in any way are not well suited for this kind of lighting alone.

Figure 11.38 shows a render that does not include the environment in direct or reflected view of the camera. At this angle, the lighting is effective and the quick rendering of the setup make this a good lighting choice. As you can see, however, in Figure 11.39, ground-based perspectives are not ideal for this type of light design.

Figure 11.38

Physically based daylight works well when the environment is not visible to the camera view.

Figure 11.39

Lower angles do not work as well with this type of environment because the environment offers little in terms of reflections or backdrops.

Hybrid Lighting

Each of the previous examples of lighting are great in certain situations, but the drawbacks are obvious, as mentioned in each case. The best solution is to take the elements that make each technique work well and implement those parts to make a complete light rig. The difficulty comes in aligning the Physical Sun element with a photographic environment. Start by loading an environment that suits your needs and enabling Physical Sun on the Directional Light. Using a guess and test method, aligning the lights can take a long time, but there is a much easier way to do this:

1. Go to the Model tab.

2. Hide your main mesh layers.

3. In the viewport options menu (the middle button in the upper-left corner of the viewport), choose GL Background → Environment. This displays the HDR environment in the real-time viewport.

4. With the cursor over the viewport, press the O key to bring up the viewport options.

5. In the Item Visibility section of this pop-up menu, enable Show Lights. This will make your light item visible in the viewport.

6. Adjust the Time parameter in the Directional Light properties (under the Physical Sun section) to get close to the inclination of the sun in the environment.

7. Adjust the North Offset value to get the angle of the Directional Light to match the environment.

8. Maneuver the perspective view so that you can look from the center of the scene toward the incoming light. This allows you to more easily see the alignment between light and environment (see Figure 11.40).

9. Repeat steps 7 and 8 to fine-tune the alignment.

Figure 11.40

By using visible light and environments in the real-time viewport, lighting can be aligned quickly.

This technique of separating elements of the environment can also be used to create another environment layer that is visible only to the camera (to act as a backdrop). This last environment, the image will need to be set up a little differently than the other images:

1. Place a regular photograph as the Environment Color layer.

2. In the Texture Locator for the photograph, set the Projection Type to Front Projection.

3. Set the Projection Camera to your render camera.

4. Position the camera so that the perspective aligns closely with the perspective in the photograph. When using front projection, the image stays locked to the camera and will not move.

You may need some color correction after the render is completed (this topic is covered in Chapter 12, "Improving Final Renders"), but the result will provide the best mix of all of the options covered in this chapter. With lighting, reflections, and background all handled by different environment items, you will have the control you need to make your model and scene look as good as possible.

Review

This chapter has covered the fundamentals of creating an outdoor scene. Even though the exercise is specific to architectural visualization, the same techniques can be used for many other applications. The clean textures designed here can easily be customized with grime and wear to create a less ideal and more realistic look. Outdoor lighting and HDR environments can be used to showcase other types of models beyond architecture. After reading this chapter and practicing the exercises, you should be able to do the following:

- Use and adapt preset content for your projects
- Create material presets for architectural purposes
- Use basic fur materials
- Apply replicators to a scene to add objects with random scale, position, and coloration
- Use high dynamic range images for lighting purposes
- Light using Physical Sun and Sky
- Combine multiple environments to gain control over lighting, reflections, and backdrop

Where to Go from Here

Using preset lighting and textures can be helpful for learning and for creating quick projects, but taking your own source photography will allow you to get exactly what you need for your project. Start taking your own photographs for texture creation, photo backgrounds, and even HDR environment creation (all you need is a chrome ball and a decent camera to start). In the next chapter, you will learn about extending texture creation beyond the basics and how to improve your renders by post-processing in an image-editing application. You can use your finished images from this chapter with those techniques to create more real, adaptable, and compelling imagery.

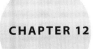

CHAPTER 12

Improving Final Renders

In many cases, finishing touches need to be added to give a render just the right look. Sometimes these effects could be rendered directly, but adding them after the render is easy and offers much better flexibility and speed. You will look at methods for creating the best-quality finished product. This chapter covers the following topics:

- **Mastering the Shader Tree**
- **Using render outputs**
- **Sweetening 3D renders by using Photoshop**

Mastering the Shader Tree

At several points throughout this book, we have covered the Shader Tree. The Shader Tree is home to all materials created in modo. You have looked at its use in creating textures for scenes of differing types and styles, but the overall amount of complexity has been relatively simple. This section covers the use of the Shader Tree to create more-complex textures. You will look at layering and grouping materials (while making good use of procedural and image-based textures), and detailing textures individually or in groups. This will broaden your perspective and help you create textures for just about anything you can imagine.

Layering Textures

From a simplified standpoint, the Shader Tree works on a layered basis. This is similar to Photoshop, in which higher layers are visible unless blended or masked. Assigning a material to a group of polygons essentially adds a mask to the image so that the given material is visible for the polygons with that material tag. Layering textures upon textures grants an enormous amount of power. Let's begin by creating a simple scene to work with:

1. Create a basic scene of a sphere sitting on the ground plane.

2. Place a shadow catcher preset object in the scene (Assets → Meshes → Basic → ShadowCatcher).

3. Insert a preset environment. (I used Outdoor Spherical 02 from the Outdoor environment presets.)

4. Enable the Global Illumination option and hide your light. Your render will look something like Figure 12.1.

Figure 12.1

A simple scene for testing work in the Shader Tree

A scene set up like this is a good way to design and test textures. Now, let's add texture:

1. Place a new texture on the ball and then assign the Concrete 02 material from the Concrete section of the Stone material presets. This will act as a good basis for layering textures. Before adding to this material, it is important to take a look at how Concrete 02 was constructed. This material has a base material, an image map set to Diffuse Color, and two instances of the diffuse image set to the Diffuse Amount and the Bump channels.

2. Select the Diffuse Amount image. You will notice purple-toned circles to the left of the properties. The exceptions are Enable, Low Value, and High Value. In these cases, the property has been unlinked from the parent value (the one that the instance was made from). Any property can have the link broken by clicking twice on the purple circle (it will appear gray). In this case, the Low Value is the only one that has been changed to decrease the amount of dark areas created by the image. Selecting the Bump channel will show that it has the same properties uncoupled. In most cases, this will not make a difference, but as a matter of practice, you will rebuild the material.

3. Delete the two instance layers (Diffuse Amount and Bump) and make two new ones by right-clicking the original (Diffuse Color) layer and choosing Duplicate. Make sure to duplicate the original texture layer (the nonitalicized layer) each time for the best results.

4. Set one of the instanced Diffuse Color layers to Diffuse Amount and the second to Bump.

5. Go to the Diffuse Amount instance and change the Low Value back to 25% (found under the Texture Layers in the Properties menu). With this done, the material is built cleanly, and any changes made to the Diffuse Color layer will adjust the instances (with the exception of the Low Value on the Diffuse Amount). Your base texture will look like Figure 12.2.

LEARNING FROM PRESETS

Presets can be excellent learning tools. Adding one to your scene will allow you to see how other artists approach problems, and you may even notice ways that these can be improved. In addition to the presets included with modo, many material presets (along with presets of other varieties) are available from the Share section of the Luxology website (www.luxology.com/asset).

Now that the material has been inspected and properly adjusted, you can move on to do extra work on it. First of all, the material looks good but does not appear connected in any way to the environment, beyond the shadow that is being cast on the ground. Real concrete often has a sealer or other coating that picks up small amounts of reflection. To remedy this, some subtle reflections will need to be added.

Figure 12.2

The rebuilt Concrete material applied to the sphere

To add subtle reflections, follow these steps:

1. Create another instance of the Diffuse Color layer and set it to Reflection Fresnel. This will likely cause the reflections to appear very shiny, like wet concrete, as seen in Figure 12.3.

Figure 12.3

Initially, the reflections give the appearance of wet concrete.

To make this effect more subtle, a few adjustments need to be made. The reflection color is white (which is too bright for a material like this).

2. Another instance set to Reflection Color will move the material in the right direction. However, that will make only a slight difference because the lighter areas in the image, which control the amount of reflection, are also controlling the reflection color. Darker values are not being considered because the darker areas do not have as much (or any) reflection.

3. Set the High Value back to 75%, and the reflections will be toned down significantly.

4. The only thing that remains is the sharpness of reflection. Enabling Blurry Reflection (found under the Material Ref tab) in the material can control this.

5. To give one last bit of variation to the surface, create one more instance and set it to Roughness. This will control just how blurry the reflections will be. Light areas will be very blurry, and as the color gets darker (and less reflective), the blur will decrease.

6. Going from completely clear to completely blurry may be a bit too strong, so set the Low and High Values to 10% and 50%, respectively.

This completes the texture and leaves it open for a lot of fine-tuning by adjusting the amount of blur, the color, the amount of reflections, the weight of the bump on the surface, and more. Figure 12.4 shows how the material blends more properly into the environment.

Figure 12.4

With the material completed, it feels much more like it belongs in the environment.

The beauty of a material design such as this is that the base Diffuse Color can be adjusted, scaled, and otherwise manipulated while keeping the related channels properly tied in. As you develop your own materials and alter presets, try to keep in mind that a sound construction from the beginning will save you a lot of time in the long run. Keep a clean structure with the material layers and you will be able to manage and manipulate it much more easily.

Grouping Materials

Layers will help you to create complex and believable materials, but when textures require depth, additional layers can add up quickly and get out of control. This is where grouping can help you create materials with complexity of a higher order of magnitude.

To demonstrate this, you will take the completed concrete texture and add more to it. Let's start by adding some chipped-off paint. Because you have already looked at the creation of some simple materials, there is no need to go into great depth on the creation of a simple painted concrete material. Find the Red Curb 01 material at the bottom of the concrete section, where the base material was located. Simply double-clicking the material to add it will work, but just adding all of the material components on top of the stack will also cause a bit of a mess. Instead, it can be helpful to start adding groups into the material:

1. Go to the Add Layer drop-down menu in the Shader Tree and choose Group. This places an empty group inside the current material.

2. Position the group on top. Then select all of the concrete layers and drag them into the new group.

3. Because grouping can get complex, it is a good idea to name the groups as you create them. With all of your concrete layers grouped, create a new group for the red paint. With the group selected, double-click the Red Curb material to populate the group with that material. At this point, you will have a red concrete material, as shown in Figure 12.5.

Now that the layers are created, the next step is properly masking the paint layer so that it looks like it is chipped. To do this, you will start with finding a procedural texture that has a proper look for the task. The quickest way to do this is to add a material to the top of the material and leave it at its default (Diffuse Color) setting. Follow these steps:

1. Start with Crackle, which is found in the Organic section of the Enhance: modo Textures. The default setting produces a large, broad texture that will not work well for chipping away the material. To fix this, the texture needs to be scaled down.

2. To scale down the texture, go to the Texture Locator tab and set the Size X, Y, and Z to 100 mm. The material is getting close, but what you are looking for is an alpha channel, so more contrast is needed. Adjusting the Bias and Gain will solve this problem.

Figure 12.5
The Red Curb mate-rial layered on top of the concrete

3. Set the Gain to 99%. The contrast will be adequate.

4. Adjusting the Bias will fine-tune the amount of white and black in the texture. Set Bias to 95%, and your material should look something like Figure 12.6.

   This could be the basis for a decent material mask, but it is a bit too geometric in nature.

Figure 12.6

The Crackle tex-ture added to the sphere, properly scaled and with Bias and Gain edited

5. Right-click the Crackle texture and choose Change Type. From the drop-down list, you will be able to choose any other type of texture to replace the current one.

    When you choose a new texture, the size will be kept but the Bias and Gain adjustments will not. By quickly adjusting those settings, you will be able to quickly audition textures. As a general rule, Gain set to 99% will work with most textures, but Bias will vary from texture to texture. Remember that this texture will function as an alpha channel, so white areas will show the red material, and black will show the underlying concrete. For this purpose, Multi-Fractal can work quite nicely. The beauty of this texture is that it can use multiple levels of fractal mathematics to provide more complexity to the pattern (thus avoiding the geometric look that was found in the Crackle texture).

6. Choose Multi-Fractal (from the Enhance: modo Textures → Noise heading). The texture can look a little simple at first.

7. Increase the Frequency and Octaves to add roughness to the areas of contrast. Set the Octaves to 4.0, the Frequency to 3.5, and the Bias to 70%. The texture will look like the image in Figure 12.7. This will work for creating chips in the paint.

8. Next, set the layer from Diffuse Color to Group Mask (located in the Shader Control heading when right-clicking under the Effect column). This effectively masks the painted group and allows the concrete to show through in the previously black areas.

    If you look closely at the image shown in Figure 12.8, you will notice that there is one real issue with this image, and that is the lack of physical depth.

Figure 12.7

The slightly modified Multi-Fractal texture

Figure 12.8

**The procedural
texture now masks
the Red Curb mate-
rial like an alpha
channel.**

The paint and the concrete appear to be on the same level, with no real height difference between the paint and the concrete.

9. Next, add an additional layer of bump map to create the missing depth. This can
be done in several ways. The simplest way is to increase the bump depth on the
RedCurb01 material layer. Setting the value to 5 mm will create a difference between
the two layers. However, this approach can be problematic because you have little control over the actual edge created by the difference between the two layers of bump. A
second approach is to create an instance of the Multi-Fractal texture. Drag this texture
above the two groups and set it to Bump. To make sure that the other bump maps still
exist, set the blend mode of this layer to Add. Your material will look like Figure 12.9,
with subtle edge highlights and shadows at the edges between the two materials.

In many cases, this type of setup will suffice but at other times, some additional
depth is needed. The problem with simple bump maps is that they do not offer anything in the way of edge contour, so when surface disturbances fall along an edge,
the illusion of depth is lost. In this case, the use of a displacement map will be very
helpful.

10. Change the instance from Bump to Displacement to get real depth on the surface. At
first, this will probably add massive depth relative to the surface. This is due to the
setting for Displacement Distance. To fix this, change the value on both materials
(the red and the concrete) to 5 mm. This will really increase the quality of the depth
beyond the simple appearance created by the bump map, as shown in Figure 12.10.

Figure 12.9

A layer of added bump makes the two materials begin to separate.

Figure 12.10

The use of displacement maps adds real depth to the surface.

Because the displacement is an instance of the Group Mask, this can be adjusted automatically when changing the Bias on the main texture layer (the Group Mask layer) to increase or decrease the amount of chipping. There is, however, a way of softening the edge without unlinking the displacement from the Group Mask. By adjusting the Gain on the instance, it will become separate from the mask, but all of the other attributes will remain linked. Setting the Gain lower will wear away the edges of the paint layer slightly and also add a little roughness to the surface of the material. This can be adjusted as much as necessary to get the proper appearance from the material. In Figure 12.11, the Gain has been lowered slightly to 95%. For these two layers, the material is now complete, and you can move on to additional layers of complexity.

Figure 12.11

Softening the displacement layer (lowering the Bias setting) helps to add some additional roughness to the surface and soften the edges of the paint.

Before moving on, save the material as a preset (right-click the material group and choose Save Preset). The preset material may need some adjusting of the scales depending on the target, but other than that, it can be applied quickly and easily to add detail to a scene.

Adding Detail to Textures

To see the next concept in action, you will look at a different scene with several materials and at the possible interactions between those materials in the same scene.

Open the file Texture_Layers.1xo from the Chapter 12 section of the enclosed DVD. This is a simple scene with individual material groups assigned to polygons, UV maps already created, and a basic lighting setup (see Figure 12.12). From this basis, you will add textures and create a completed scene. Each color represents a different texture.

Because the individual texture groups are color coded, it is easy to select them in the preview render window (by clicking). This is a good idea when setting up blank materials because this visual cue will indicate which polygons have had a texture applied and will therefore make for quick identification for texture editing. Using a mixture of the material presets that you created and the presets that ship with modo, you can fill out the scene pretty quickly. You may need to adjust texture placement (in the Texture Locator). In a case like this, all of the textures can be applied with either Planar or Cubic projection. To change the mapping methods for a material, follow these steps:

1. Select the image map that is applied (in many cases, there will be instances applied to other channels).

2. Consider the surface the texture is applied to and decide whether it faces just one axis (for example, the side walls or the street) or has elements that face in multiple directions (for example, the curb or the back wall).

3. Select the appropriate projection method (Planar for single axis or Cubic for more than one).

4. Once the mapping is applied, the Size will determine the scale of the material and should be set to the scale that a single tile of the image should be.

5. Check the orientation to make sure that the image is not rotated vertically when it should map horizontally, and vice versa.

6. If the image is not oriented correctly, use Rotation for the same axis that is used in the Projection Axis and rotate the image until it is properly aligned (probably 90° or −90°, depending on the initial orientation).

Figure 12.12

This basic scene will serve as an excellent example for practicing texture detailing.

If all of your texture layers are instances of a single image, only one image (the original) needs to be set. If there are specific images for each input, each image will need to be aligned manually. After using this method on a few surfaces, everything but the curb and the door are ready to go for this stage, as seen in Figure 12.13.

Figure 12.13

Simple Planar and Cubic projections handle most of the textures in this scene.

For the door, you will use a specific nontiling image that will fit precisely to the shape of the door. In this case, I am using a sample material from the first volume of textures from Arroway Textures (www.arroway.de). This particular texture comes with a diffuse (color) map, a specular map, and a bump map.

For the door:

1. Start by applying the diffuse image. Set the texture Projection Type to Planar and set the Projection Axis to Z.

2. Click the Auto Size button (beneath the Size value inputs), and the texture will automatically be scaled to the dimensions of any polygon(s) that hold the material. In this case, you have just the single polygon, so it will snap perfectly into place.

3. Repeat the process with the bump map (designated with a *b* at the end of the filename), and the specular image (with the *s* designation).

4. To increase the usability of this texture set, the specular image can be used to affect reflectivity as well. To do this, go to the base material for the door and select the Match Specular check box above the reflectivity settings.

5. At first, the reflections are a bit overwhelming. Turn on the Blurry Reflection setting, and the look improves significantly.

6. Finally, create an instance of the Specular Amount image and set it to Diffuse Amount. The finished door offers some nice variation in diffuse and reflective properties, as shown in Figure 12.14.

Figure 12.14

Using packaged image maps can help create textures very quickly.

COMMERCIAL TEXTURES

Texture sets can be a quick and powerful way to add photographic detail to your scenes. Many companies such as Arroway Textures even offer free samples to try in your materials. These can be a worthwhile investment if you find yourself creating a lot of materials beyond those that ship with the application.

The last texture remaining is the curb. This is a great location for the layered paint/concrete material created in the previous section. Just as with the other presets, you will need to make some adjustments to the scale and orientation of both the base concrete and the paint layers. With some adjustment, this material will be properly assembled. As you can see in Figure 12.15, something in the paint chips needs to be adjusted to get the curb looking right.

Figure 12.15
The chipped paint and concrete material works well in this scene with some minor adjustments, but the paint needs a bit more detail.

The problem we face at this point is that the chips are spread randomly throughout the surface of the curb. In the real world, this kind of wear appears more frequently on the edges of materials, where more abrasive contact is usually found. To constrain the chips to the corners, you will use an Ambient Occlusion material as the layer mask on the Group Mask:

1. Add the texture to the material, which is found in the Processing section when adding Shader Tree layers.

2. At first, this will be added to the Diffuse Color layer. Using this default setting to modify the texture layer will give better control and quicker feedback. You will immediately see that the Ambient Occlusion texture does not appear in the real-time viewports and that the only way to see it is in the preview render window (or by doing a full render). If this gets a bit too slow while editing, you can turn off the Irradiance Cache updates while texturing. This is done with the IC: Update button at the upper-left side of the preview window. Turning this off will decrease redraw time and help you adapt the texture more quickly.

3. When first applied, Ambient Occlusion has the Type set to Uniform. This produces a result that is too soft for our use. Changing the Type to Concavity & Convexity will put the textures at the edges and creases. The texture will show a lot of noise because the material has a displacement map.

4. To fix this noise, change the displacement map to Bump (and set the blend mode to Add). Because this will be acting as an alpha, the Occlusion should be inverted to show white on the edges and in the creases, as shown in Figure 12.16.

Figure 12.16

The Occlusion texture can essentially mask off sections of geometry based on the shape of the mesh.

This texture will be used to mask off the chips in the paint as well as the bump map for the chips.

5. Create two instances of the texture layer. Then drag the original directly on top of Multi-Fractal Group Mask in the Paint group, and the instance onto the bump map (the other Multi-Fractal texture). The second instance will be used shortly and can be hidden for now. This will mask the chips in the paint to a more controlled area.

6. To edit the Occlusion at this point, click the + next to the group mask. You will see the Occlusion texture inside. Editing the Occlusion Distance, Variance, and Variance Scale will allow you to fine-tune the masking of the chipped-off areas. Figure 12.17 shows the texture with some minor adjustments to these settings.

7. Now, you can unhide the second Occlusion instance. This will be used to add some additional wear to the edges.

8. Drag this texture to the top of the material and deselect the Invert option.

9. Set the layer blend mode to Multiply and decrease the Opacity until the edges look properly darkened without the effect being overdone. I used a setting of 20% Opacity.

Figure 12.17

Using layer masks can help control the area where textures appear. Here the chipped off paint areas are being confined to specific areas of the geometry.

The material is working now, but the curb paint is looking a bit too saturated.

10. To fix this, add a Process texture into the Paint group and decrease the saturation. With the last texture in place, the initial pass is completed, and the scene will look like Figure 12.18.

Figure 12.18

All textures are in place and ready for additional editing.

Now there is one last thing that can help add some extra polish to the look of the image, and that is grime. So I guess it is the opposite of polish, really, but it will help to complete the scene. You can add the well-worn look to textures and images in various ways: with procedural texturing, by hand, or using photographic references.

Procedural Grime

Creating grime with procedural textures can be quick and adaptable:

1. To make the initial setup easier, create a new material in the Shader Tree and place it at the top, just under the Base Shader. This will make the scene all white with lighting only and provide a base for adding the details. After the work is complete, the material can be hidden or deleted, and the grunge will sit on top of the rest of the materials. This will be the common setup for all of the detail texture editing.

2. Now, start by adding another Ambient Occlusion layer. Set the Occlusion Distance to a high number. Somewhere around 10 m will make a good starting point. Adjust the Variance and Variance Scale to suit your needs. Figure 12.19 shows the values set to 40% and 2 m.

   This can be adequate in certain situations, but a bit more detail can help make this solution work.

3. For the moment, hide the Occlusion layer and add a Dirt procedural texture. This will cover the entire scene and be far too busy for these purposes.

Figure 12.19

Ambient Occlusion can help add wear to the textures in the scene.

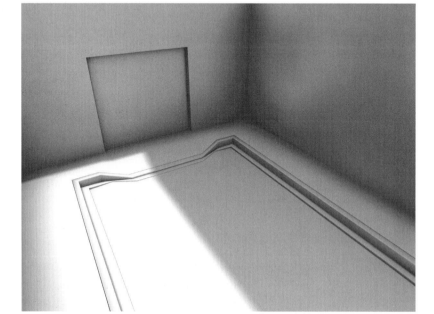

4. At this point, the Ambient Occlusion layer can come in handy once again. Unhide the layer and invert it. This can be used as an alpha channel by dragging it on to the Dirt layer.

5. Set the Dirt texture's blend mode to Multiply, and it should be ready to go. Figure 12.20 shows the result on the blank scene.

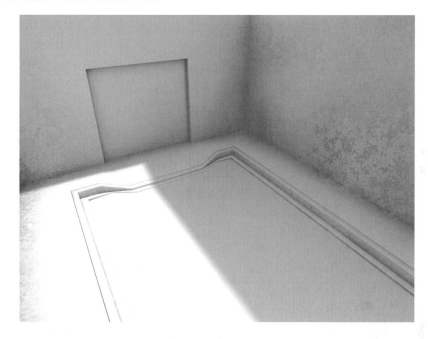

Figure 12.20

Dirt with an Ambient Occlusion mask (alpha) creates grime in areas of the geometry where grime would likely gather.

6. After hiding the white stand-in material, the dirt will be applied to the entire scene, as shown in Figure 12.21. The Dirt and Occlusion texture layers can be edited to adjust the look further. The benefit of this kind of detailing is that it is not dependent on resolution (as the next types will be). On the down side, relying on generated patterns can leave little control or turn out being too obvious, depending on the situation.

Painted Grime

Another method for this type of work is painting the details by hand. For this method, a pressure-sensitive tablet is highly recommended. Follow these steps:

1. To get started, place the white material back in the scene (or unhide it if it was not deleted).

2. Next, you will need a blank image texture to paint on. There are several ways to do this. For this case, go to the Paint interface tab and then the Utilities section of the toolbox and click Add Color Texture. This brings up a dialog box to save the new image file.

Figure 12.21

When applied to the scene, this method can provide some excellent detail.

3. Place the file with the rest of your project and save it as a Targa file to avoid any compression artifacts.

4. For this case, a resolution of 2048×2048 should provide enough resolution to work with and allow for decent performance on most computers.

5. With this image map selected, you can paint directly on the model. Go to the Paint Tools section in the toolbox and select the Airbrush. The standard brush tip that is selected when a brush is activated is a soft round one that is not adequate for this type of painting.

6. Select the Procedural Brush to get a more randomized effect.

7. Set the FG color (the color that you will paint with) to black or another dark color and begin to paint in grime around the scene.

8. Right-clicking will change the brush size. After a few minutes of painting, you can have something like Figure 12.22.

SAVING PAINTED IMAGES

While you are painting, your image will not be automatically saved. To save the image, you can either find the image in the Images tab (in the same section as the Shader Tree and Items list) and then right-click and choose Save, or you can choose Save All from the File menu. Remember that simply saving the scene file will *not* save the painted image!

9. Using the Nozzle (located below the brush tips) and the Jitter options (located under Tablet Nozzle in the tool options) adds more randomness as you continue to refine the texture. When you are finished, you can have an image with specific areas of grime to fit your needs. Figure 12.23 shows an example of the painted texture on the scene.

Figure 12.22

Hand-painted grime can be placed precisely where you want it.

Figure 12.23

Painting textures by hand can take some time but can enable you to create precise areas of detail and have excellent control over your texture.

Image-Based Grime

The last way that you will look at adding grime-based detail is by using photographic references and applying them to the image. This can be done directly in modo by using Image Ink. However, for this exercise, you will work on the UV image in Photoshop. For this method, I will be using grime textures from the DV Garage Surface Toolkit (www.dvgarage.com). This is a really amazing set of grime and grunge maps of many types and comes in handy for any complex texture work. There are also kits available for adding water damage and even graffiti.

Export the UV map to an EPS file, as you did when previously working with UVs in Photoshop (choose Export UVs To EPS from the Texture menu in the menu bar). Then open the EPS file in Photoshop at a resolution of 2048×2048 and place grunge images in appropriate areas around the scene. You can also use Photoshop paint tools to add further detail by hand, similarly to the way it was added directly to the model in the previous example. The results here can be quicker than painting everything by hand and can provide compelling results. However, having good reference images is crucial to making this work well. The end result will look something like Figure 12.24. Notice the photographic quality of the details. This type of detail can take a long time to accomplish either by hand or by using procedurals.

By using a combination of the methods covered in this section, you will be able to add subtle realism and life to your rendered images. Obviously, this kind of wear may not be suitable for every render, but when a project requires a more "lived-in" feel, this is a great way to start.

Figure 12.24

Image-based textures can be used to quickly create realistic wear and grime if you have good reference imagery.

Using Render Outputs

In many cases, after clicking Render, your image is completed and ready to present. However, much can be accomplished after the render is completed. To do this, a fair amount of preparation needs to be done to get the most out of post-processing. Unlike post-processing, post-processing 3D rendered images can offer many options and tools for making the job easier and affording you possibilities that are not available when working on photographs. In modo, render outputs can be added either by duplicating an existing output and then right-clicking to change the actual output or by selecting Render Output from the Special section of the Add Layer drop-down menu at the top of the Shader Tree.

Render outputs tell the rendering engine what kinds of images need to be produced. Some options are used directly, others are used for image diagnosis, and still more are used indirectly to enhance the final output in post-processing. Here you will consider some of the most useful render outputs and then look at how they can be utilized in post-processing. The outputs covered here are Final Color, Diffuse Shading (Total), Transparent Shading, Reflection Shading, Specular Shading, Alpha, Surface ID, Depth, and Ambient Occlusion. The first five of these are essentially components of a final render and the other four are used to derive some additional effects for the editing of final images. To continue, you will look at each of these groups in more depth.

Component Outputs

A typical rendered image can be broken down into four main components: diffuse, reflection, specular, and transparency. You may recognize these as elements of materials that have been created throughout the course of this book. Just as these elements are combined to make a finished texture, they also make up the finished render. The Final Color output is commonly known as a *beauty pass*, because it features all of the components of a fully lit and textured scene. In many cases, this will probably be enough for editing purposes. You may be wondering why the individual components are necessary if the Final Color output contains all three of them. The reasons are flexibility and speed. By having the diffuse, reflective, specular, and transparent elements separate, they can be adjusted without affecting the other elements. To further explore these elements, you will add a preset car into the scene. Figure 12.25 shows a final render of the alley scene with an Alpha Romeo from the modo stock content inserted into the scene.

GAMMA OUTPUT

Many people render with outputs and then get discouraged when they open the layers in Photoshop and are unable to get the look of the final render. When rendering a final output, the Gamma defaults to 1.6. Render outputs are set to 1.0 by default. You can adjust this setting in the properties for each output, in the render window for each layer after the render is complete, or in Photoshop after opening the layered file. It is usually best to adjust the gamma in the properties for each output before rendering so that it is correct from the start.

The Diffuse Shading (Total) output provides an image with all of the diffuse values from the finished render (see Figure 12.26). This is a good place to start when adjusting coloration of objects after render.

Reflection Shading and Specular Shading deliver the effects of reflection in the scene. The Reflection Shading output is shown in Figure 12.27. Notice that blurry reflections are taken into account in this render, but it should be mentioned that blur can be added in post-processing when the reflections are separated from the rest of the outputs.

Figure 12.27
The reflective elements of the same scene are shown in this output.

Transparent Shading can be a little tricky. This output provides us with any section of the scene that is touched in any way by a transparent material. Transparent windows that show the backdrop behind fall into this category. Transparent Shading also handles the headlights along with the entire interior of the car. Because the inner pieces of the headlights and interior of the car have some transparent material between them and the viewer, they will appear here even though they are assigned opaque materials lit by the scene light or environment. The Transparent Shading output is shown in Figure 12.28.

Figure 12.28
Any pixel in the rendered image that has a transparent element between itself and the camera will be included in the Transparent Shading output.

Editing Outputs

The other mentioned render outputs are used in the editing process to add flexibility or additional effects to the final render. The Alpha output simply separates the visible objects in the scene from the background. Surface ID tags each material in the scene with an individual color (see Figure 12.29). This can be helpful for mask creation when editing.

Figure 12.29

Surface ID can help you quickly select and edit materials in a final render.

The Depth output provides a gradient based on the distance each pixel falls from the camera. White pixels are closest to the camera, and black pixels are at or beyond the Maximum Depth setting. When using Depth, it is important to adjust the Maximum Depth so that as much contrast as possible appears in the render. When set too low, more of the scene will appear black, and when set too high, the scene will appear as having too much white. For the example in Figure 12.30, Maximum Depth was set to 14.4 m.

Finally, the Ambient Occlusion output can be used to add some additional shadows to a bright scene and can help accentuate fine geometric detail (such as grooves and cracks). One important thing to check in this output is the Occlusion Rays setting. The default setting will result in a very grainy and nearly unusable render, while a setting of 256 Occlusion Rays will provide a reasonably smooth finished image. If your scene is an interior or has a very dark occlusion map, increasing the Occlusion Range setting can allow more light into the render pass. Figure 12.31 shows the Ambient Occlusion output with default settings and the Occlusion Rays boosted to 256 for a cleaner render. As with several of the other outputs, this should have the Gamma adjusted to 1.6 for the best initial results.

When used in conjunction, these render outputs can greatly improve the look of a finished render or allow for greater flexibility after the render has been completed.

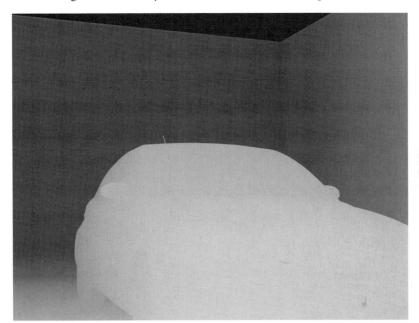

Figure 12.30

Properly setting Maximum Depth will help you get the most out of a Depth output.

Figure 12.31

Ambient Occlusion can be used for a variety of purposes in post-processing.

Sweetening 3D Renders by Using Photoshop

With a rendered image completed and outputs ready (either exported separately or included in a layered PSD file) you can start post-processing. In this section, you will look at some simple adjustment and corrective editing as well as some features that can be added to stylize the finished render. Many of these effects can be achieved in a render without post-processing, but the ability to do these things and adjust them in seconds as opposed to waiting on new renders can be a great benefit to any workflow.

To start working with render outputs, place the Diffuse layer underneath the Transparent Shading and the Reflective Shading layers. Start by setting the Transparent and Reflective layers to a Screen blending mode. If you have a Specular layer, this can also be layered and set to Screen. Once this is done, your image should look nearly identical to the beauty pass (if not indistinguishable). In the case of Figure 12.32, I left out the Specular pass because I did not like the effect on the finished render. Alternately, you could keep that layer and simply reduce the opacity to lessen the effect.

Figure 12.32

When composited correctly, the individual render passes display all of the results of a complete render but with more control.

Making Basic Adjustments

Just to give a feel of the possibilities that exist here, you will make some changes to the scene, starting with the car paint. Say you are sitting with a client who says he loves the render *but* wants the red car to be blue and to have more reflectivity. If you are not prepared, you could open the scene file, make some tweaks, and wait for the preview render to give the client an idea of the changes made. If you are set up with proper render outputs and a little Photoshop work, you could make those changes in seconds while the client watches! To set up the Surface ID for quick image adjustments, follow these steps:

1. Using the Surface ID layer (having it selected even if it is hidden by other layers will do the trick), use the Magic Wand tool with a Tolerance setting of about 8 and the Contiguous option deselected, and then click in the middle of the paint material. This should make a clean selection that includes only the car paint.

2. With this selection made, create a new Hue/Saturation adjustment layer. You will see that the layer has an attached alpha channel. Now drag the Hue slider to the left until the appropriate blue tone is reached.

3. Hold Ctrl/Command and click the layer mask for the recently created adjustment layer to reselect the paint.

4. Select the Reflection layer and press Ctrl/Command+J to duplicate the portion of the Reflection layer that pertains to the car paint. Because the layer is already set to Screen, the reflections will be magnified. If the result is too strong, simply reduce the opacity of the new layer. If it still isn't enough, duplicate the new layer, and the effect will be increased even more. After less than a minute of editing, Figure 12.33 shows color and brightness changes to the car paint, both walls, and the curb, as well as an adjustment to the reflectivity of the car paint.

Figure 12.33

Editing color, brightness, and reflective values can be done nearly instantly with a properly designed Photoshop file.

Even with a very fast computer and a very experienced 3D artist, the client would not see results of this quality for a significantly longer time. Imagine the possibilities of doing this on a high-resolution render that took all night to process. Working intelligently and using your options can help you stay ahead of your competition and keep your clients or supervisors satisfied!

Finishing the Image

With coloration, reflection, and other basic elements fine-tuned, the image can be further adjusted. Adding depth of field (camera focus), sharpness, bloom, and some vignette effects to the image will create a finished image that really pops. The purpose of these edits is to further the focus on the subject and to add interest to the finished look. Certainly these techniques do not represent the only way to finish an image. Much of the fully finished look will depend on your taste and the needs of the project or client. By learning these principles, however, you should be able to adapt to the situation and get just what you want out of your rendered images.

Before starting this process, I should note that I found the headlight lenses to be too transparent in the previous section. To fix this, duplicate the Transparent Shading layer. In one version, paint out the headlights (in black); in the other, paint out everything else. Then the transparency can be lowered simply be decreasing the opacity of the layer with the headlights to give them a more fogged or tinted feel, as you will see shortly.

Let's start by adding the camera focus to the image. For this, you will use the Depth Output layer in conjunction with the Lens Blur effect under the Filter menu in Photoshop. If you have ever used this blur effect on its own, you probably noticed that unlike the Gaussian blur, it features a more lens-shaped blur (especially noticeable in small, bright areas) and some additional features such as adding a bloomlike effect to bright spots and adding some noise to simulate grain. The real power of the Lens Blur effect comes when there is a grayscale depth channel that is used to define the area of focus. To use Depth Output with Lens Blur, the layer needs to be a channel:

1. Select and copy the depth layer. Then go to the Channels tab, make a new channel, and paste the copied layer into this channel.

2. If you have made multiple layers to edit colors and other properties from the previous section, it is best to get a flattened version to work with at this point. This can be done by simply selecting the entire canvas and copying the merged layers (Ctrl/Command+Shift+C).

3. Then paste the merged copy layers on top of the others. Select the merged copy layer and run Lens Blur.

4. Set the Depth Map Source to the newly created depth channel (Alpha 1 if you did not rename it).

5. Now you can simply click an area in the preview window to set that as the area of focus. In Figure 12.34, the focus is set around the windshield wipers and a slight Smart Sharpen was added (set to 125% and a radius of 0.5 pixels).

Figure 12.34

Adding depth of field with the Lens Blur tool can save a lot of render time and gives you the ability to adjust the focus quickly and easily.

As I mentioned, a Smart Sharpen effect was added to the image. This helps to improve the sharpness on the focus area. For this kind of sharpening, it is important to use a radius of 0.5 pixels, as this will allow you to get crisp results without an unwanted halo effect around the areas of contrast.

Next, you will move on to adding some bloom. This is done by creating a duplicate of the layer, adjusting the colors, blurring the layer, setting it to Screen mode, and then adjusting the opacity to fine-tune the strength of the effect. In this case, using Smart Sharpen on the main layer is key to keeping the details visible. There are two common ways to adjust the coloring of the duplicated layer: Levels and Exposure (best accessed by choosing Layer → New Adjustment Layer). By adjusting the levels and pulling up the black input, the focus will shift to the brighter areas and give a good, even bloom effect. Sometimes this will cause the saturation to increase too much, so you may need to decrease the saturation before continuing. For a more aggressive and edgy look, adjusting the Exposure works well but is a bit more complex. There is a fine balance of adjusting the

Exposure slider to the right, the Offset slider to the left, and the Gamma Correction slider to the right. As you make the corrections to the layer, remember that the point here is to keep the areas where you want the bloom to appear and push the rest to dark colors (or black).

Figure 12.35 uses the Exposure method with an 8-pixel Gaussian blur and the layer opacity set to 40% (and in Screen mode). You can adjust this as you see fit to get the right finished look. You may also wish to desaturate or even tint this layer to achieve some interesting effects.

Figure 12.35

With bloom added, the image starts to take on more character.

The final step for this particular image is to add a sort of vignette effect by first creating a heavily blurred, dark border to draw focus toward the car. In this case, I added an alpha channel to keep the shading from affecting the car itself (this could also be done by erasing the border in the area where the car is). To heighten the effect of the shading, I am also going to use the Ambient Occlusion layer. The first step is to adjust the levels on the layer so that the car is mostly white (pull down the white input level). You may also wish to pull up the black output level to keep the shadows from being too dark. Also, make sure to apply the Lens Blur and Smart Sharpen effects that were used on the main color layer. This will ensure that the details align properly. Change the layer blend mode to Multiply and adjust the opacity to get the right effect for your needs. Adding an Exposure adjustment layer over the top of the entire image will allow you to make good final adjustments to the image, as shown in Figure 12.36.

Figure 12.36

**With the vignette,
Ambient Occlusion,
and a final Exposure
adjustment layer,
this image is
complete.**

Review

This chapter serves to give you more depth of skill when working with textures and final renders. A solid understanding of materials and how they are created will help you make surfaces for any type of model with some practice. Taking a complete render and finishing or "sweetening" it in an image editor will help you to go beyond the basics of simple renders. This will make them more flexible and give you additional possibilities for adding a finishing touch. In the end, the style that you choose to create is your own. These techniques, like imaging and 3D applications in general, are simply tools that you can use to bring your creative vision to life. After reading this chapter and practicing the exercises for each section, you should be able to do the following:

- Create layered materials that are easily editable
- Create complex material groupings that can be blended and masked to add more depth to the surface of your 3D models
- Create proper render outputs for post-processing
- Use rendered assets to edit image attributes in real time
- Finish your image by using render outputs and an image-editing application

Where to Go From Here

Using these techniques can improve the quality and adaptability of any render. Savvy Photoshop users will even record macros for handling the more repetitive tasks. Spend some time going through the scenes created for previous chapters. Using render outputs and more complex materials, retouch those scenes and renders to see what improvements you can make. Above all, use your own artistic sensibilities. The goal of this chapter is to get you started. Adding your own style and techniques to the ones mention here will help you to take your 3D renderings to new heights.

ON THE DVD

As with the other chapters, the DVD includes video walk-throughs of the exercises in this section. In addition, there are sample materials from the DV Garage Surface Toolkit to help you get started adding organic complexity to your textures and materials.

CHAPTER 13

Animation

Animation skills are not only for creating explosive visual effects scenes or bringing impossible characters to life. A solid understanding of basic animation skills can improve productivity, enhance your workflow, and give you more options in your creative endeavors. Knowing where to start is key to making your first foray into animation a positive experience. This chapter covers the following:

- **Creating keyframes for animation**
- **Using the Graph Editor**
- **Setting up motion paths and constraints**
- **Rendering sequences and composing in After Effects**

Creating Keyframes for Animation

Figure 13.1

Any attribute with
a gray circle can be
animated. Click the
gray circle to enable
animation.

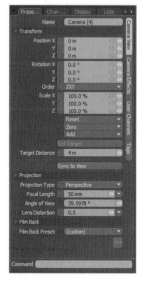

At its core, *animation* is the process of creating changes in a scene over time. Keyframes are the frames set by the user. For typical animated motion, these frames represent the key points in time that define motion or changes. Think of these as the plotted points that define a curve. These can be used in two ways: to define animated motion (as mentioned) and to set up values for rendering individual frames in succession.

Keyframes can be set on almost any attribute in modo (position, rotation, scale, color, reflectivity, and so on). This means that almost any attribute can be animated via simple keyframes. To set keyframes on an attribute, animation needs to be enabled. Every attribute that can have keyframes set has gray circles located to the left of its value field. Figure 13.1 shows an example of a mesh attribute tab with the keyframe fields highlighted.

If the animation checkbox is left unselected (remaining gray), any changes made to the attribute will be set at a value regardless of time. When mousing over the keyframe toggle circle, a small pop-up will appear showing a color key for the values of these check boxes. Values for the keyframe colors are as follows:

- Empty = Default value (this value has not been modified in any way)

- Gray = Constant value (will not change over time)

- Red = Animated channel with a keyframe at the current frame

- Green = Animated channel with no keyframe at the current frame

- Blue = Mixed values (this appears when multiple items are selected that do not have the exact same keyframe values)

- Purple = A value that is not directly animated but instead derives its value from a relationship with another item or attribute

For the most part, Gray, Red, Green, and Blue are the types of keyframes commonly used for basic animation, as you will see in this chapter. Using these basic ideas, you will create two simple animations.

Animated Product Shot

Still shots for products can provide excellent details for high-quality images. Many times, however, an animation can help show additional details or angles to enhance the presentation of a product. With the increase in dynamic content available, the addition of a short animation to a product presentation can help you to better present your concepts, products, and ideas. This can be done by animating the camera, animating the product (for example, with a turntable), or a combination of the two. For this demonstration, I am going to use the bottle created in Chapter 5, "Subdivision Surface Modeling," Chapter 6, "Textures for Visualization," and Chapter 7, "Studio Lighting and Rendering."

Animated Camera Sweep

Let's start by animating the camera. In situations like this, it is helpful to create a new camera for animation, leaving the original camera for still shots. You can either right-click the camera in the Items list and duplicate it there or you can choose Camera from the Add Item menu in the Items list. It may help to rename the camera to keep things organized. Before animating anything, it is a good idea to plan out the necessary animated properties. A simple storyboard or sketch of the motion can help you figure out what is necessary. In this case, you will move the camera across the scene from right to left, as shown in Figure 13.2.

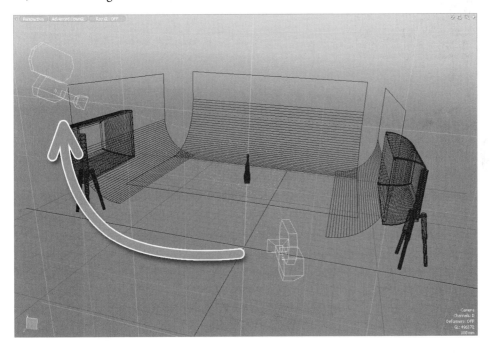

Figure 13.2

This illustration shows the necessary camera move.

From this figure, you can see that the camera will require keyframes on the position at the beginning, middle, and end of the sequence. In addition, the camera angle (rotation) needs to change in order to keep the subject in view. If the camera is to move (or dolly) horizontally, only the X and Z position values need to be animated. If the camera will move up or down at all, the y-axis needs to be included. Click each of the circles for these properties to enable animation (and set an initial keyframe). The initial key can be changed, so don't worry if the camera is not already in the proper starting position. In addition, the rotational values will need to be animated in order to keep the subject in the camera view, so enable animation for those attributes as well. The bulk of the animating will take place in the Animate tab, so click that tab to continue.

THE ANIMATE TAB

When accessing the Animate tab, you will be greeted by a large central viewport, an animation timeline (at the bottom of the screen), the typical Items and Properties tabs (at the right), and an extensive list of animation options (on the left). Don't be daunted by all of the options that appear. Most of what you need to create simple animation is in the familiar viewport, Properties tab, and the simple timeline at the bottom of the screen.

In the Animate tab, you will notice that the timeline goes from 0 to 120. These are frame numbers representing 5 seconds of animation. By default, the frame rate is set to 24 frames per second (fps), which is the frame rate for film. If you would like to change that to something else (such as 30 fps, which is common for many multimedia uses), simply do the following:

1. Click the Options button in the center of the screen beneath the timeline.

2. From there, you will find a pop-up menu, and one of the options is Frame Rate.

3. Choose several standard rates or Custom to enter any value you need.

4. For this case, set the frame rate to 30.

You will notice that the timeline now shows 150 frames, which means that there are still 5 seconds of animation available. If more time is needed, the number of frames can be changed in the fields in the far right under the timeline. The first of these two fields shows the number of frames visible in the timeline, and the second is the total number of frames in the scene. Please note that the visible frames cannot exceed total frames, so the second field needs to be set first. For this simple animation, 5 seconds should be plenty of time, so no adjustment is needed.

Now you are ready to begin setting up the actual animation. Start by positioning the camera to the right and looking down slightly on the bottle, as shown in Figure 13.3. Because keyframes are already enabled for the camera position and rotation, this will automatically set the initial value. Move the timeline to frame 150 and then move the camera to the other side of the bottle and lower it slightly, as seen in Figure 13.4. By default, keyframes are automatically set so the initial pass of animation is set. You will see a green line appear in the timeline, which indicates the presence of animation.

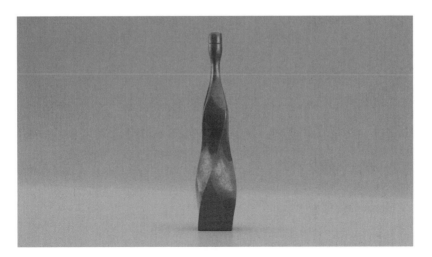

Figure 13.3

The starting camera position for the animation

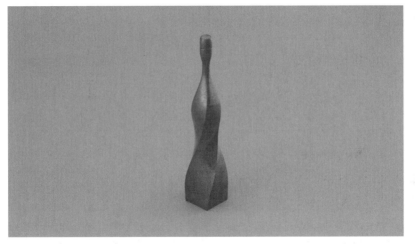

Figure 13.4

The ending camera position for the animation

CLEANING UP THE CLUTTER

Sometimes a 3D viewport can become cluttered when dealing with a lot of information (models, lights, camera, multiple textures, and so on). To deal with this, you can hide some unnecessary data from the display. With the mouse over your main viewport, press the O key. This brings up a menu for visibility and control over items displayed in that viewport. Texture locators have a way of cluttering up a scene. So, in the Visibility section, deselect Show Texture Locators. This should dramatically clean up the viewport and make it much easier to see your project. You can also disable other items as needed. Just keep visible what is necessary for your current task, and it can help you keep tabs on the project.

To see the animation, you can either click and drag in the timeline (called *scrubbing*) or simply click the Play button under the timeline. By default, the playback will move in real time (30 fps in this case). This will be the case even if your graphics card is capable of playing at a higher speed or a large scene begins to slow it down. In the latter case, the playback will skip frames to maintain the playback speed. If seeing every frame is important, you can deselect the Play Real Time option in the Options menu (where the Frame Rate setting is located). This will cause playback speed to be maximized based on your hardware configuration. Letting the playback loop as you watch is a good way to quickly assess the current state of your animation and decide where fine-tuning may be needed.

In this case, you will notice that the focus tends to drift a bit in the middle of the animation and the bottle falls out of view, as shown in Figure 13.5. You can fix this by adding a keyframe to adjust the position of the camera, the rotation, or both. At frame 75, adjust the camera so that the bottle is back in focus, as shown in Figure 13.6. When you do this, a keyframe will automatically be added, and the animation will be updated to include the new keyframe.

Figure 13.5

At the middle of the animation, the subject is not as well centered as it is at the beginning and ending keyframes.

DIVIDING THE VIEWPORT

In the top-left corner of every viewport, there is a small dot that turns orange to indicate which viewport is active if you have multiple views onscreen (such as in the Model Quad or Render tabs). Holding the Ctrl key and then clicking and dragging divides the viewport in the direction of the drag. In other words, dragging downward divides the viewport into two views stacked on top of each other (with the new viewport at the bottom). Dragging to the right creates a new viewport to the right. In this manner, the screen can be divided into any configuration imaginable. From here, a right-click on that same small circle allows you to duplicate, detach, delete, or perform other operations to further customize your workflow. If you get things too messed up, you can always return to the default setup by going to the Layouts section of the Layout menu and choosing 501 Default Layout.

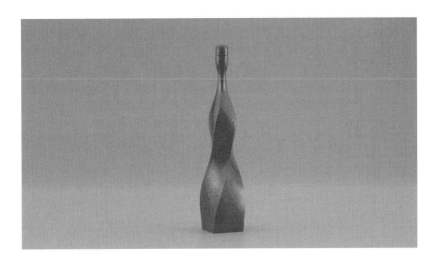

Figure 13.6

Adjusting the camera at frame 75 to keep the subject well centered will help smooth out the animation.

Turntable Animation

Although there is a turntable option under the Render menu, it is actually a holdover from previous versions of modo that have no animation capabilities, and it is not recommended for use to create turntable animations. Instead, a short setup will allow you to create more-predictable animations with a lot more control. The bottle can be animated directly just by selecting it (in Items mode) and animating its properties. This will usually yield decent results, but another method offers more flexibility and also illustrates some ways of creating more-complex animations later on. *Locators* (or nulls in some other 3D programs) are items that can be used for grouping, organizational, and animation purposes. By creating and animating locators, you are able to more easily control your animation and expand your options in the future. To create a locator, move to the Items list and select Locator from the Locators section of the Add Item menu. This places a locator in your scene at the origin (see Figure 13.7).

Because you want to make sure that the rotation happens from the center of the bottle, the locator needs to be aligned to the center of the bottle. This ensures that the bottle will not rotate awkwardly off-axis when it is attached to the locator. To do this, you will use the Work Plane and its ability to align to any portion of the scene:

1. Select the bottle mesh layer and go to Polygons mode.

2. Select a loop of polygons around the base of the bottle to define the area that will be used as the new center.

3. Select Align Work Plane To Selection under the Edit → Work Plane menu. The Work Plane will be centered on the current selection of vertices, edges, or polygons.

    This can be useful for many advanced operations, but in this case you will use the recentered Work Plane to snap the locator to the base of the bottle.

4. Go to Items mode and select the locator.

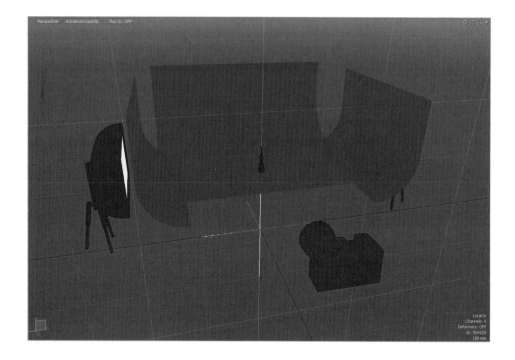

5. Move to the Animate tab and choose To Work Plane Position under Set in the Setup section of the Commands tab. If the To Work Plane Position button is not visible, make sure that the left-hand vertical tab is in the Setup section and not the Modifiers section. Once clicked, the locator will appear at the base of the bottle.

6. At this point, your locator should be perfectly positioned for the animation (see Figure 13.8). The Work Plane can be reset to the default position be choosing Reset from the Edit → Work Plane menu.

7. For this animation, the locator needs to be animated only for the Rotation attribute in the y-axis. Click the corresponding property to enable the animation. Set the value to 0° at the first frame of the animation and 360° for the last frame.

CAMERA VIEWS AND RENDERING

Selecting a camera to view from in a viewport is simple. Choose the desired camera from the Camera section of the View menu located at the top-left corner of each viewport. Remember that any camera can be activated in this manner, but the render camera must be chosen from the Frame section of the Render Properties viewport.

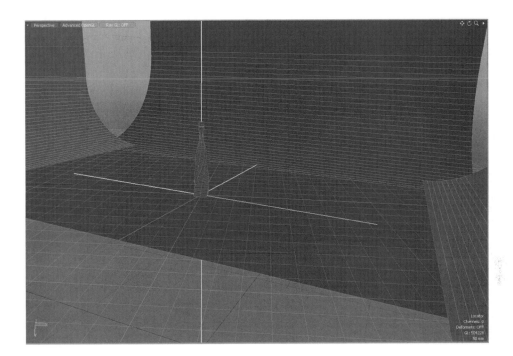

Figure 13.8

The locator is now aligned to the geometry of the bottle and is ready for animation.

8. Move to the stationary camera to get a cleaner look and then click the Play button. The locator rotates smoothly and comes to a stop each time the animation cycles. For a more continuous loop, the graph for this animation will need to be adjusted. You will handle this in the next section on the Graph Editor, but for now, the animation is complete.

9. To apply this to the bottle as well, simply drag the bottle mesh layer onto the locator layer. Rename the locator something more appropriate, such as **Turntable Rotation** or something that will help you to keep organized. The locator will now have a small arrow next to it and if clicked, the bottle layer will appear as a child of the locator.

10. Click Play again. The bottle rotates in conjunction with the locator.

There are other ways to link animated properties, but this is the simplest and most direct. Other options are discussed later in this chapter.

Turntable with an Animated Camera

If you choose the animated camera at this point and preview the animation, the effect may be a bit dizzying. Because the bottle rotates one way and the camera rotates against it, the countermotion becomes a bit too busy. To fix this, you will design a second camera move that will simplify and clean up the presentation. In this case, you are not going to animate the position or rotation of the camera but instead will have the camera zoom in very slowly as the bottle rotates. To do this, the camera Focal Length needs to be animated. To animate this property, select the camera and do the following:

1. The default Focal Length is 50 mm. This is probably a good ending length, so move to frame 150 and enable animation for the Focal Length (found in the camera properties).

2. With the keyframe set, maneuver the camera to give a nice close shot of the subject (an example is shown in Figure 13.9).

3. When you have settled on your ending frame, move back to the first frame.

4. Because the keyframe was already set at the end, making an adjustment here will place another keyframe and animate the camera. Because you don't want the camera to move at all, simply adjust the Focal Length. In Figure 13.10, the value is decreased very slightly to 45 mm.

The effect when played back is a simple, slow camera zoom. As a side note, for this render I am setting the camera render frame to a portrait aspect ratio by adjusting the Frame Width and Height in the Render Properties viewport. Adjust the settings as you see fit to tweak the animation, and you are finished.

Combinations of these options are easy and follow the same basic principles as the shots described here. Adding a slight camera tilt and move to the last shot can provide an interesting look. Pulling the camera out while zooming in can also give an interesting perspective on the subject. There are endless ways to put these principles to use. Adjustments are easy to make as long as the initial creation is kept as simple as possible.

Figure 13.9

Ending camera position with Focal Length set to 50 mm

Figure 13.10

The camera in the same position and Focal Length decreased to 45 mm

Remember to add keyframes only as you need them. A common mistake is to add keyframes in too many places. This is a sure method for creating jerky, unnatural, and rough-looking animations. Start with the first and last frames and then add frames in the middle as needed to get the right camera motion without unnecessary work or roughness. Some animations will require more adjusting than simple keyframes can easily handle, and that is where editing the space between keyframes becomes necessary.

Using the Graph Editor

Keyframes really represent only a part of the story of an animated sequence. A process commonly known as *tweening* creates the rest of the frames. This terminology comes from traditional animation, when keyframes were created to rough out and time the motion and then (after approval) additional frames were created to fill the space between the keys. The computer now handles this process, and this fact allows the animator (you) to have more-direct control of the tweening process. The motion between keyframes can be linear, eased in, eased out, or a combination. In addition, the amount of easing can be defined precisely through the editing of a graph of each attribute. By default, the keyframes will automatically ease in and ease out.

To start looking at this aspect of animation, let's consider the animation graph for the turntable locator. Select the locator in the Items list and then bring up the Graph Editor, which is located both in the bottom of the Animate tab to the right of the Options button and at the top of the Options pop-up itself. When an item is selected, a graph showing the animated attributes for that object appears, as shown in the graph of the turntable locator in Figure 13.11.

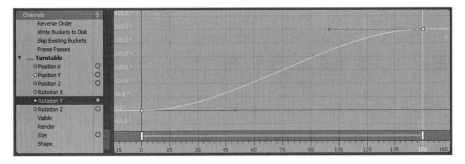

Figure 13.11

The animation graph for the turntable locator

As you can see from this example, the ease-in and ease-out is very pronounced. The graph represents the y-axis rotation over the course of the animation. In order to make a continuous turntable that could be looped repeatedly, the easing needs to be eliminated:

1. Select the first keyframe and right-click to reveal options.

2. Under Incoming Slope, choose Linear Out.

3. Then select the second keyframe, and for the Incoming Slope choose Linear Out. The resulting graph will look like Figure 13.12.

Figure 13.12

With both incoming and outgoing tangents adjusted to be linear, the animation will play seamlessly.

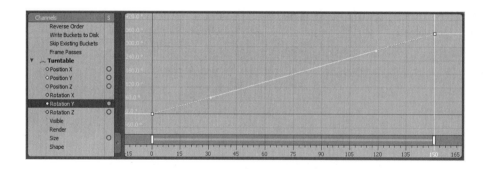

With this continuous motion, the looping animation will now be seamless. Test this by choosing your stationary camera and clicking the Play button. The animation will loop without slowing down and starting back up with each loop.

Now you will look at something a little more complex. The first animated camera featured three keyframes that were used to keep the bottle in view. The adjustment can be made without the additional keyframe if the curves are properly set. For this animation, you will remove the animation from the bottle. Because the actual animation is on the locator, the animation can be removed simply by dragging the bottle out of the locator. Once this is done, the bottle will not spin until it is placed back under the turntable locator. Now change the view to the first animated camera. Select the camera in the Items list and open the Graph Editor. You will see highlighted values for the three Position and Rotation axes (channels) and graphs for each value, as shown in Figure 13.13. If all of the curves are not in view, press Shift+A to center the current selected attributes in the Graph Editor window.

Figure 13.13

The motion graph for the first animated camera

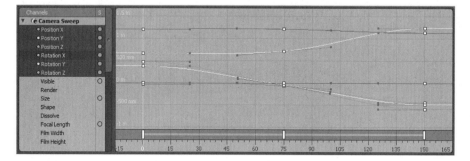

GRAPH EDITOR COLORS

In the Graph Editor, color-coding is based on the same red, green, and blue values seen in all other parts of the user interface (in viewport axes and tool handles, for instance). X values are shown in red, Y values are green, and Z values are blue. Remember this to keep the graph straight when editing the curves.

Start by deleting the keyframe in the middle. To do this, drag across the keyframes to select them and press the Delete key. The graph will automatically adjust, and the tangents will keep the curves smooth (see Figure 13.14). Start by selecting all of the keys at frame 0 and setting them to Linear Out. Then set the keys at frame 150 to Linear In. From here, select the individual attributes to simplify the graph by making only the selected curve visible in the window. Now you will address the easing issue in two steps: removing it completely and then adding back in just what is necessary to keep a clean camera move. Select all of the remaining keyframes. Then right-click anywhere in the Graph Editor and choose Linear. This will make every aspect of the movement completely linear and have no easing at all, as shown in Figure 13.15.

From this simplified standpoint, it will be easier to fine-tune the motion. First you will adjust the motion so that the camera does not get as close to the camera as it moves by. To do this, the Z position graph needs to be altered so that it arcs toward the final position. Select the Position Z attribute in the Channels list of the Graph Editor to show just the Z curve. Select both keyframes and choose Manual from the right-click menu. When set to Manual, the curve tangents will become editable again. Drag the tangent for the first keyframe so that it goes almost straight out from the keyframe (horizontal) and drag the tangent for the second keyframe nearly upward. The resulting curve will be a half arc, as seen in Figure 13.16.

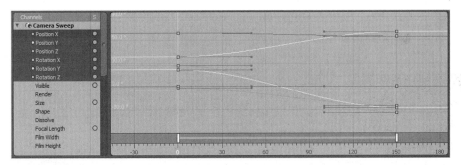

Figure 13.14

The graph for the camera move with the middle key- frame removed

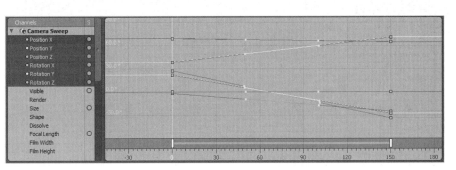

Figure 13.15

Linear interpola- tion will be ideal for most of the keyframes in this animation.

Figure 13.16

Figure 13.16

The proper curve adjustment for the Position Z channel

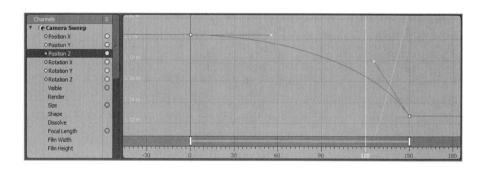

The Position X channel will control the camera move from right to left. As it currently works, the camera waves back and forth and does not keep the subject in view very well. Change the keyframes to Manual (just as with the previous channel) to make them editable. In this case, a very soft S-curve will help the motion, so pull the tangent for the first keyframe just below the curve and the tangent for the second just above the curve, as shown in Figure 13.17.

Figure 13.17

The proper curve adjustment for the Position X channel

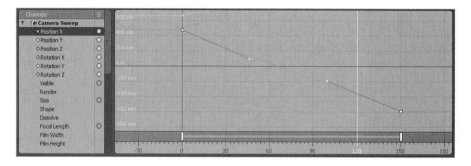

Finally, an adjustment to the Position Y channel will help the vertical motion keep the subject from dipping below the bottom of the screen. In this case, another S-curve is appropriate. Pull the first tangent slightly above the curve and the second tangent below the curve (at a slightly larger distance from the curve than the first tangent). The curve should look like Figure 13.18.

Figure 13.18

The proper curve adjustment for the Position Y channel

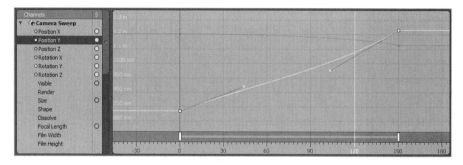

A good way to get a clear idea of the effect of the tangent on the motion is to start playback and then adjust the curve while the animation plays. Creating a balance between the tangents takes a little fine-tuning, but taking the process one attribute at a time will help simplify the process. It should be noted that this camera move could have been adjusted with changes to the Rotation channels while leaving the Position channels with linear interpolation. As a good practice, fine-tune the camera move by using the rotation curves instead of the position ones. This will allow you to see how fine changes in curves can make a big difference in your animations.

Setting Up Motion Paths and Constraints

Keyframes offer a good, straightforward solution for setting up animation by allowing you to set and frame important points. At times, however, creating a perfectly smooth motion path is key to the success of a sequence. In these cases, creating a path for objects to follow can help speed up the process of creating smooth animation. Animating on curves offers a number of interesting possibilities for creating fluid motion and even interpolation between start and end points. Additionally, this will allow you to create camera moves that would be difficult, if not impossible, to achieve with keyframes alone. Perhaps best of all, creating this style of animated motion is quick and easy once you have a firm grasp of the process. With a little practice, you will be able to create, edit, and refine a motion path in a matter of minutes.

The first stage of this process is to create a curve to use as the animation path. Curves are created from the Curves palette, which is located in the Geometry menu. When selected, the Curves palette will appear (see Figure 13.19). This palette contains a lot of options, but we will concerns ourselves with the first three in this case.

Figure 13.19

The Curves palette

CHOOSING CURVE TYPES

The basic two types of curves available are *direct curves* (which flow smoothly between points) and *Bezier curves* (which have handles to control the interpolation). For the most general-purpose use, the straight curves are more versatile and can be used directly in many applications. However, Bezier curves are easier to edit and create complex shapes with fewer points. In the case of path animation, either type works well, so Bezier is usually a good choice for animation paths.

Select the Bezier tool from the Curves palette and place three points in a semicircle around the subject, as shown in Figure 13.20. It is important to note that Bezier curves change slightly after the tool is dropped. If a point has been placed, it will retain the handles for control of the curve, but they will appear as simple vertices. If the very first point plotted was not adjusted (in other words, the tangent handle was not moved from the default position), the first point on the curve will not have an editable Bezier handle after the tool is dropped. Additionally, it is important to realize that the tangents are broken once the tool is dropped. This means that editing handles individually can result in a break in the curve, as shown in Figure 13.21.

The broken handles are easily fixed by using a simple technique. To properly edit a Bezier curve, follow these steps:

1. Select all of the vertices related to the control point you wish to edit (the control point and the two handle vertices).

2. Set the Action Center to Selection.

3. Use the Move tool to position the control point.

4. Use the Rotate tool to adjust the orientation of the control point.

5. Use the Scale tool to adjust the tension of the curve around the control point.

The first thing you will notice is that the curve was created at the Y = 0 position. Select all of the vertices related to the curve and move it up to a Y position around the middle of the bottle. Spend a few moments adjusting the curve so that the path arcs upward in the middle and then back down at the end, as shown in Figure 13.22.

Figure 13.20

An arc created around the subject using a Bezier curve

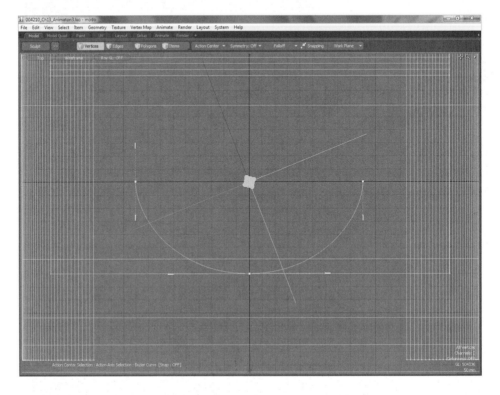

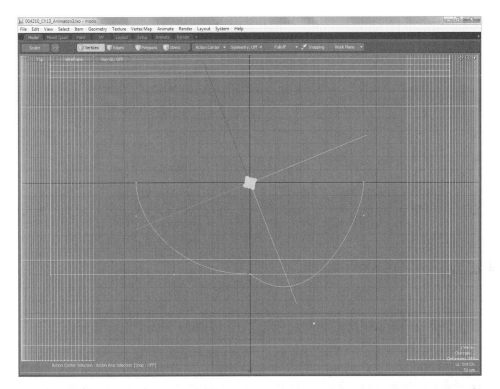

Figure 13.21

The tangents on Bezier curves break when the tool is dropped.

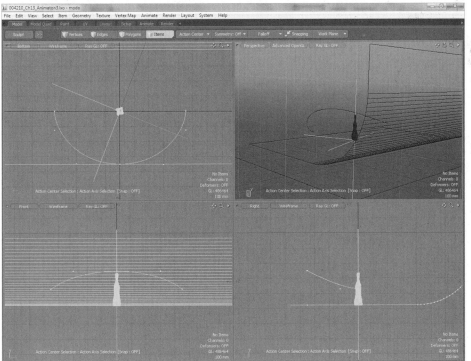

Figure 13.22

The finished path for the camera to follow

Once again, the best way to proceed with the animation here is to animate a locator and then attach the camera to that locator. To set up the curve path for the locator, do the following:

1. Create a new locator (rename it if you want to keep organized).

2. Select the locator and then Shift+click on the curve layer in the Items list (this can also be done in the viewport but is usually easier to do in the Items list).

3. Go to the Animate tab.

4. Select the Modifiers section from the Commands tab.

5. Under Constraints, click Path to attach the locator to the curve in the layer (remember that you can have only one curve in a layer for this to work).

With the locator attached to the curve, you will see a + sign to the left of the locator. Click this to reveal the Path Constraint. When selected, this will reveal properties to control the location (and animation) of the locator along the path. Set the Path Percentage to 0% at frame 0. Enable animation for Path Percentage, move to frame 150, and set the percentage to 100. Scrubbing the timeline will show the locator moving smoothly along the path. There are a few options offered in the Path Constraint properties that may be useful, so we will cover them here:

- *Path Offset* works similarly to the Percentage option and can allow some variation to the overall position along the path.

- *Wrap* allows you to loop continuously around the path, if you have a closed path.

- *Roll* controls the bank of the locator (or any attached item). Positive numbers cause the item to bank with the curve, and negative values bank against the curve.

- *Axis* determines which axis is aligned along the path.

- *Negative Axis* flips the axis so that it faces backward along the path.

- *Local Up Vector* causes the alignment to be relative to the curve layer. (This takes effect if the mesh item containing the curve has been rotated.) Note this is not often used in simple path animations.

- *Up Vector* presents a set of fields that defines the upward direction of the path alignment. Changing the value for the axis that is horizontally perpendicular to the axis will change the bank of the attached item. This item is also not used frequently in simple animations.

There are several ways to attach the camera to the locator. Create a new camera to start off this section. The simplest way to attach the camera is to drag the Camera item onto the locator. This creates a hard link between the two objects and links both the position and the rotation. Changing the Axis on the path to X and turning on Negative Axis will cause the new camera to point toward the center of the path (and the subject).

Scrubbing the timeline will show an animation in which the camera moves around the bottle and tilts as the path moves up and down. Adjusting (and keyframing) the roll can keep the bottle in view, but the tilt on the camera remains, making this a bit awkward for our purposes. Figure 13.23 shows this camera move at frame 45 of the animation. To get a better result, you will use another type of animation constraint that will offer more options.

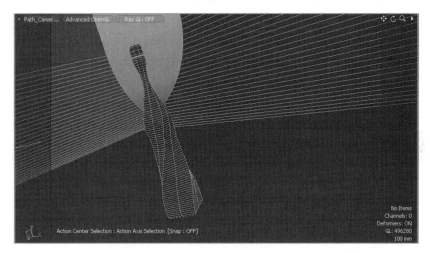

Figure 13.23

The hard-linked camera and locator cause some tilts in the camera, which make it awkward for this use.

Making two constraints will allow you to create a more flowing and natural camera move. To set up the first constraint:

1. Select the camera and drag it out of the locator.

2. Shift+click on the locator.

3. Go to the Animate tab.

4. Select the Modifiers section.

5. Under Constraints, click Position.

The camera is now attached to the locator for position only. This means that no path alignment or roll on the locator will affect the camera. Now you will need to get the camera to point at the bottle. You could keyframe the y-axis rotation (to keep the camera faced in the right direction) and the x-axis rotation (to keep the bottle vertically in view), but that will leave it with some roughness and take a lot of time to fine-tune. Our purpose here is to do this job as simply as possible. To get the camera pointed at the bottle, do the following:

1. Create a new locator.

2. Position the locator in the middle of the bottle mesh.

3. In the Items list, select the camera.

4. Shift+click the new Target locator.

5. Click the Direction option (from the Constraint section of the Animate tab).

The camera now points at the bottle (the locator, actually), no matter where the camera moves. Scrubbing the timeline at this point will provide a good, smooth animation with no awkward tilting issues. Figure 13.24 shows frame 45, which was problematic in the previous version. The alignment is good, and the bottle is perfectly in view.

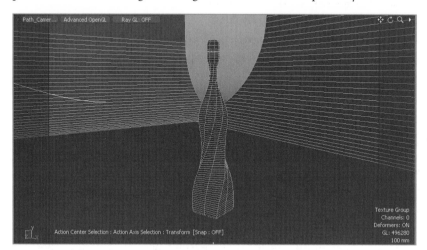

Figure 13.24

With the camera targeting the locator, the alignment of the camera is now smooth throughout the sequence.

Different projects will call for different animation styles and needs. Learn and internalize these simple methods, and they will help you to quickly add some motion to your next project.

Rendering Sequences and Composing in After Effects

Once your motion is complete and you are ready to create a finished presentation, you will need to render out the frames. Choosing the Render Animation option from the Render menu accesses sequential frame rendering. The subsequent dialog box allows you to choose the starting and ending frames and the type of files to be created.

Saving the file as a movie will allow you to get an instantly playable animation, but this has some serious drawbacks. The main issue with rendering to a movie file is that the file is not completed until the final frame renders. In other words, if your computer slaves away rendering 999 out of 1,000 frames in a weekend-long render and a power outage occurs before the last frame renders, you will lose the entire rendering—not a problem that many people would like to have.

The better option is to render image sequences. The Image Sequence option will render the number of frames specified in the format of your choice. If an alpha channel is enabled in Render Outputs, it will be included as an embedded channel in the images (if rendering to a file type that supports alpha channels). If you have multiple render outputs, the Layered Images option will be of most use. This will allow you to save a sequence of layered PSD files (as well as a few other formats), which can be directly imported into Adobe After Effects or another video-editing program.

Setting Animation Options and Render Outputs

When preparing an animated sequence, you should consider a few options. Motion Blur, Global Illumination, and Antialiasing need to be planned depending on the purpose of the animation and the render time for the project. If the animation is something like a turntable, in which viewers may wish to pause and inspect individual frames, then motion blur is probably not the best choice (plus it does increase render time). In other types of animation (or when outputting to a video that does not usually pause), the motion blur can help add some realism and make the motion appear smoother. Gauge this option based on the project needs and render time that can be spent on the entire number of frames to be rendered.

When rendering a sequence with Global Illumination (which will often be the case) and a static scene with an animated camera, the Walkthrough option can be very useful. Click the Walkthrough Mode button in the Global Illumination section of the Render Properties viewport. This option will calculate the full Irradiance Cache (high-quality light samples) for the first frame, but in subsequent frames, only the areas of the frame that were not in the previous frame will have the Irradiance Cache calculated. This can result in some tremendous time savings depending on the scene. I personally have seen render times go from 90 minutes for a first frame (of a high-definition architectural walk-through) down to less than 40 minutes for additional frames with no visible loss in quality. In addition to the Walkthrough mode, you should take some time to adjust the Global Illumination settings. Refer to Chapter 12, "Improving Final Renders," for reference on optimizing these settings.

After you have set the preceding options and have optimized them as much as possible, checking the Antialiasing settings will help you get the best speed out of your renders. Remember that in the case of animation, a little less refinement is needed. This is especially important if the animation is to be accompanied by higher-resolution still frames. In many instances, a setting of 8 Samples/Pixel is fine for animation (though this can go higher if Depth Of Field or Motion Blur are in effect, as these settings require higher antialiasing to get the smoothest possible result). Making adjustments of this type can be helpful. Figure 13.25 shows a rendered image with the settings for a nice quality still and a render time of just under 1 minute and 10 seconds. Figure 13.26 has the settings optimized for animation and a final render time of just over 19 seconds.

Figure 13.25

Before optimizing the scene for animation, the rendered frame takes 1:07 to render.

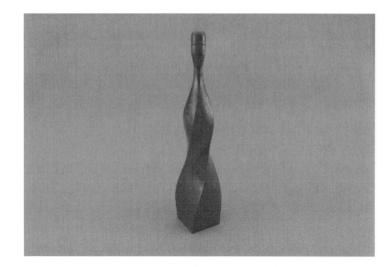

Figure 13.26

With some render options adjusted for animation purposes, the render time drops to just over 19 seconds.

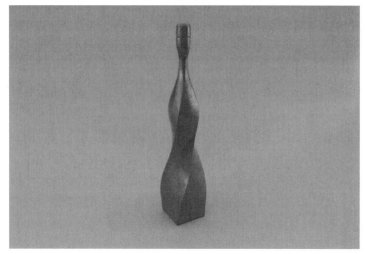

Animated sequences can utilize the same options of Render Outputs that can be used in still renders (as demonstrated in Chapter 12). Set up the necessary render outputs to make later edits on the animated sequence. Just as in the previous chapter's discussion of still render output layers, useful options include Surface ID, Diffuse Shading (Total), Reflection Shading, Transparent Shading, Ambient Occlusion, and Depth. These can all be saved as layers in a Layered Image animation render. Saving these images as a sequence will not give you an instantly playable movie, but with a small amount of work, a rendered movie can be output from After Effects by using just the standard Final Color output or with more options using composited layers.

Composing Final Animations in After Effects

Once you have rendered a finished animation sequence, you need to assemble the frames to create a final movie. Included on the DVD is a rendered turntable sequence for you to use if you don't want to wait on a fully rendered animation sequence just to practice movie creation. To get your animation into After Effects:

1. From the Import section of the File menu, choose Multiple Files. This brings up a standard file import dialog box.

2. Navigate to the location of your rendered sequence and select the first file in the list.

3. Make sure that the Photoshop Sequence check box is selected and then click Open.

4. Change the layer import from Merged Layers to Choose Layer.

5. Select the first render output from the drop-down menu and then click OK. The layer sequence is placed in the Project list, and you are then returned to the import menu.

6. Repeat steps 2–5, choosing a render output layer until all of the desired layers have been imported. When this is complete, click Done on the import screen to stop importing files.

When your image sequences are in the Project list, you will need to create a Composition to house the animation. Start a new composition (choose New Composition from the Composition menu). In this dialog box, set the frame width and height to match the image resolution (480×480 pixels in this case), set the Frame Rate to 30, and the duration to 5 seconds. After you have created a new composition, you can place the rendered frame sequences in the timeline directly or drag them onto the composition in the Project pane. Choose Make Movie from the Composition menu, choose a file location, and click Render in the Render Queue pane to render out your sequence as a movie.

AFTER EFFECTS

If you are new to Adobe After Effects, you can reference its short series of focused tutorials aimed at getting you moving quickly in the program. Like this book in general, these do not cover every feature of the application but will give you targeted information that will allow you to use the aspects of the program that are key to getting your job done and making it look good fast. These tutorials cover the basics of navigating in After Effects as well as ways to import and compose rendered output channels to create a nicely composed final animated sequence.

Review

Animation can add a lot to a finished project. By including motion sequences with the finished deliverables, you can increase your options and the options you can give to your clients. Animation can be a huge topic (easily taking up an entire book on its own). This can be daunting to the beginner, but with a few simple techniques and some creative implementation, animation can add depth, value, and life to your projects without eating up large amounts of time. After reading this chapter and practicing the exercises, you should be able to do the following:

- Create simple animations using keyframes
- Fine-tune your animations through the use of the Graph Editor
- Animate by using locators and parenting
- Use motion paths
- Use constraints to keep animation controlled
- Compose final animations by using After Effects

Where to Go from Here

Animation can be helpful for any project. If it is something that you would like to learn more about, consider using it in more capacities. Remember that nearly any attribute can be animated in modo, so animation can be used for many different situations. In addition to animating transformational and other attributes of items, many other things can be animated. Morphs can be used to animate deformations of objects (these can be anything from simple changes in the mesh formation to different facial expressions on characters). For more information on animation, numerous video tutorials are available at www.Luxology.com as well as on the section of my website dedicated to this book, located at http://3dforGD.sm-graphics.com.

About the Companion DVD

This appendix summarizes the content you'll find on the DVD. If you need help with copying the items provided on the DVD, refer to the installation instructions in the "Using the DVD" section of this appendix.

- **What you'll find on the DVD**

- **System requirements**

- **Using the DVD**

- **Troubleshooting**

What You'll Find on the DVD

You will find all the files for completing the tutorials and understanding concepts in this book in the Chapter Files directory on the DVD.

Working with files directly from the DVD is not encouraged. Copy the entire folder for each chapter to your local drive to ensure that the example files function properly.

Please check the book's website at www.sybex.com/go/3dforgraphicdesigners, where we'll post updates that supplement this book should the need arise.

System Requirements

You will need to be running Luxology modo and Adobe Photoshop to fully use all the files on the DVD (the software is not included on the DVD). Go to www.Luxology.com to download a 30-day trial version of the software. The projects can be completed with any 3D program as long as you are familiar with the toolset.

> This DVD does not include the modo software. You will need to have modo installed on your computer to complete the exercises in the book.

Make sure your computer meets the minimum system requirements shown in the following list. If your computer doesn't match up to these requirements, you may have problems using the files on the companion DVD:

- A computer running Microsoft Windows 7, Windows XP (SP2 or newer), or Windows Vista, or Apple OS X 10.5.2 or newer
- An Internet connection
- A DVD-ROM drive
- Apple QuickTime 7.0 or later (Download the latest version from www.quicktime.com.)
- At minimum, you will need a fast processor, a minimum of 2 GB of RAM and a dedicated graphics card (integrated graphics cards do not offer optimal performance for 3D applications).

Most modern computer systems will run modo and other 3D applications for at least basic functions relatively well.

For minimum requirements, see the website of your 3D program. If you are new to 3D and using modo (or trying modo as a new 3D solution), visit the Luxology website.

Using the DVD

For best results, you'll want to copy the files from your DVD to your computer. To copy the items from the DVD to your hard drive, follow these steps:

1. Insert the DVD into your computer's DVD-ROM drive. The license agreement appears.

Windows users: The interface won't launch if Autorun is disabled. In that case, choose Start →
Run (for Windows Vista, choose Start → All Programs → Accessories → Run; for Windows 7, type
run into the Search Programs And Files box and click the Run program icon). In the dialog
box that appears, type **D:\Start.exe**. (Replace D with the proper letter if your DVD drive
uses a different letter. If you don't know the letter, see how your DVD drive is listed under My
Computer.) Click OK.

2. Read through the license agreement, and then click the Accept button if you want to
   use the DVD.

The DVD interface appears. The interface allows you to access the content with just one
or two clicks. Alternately, you can access the files at the root directory of your hard drive.

Mac users: The DVD icon will appear on your desktop; double-click the icon to open the
DVD, and then navigate to the files you want.

Troubleshooting

Wiley has attempted to provide programs that work on most computers with the minimum
system requirements. Alas, your computer may differ, and some programs may not work
properly for some reason.

The two likeliest problems are that you don't have enough memory (RAM) for the
programs you want to use or that you have other programs running that are affecting the
installation or running of a program. If you get an error message such as "Not enough
memory" or "Setup cannot continue," try one or more of the following suggestions and
then try using the software again:

Turn off any antivirus software running on your computer. Installation programs sometimes mimic virus activity and may make your computer incorrectly believe that it's
being infected by a virus.

Close all running programs. The more programs you have running, the less memory is
available to other programs. Installation programs typically update files and programs; so
if you keep other programs running, installation may not work properly.

Add more RAM to your computer. This is, admittedly, a drastic and somewhat expensive
step. However, adding more memory can really help the speed of your computer and
allow more programs to run at the same time.

Customer Care

If you have trouble with the book's companion DVD, please call the Wiley Product
Technical Support phone number at (800) 762-2974. Outside the United States, call

+1 (317) 572-3994. You can also contact Wiley Product Technical Support at `http://sybex.custhelp.com`. John Wiley & Sons will provide technical support only for installation and other general quality control items. For technical support on the applications themselves, consult the program's vendor or author.

To place additional orders or to request information about other Wiley products, please call (877) 762-2974.

Index

Note to the Reader: Throughout this index **boldfaced** page numbers indicate primary discussions of a topic. *Italicized* page numbers indicate illustrations.